Praise for *The Delta Model*

"The Delta Model is an invaluable tool that reinforces the importance of customer centricity as the critical lever for success in our high-speed globally linked world. It provides a powerful roadmap for the change process necessary to bring the results to the bottom line."

Randy Zwirn, CEO and President, Energy Services Division
Siemens

"I have known Arnoldo Hax for many years, and have long admired him-as a friend and as an amazing professor of infinite intellectual generosity. His methodology to approach companies' complex issues through his Delta Model is undeniable, comprehensive, effective, and allows you, with crystal clear arguments, to continuously review your business strategies."

John Graell, CEO Molymet

"The Delta Model encompasses the next major evolutionary step in strategic planning... It embraces the networked reality of today's relationships between the enterprise, its targeted customers and the complementors."

Terry Bussear, Director, Market Strategy
Baker Hughes Inc.

"Once you fully understand the power of [the] Delta Model, it becomes a valuable tool to help analyze, understand and improve your organization."

Jaime Sagarduy, Project Manager, Ikerbasque
Basque Foundation for Science (Spain)

"Disciplined strategy with heart and soul."

Richard Naimark, Senior Vice President
American Arbitration Association

"For those in the public or not-for-profit sector who question the relevance of business strategy and the Delta Model to their organizations, think again."

Chad Fleck, Innovation Counselor, Foreign Affairs and International Trade
Government of Canada

"An approach grounded in reality. It moves the focus from competition to your most important assets: your customer, supplier and partner base. Innovate, don't imitate."

John S. Lohse, Business Manager
Toyota of Killeen (Texas)

"The Delta Model is much more than theory. It is a framework with which to vision your preferred future state."

Howard Slaff, Director, Marketing
Baker Petrolite Polymers

"If you are looking inward, you are not looking forward. Dr. Hax forces you to look at the world through customer's eyes."

Michael Hardman, President
The Hardman Group

"Excellent overview of a strategic planning model that can be applied in any business or industry."

Lorenzo Salvaggio, Vice President and General Manager
Alcan Packaging

Arnoldo C. Hax

The Delta Model

Reinventing Your Business Strategy

 Springer

Arnoldo C. Hax
Sloan School of Management,
Massachusetts Institute of Technology
50 Memorial Drive
Cambridge MA 02142
USA

ISBN 978-1-4419-1479-8   e-ISBN 978-1-4419-1480-4
DOI 10.1007/978-1-4419-1480-4
Springer New York Dordrecht Heidelberg London

Library of Congress Control Number: 2009938824

Printed on acid-free paper

Springer is part of Springer Science+Business Media (www.springer.com)

To my beloved wife, Neva, the center of my life and my great source of bonding.

Preface

Often I am asked how the Delta Model was originated. What made us spend some time and effort in attempting to produce an alternative way to look at the formulation of strategies for a business firm when there were a considerable number of respectable and widely acclaimed models to accomplish this? The answer to that question is somehow embarrassing. It originated at a Convocation of Alumni that we conducted at MIT many years ago. It is a long tradition of the Sloan School to have yearly meetings with our former students, typically targeting those who have graduated multiples of 5 years ago, such as 5, 10, 15, and so forth. On one of those occasions I was the Deputy Dean of the School, which placed me as an important participant and host of the program. After 2 days of nice social and academic activities, crowned by what we believe to have been exciting seminars conducted by our faculty, it was time for me to close the meeting at a Saturday lunch with the proverbial warm send-off with the expectation of seeing again all those sweet old faces. However, when I was ready to depart and go home, two directors of Unilever who have come from London to attend the convocation and who were very close friends of mine said – "Arnoldo, don't go away. We want to talk to you." We proceeded to sit down and they started with this comment that I will never forget: "Arnoldo, this was not worth the ticket!" It was hard for me to accept such a reaction. After all we had convened with three Nobel Laureates – Paul Samuelson, Robert Solow, and Franco Modigliani. We have paraded our best and brightest faculty, old, young, and in-between. What else would they want?

Their reaction was something like this. "You are doing some very impressive things and no doubt you have a remarkably talented faculty. However, when we go back to work on Monday morning, nothing that we have heard will make us do things differently. You are not connecting with the realities of our lives and we don't seem to get any help from any of the other respectable academic places as well. The existing frameworks don't seem to work effectively for us."

As you can well imagine this was quite a blow for me. The conversation continued for about 2 hours and I was feeling increasingly uncomfortable. However at the end we agreed that we were going to establish a group composed by a select set of distinguished alumni and we were going to identify an equally top set of senior faculty to engage in a dialog to understand these issues more clearly. We labeled this initiative "The Delta Project" – Delta being a word and a Greek letter that stands for transformation and change. The original executive members of the Delta Project were Iain Anderson, the Chief Strategist of Unilever; Skip LeFauve, the CEO of Saturn; Judy Lewent, the CFO of Merck; Gerhard Schulmeyer, the CEO of Siemens, USA; and Bert Morris, the COO of National Westminster Bank. We listened to them attentively. After that, we developed the Delta Model to attempt to address the questions that emerged from these meetings.

It has been 10 years since we developed the first version of the Delta Model. I wrote a book, coauthored with my dear friend, Dean Wilde, titled *The Delta Project: Discovering New Sources of Profitability in a Networked Economy* (Palgrave, 2001), where we lay out the foundations of our new approach to strategy. I am now revisiting this subject in a new book since much has happened since the first book was published. In particular, I have been conducting an enormous amount of research with my students at MIT that has allowed us to test a wide variety of hypotheses and to apply the model in an extraordinary array of industrial settings. I have been also engaged in consulting activities literally around the world in companies of all sizes and business endeavors. The model has been enriched both conceptually and, most importantly, by the development of pragmatic tools that we have created to allow executives to implement successfully the Delta Model in their organizations. This book is intended to share these advances with you. But before we get started I want to put up in front what were the central questions that our Delta Project friends were longing for answers.

The Key Unanswered Questions

We were never told in the Delta Project discussions what were the specific issues that managers were missing from the existing strategic management frameworks. However, it was clear that there were three major concerns:

1. How to change?

Often the status quo is not an acceptable course of action. The environment is changing around us and we need to make not just incremental improvements over what we are doing, but rather to rethink, reinvent, and reengineer what our strategies should be. The conventional frameworks start the process of reflection on our past, and that is often the wrong way to make you think of change. We want to create discontinuities not to reaffirm what we have done. By providing too much emphasis on competitor's behavior, the conventional frameworks tend to anchor us in the existing industry practices.

We have found that the obvious answer to initiate a process of change is to start with the customer. What can we do to help the customer improve its business? How can we look into its full life cycle and detect novel ways of providing something that is truly unique? By focusing on the customer, we find it is much easier to detect opportunities to be truly unique and promote change.

2. How to pursue profitable growth?

Profits are revenues minus expenses. It does not require much creativity to reduce costs; there are always ways to curtail our expenditures. What is more demanding is to find ways of increasing our revenues profitably. Are there a lot of potential revenues and economic growth which are left under the table because of our inability to detect those opportunities? How could we assess the potential for growth?

One practice that is commonly used is sales forecast. I find that completely unacceptable – first, because sales should not be a subject of forecast. We forecast events over which we have no control, such as the weather. On the contrary, sales are something that we truly can and should influence. Second, sales forecast means an exercise of extrapolation of the past into the future. Again, this is unacceptable if we want to challenge our previous performance and if we want to engage in new forms of management that, hopefully, can make our past irrelevant – for the better.

Where is the answer? Again this resides on the customer. If we were to look at each customer individually, we will detect what potential exists by treating them differently, meaning offering more creative value propositions. This will allow us to examine "white spaces" – untapped opportunities – from the bottom up to come up with a much more effective growth strategy than the one resulting from competitive analysis.

3. How to spark creativity?

What we are saying, in various ways, is that we need to find mechanisms that allow us to be more creative, the so-called thinking out of the box. When I was using the conventional frameworks, I rarely found them to be the source of inspiration conducive to creating an innovative strategic environment. It might be my limitation while using those frameworks, but I doubt it. The emphasis on creating "competitive advantage" was focusing on the competitors. That is not the best way to do it. Instead, attempting to understand the granular needs of the customer and to seek the best ways to satisfy them provides the answer.

As you now realize I support a customer-centric approach. This concept is not new, but what is new in the Delta Model is that we have been able to articulate extremely powerful concepts and tools to allow us to make this a reality. I hope that after reading the book you will agree.

Cambridge, MA   A.C. Hax

Acknowledgments

This book represents in many ways the culmination of my academic and professional work. The ideas expressed here were supported by a great number of people, whose association has enriched me deeply throughout my life, including my closest collaborators and friends, my academic colleagues, my business associates, my students, and especially my family. It is my duty and privilege to recognize the names of some of these people – all of whom I owe my deepest gratitude.

Let me start with the most critical ones who are my friends Dean Wilde and Nicolas Majluf. Dean was the coauthor with me of the first book on the Delta Model and I owe him a great intellectual debt. Nicolas Majluf has been my closest friend and partner and he provided the most critical assistance to get this book started by helping me to articulate the first draft.

I also would like to provide a singular recognition to my dear friend Iain Anderson, a former Director of Unilever who was in charge of strategy and technology in that institution. I worked with Iain more than a decade to apply my strategic management principles to the wonderful organization that is Unilever. He was a source of continuous inspiration and the driving force behind my attempt to influence the strategic thinking at Unilever. I literally worked with almost all of the regional and category managers there, including Roy Brown, Johannes Eenhoorn, Jeff Fraser, David Landers, Martin Nicholas, John Ripley, Russell Sherwood, Tom Stephens, Charlie Strauss, Vikram Tandon.

Unilever was the central recipient of my methodology in strategic planning – so much so that Hax became a verb. I heard often the expression "We've just been Haxed." I leave up to your imagination to figure out the true meaning of that statement. Another Director of Unilever, T. Thomas, was the first to bring me to Unilever, which stated my remarkable association with this firm. Finally the Chairman, Niall FitzGerald, brought me into the Executive Council to do the corporate strategy of this colossal institution.

The Delta Model was tested repeatedly while helping organizations to develop a forceful strategy. There were many important executives that helped me to advance my strategic planning concepts and methodologies while I was attempting to help them in improving the strategic thinking in their organizations. Those who play the most critical roles through many years of interaction have been Maria Silvia Bastos, President of CSN and Icatu Hartford; the late Hernán Briones, CEO of Investa;

Francois Corbin, President of Industrial Tires U.S.A. of Michelin; Gary Cowger, former President of North American Operations at General Motors; Guillermo Crevatin-Zettler, President of Industrial Tires Europe of Michelin; José Luis del Rio, President of Derco; John Graell, President and CEO of Molymet; Albert Holzhacker; President of Dixtal Biomedica; the late Skip LeFauve, the CEO of Saturn; Judy Lewent, the former CFO of Merck; Marcos Lima and Juan Villarzú, both CEOs of Codelco at different times; Josep Manent, CEO of Instrumentation Laboratories; Isabel Marshall, Head of Strategy at Codelco; Charles Miller Smith, former Chairman and CEO of Imperial Chemical; Michel Orsinger, President and CEO of Synthes; Prashant Prabhu, President of Michelin Asia-Pacific; Felipe Prosper, President of IDOM; Sergio Regueros, Regional Director for Latin America of Telefónica España; Hector Ruiz, CEO of Advanced Micro Devices and formerly the President of Motorola Semiconductors; Gerhard Schulmeyer, President and CEO of Siemens Corporation; Brian Shaw, former executive of Castrol; Alex Zalesky, Executive Vice President of International Business at Sherwin Williams; Randy Zwirn, President and CEO of Siemens Westinghouse Power Corporation. I would like to especially acknowledge Hansjörg Wyss, Chairman of Synthes, who relentlessly read and commented on the Delta Model and provided me at Synthes a magnificent environment in which to test my ideas.

In the not-for-profit organization work I want to recognize the very constructive experiences I have had working with my original alma mater, the Catholic University of Chile, and in particular the support I have received from its Rector, Pedro Rosso; the Provost, Carlos Williamson; the Academic Vice President, Juan José Ugarte; and the Director of Planning, Rodrigo Fernández Donoso.

It would be unthinkable for me not to recognize at this point my colleagues at the MIT Sloan School of Management with whom I have shared extraordinary experiences throughout my 37 years at this exceptional place. I have learned from them not just academic knowledge and concepts but the full meaning of the words integrity and professionalism. Among them I would like to cite: Gabriel Bitran, Charlie Fine, Steve Graves, Rebecca Henderson, Jake Jacoby, Simon Johnson, Don Lessard, John Little, Rick Locke, Tom Magnanti, Tom Malone, Bob McKersie, Stew Myers, Bob Pindyck, Roberto Rigobon, Ed Roberts, Ed Schein, Dick Schmalensee, Michael Scott Morton, Maurice Segall, Abe Siegel, Lester Thurow, Glen Urban, Jim Utterback, John Van Maanen, Peter Weill, Eleanor Westney, and the late Rudi Dornbusch and Franco Modigliani. I would like to single out Bill Pounds who had a very special meaning in my life as a mentor, as a counselor, and as a permanent constructive critic of my work. His continuous advice – both personal and professional – has been invaluable throughout my life.

I have also worked during 3 years at the Harvard Business School, an exemplary place that has contributed greatly to my professional upbringing. In particular, I would like to acknowledge the great impact that I have received from Michael Porter, arguably the most influential academic in management in our generation, Jim Austin, Joe Bower, Pankaj Ghemawat, Bob Hayes, Bob Kaplan, Cynthia Montgomery, Steve Wheelwright, David Yoffie, and most special for me, my dear friend Steve Bradley who brought me to Harvard.

Obviously, after so many years in academia I have literally an army of former students. I would like to single out those who made direct contributions to my thinking of the Delta Model. Among them I could cite: Juan Pablo Armas, Rodrigo Canales, Dan Candea, Nicolás Droguett, Todd Gershkowitz, Liz Haas, Ann Mary Ifekwunigue, Uday Karmarkar, Rafel Lucea, Ariel Magendzo, Enrique Perez, Omar Toulan, Chris Voisey, and especially those whose contributions I have cited in the text of this book which are Carlos Brovarone, Richard Chao, Hai Thoo Cheong, Kelvin Chia, Yoshiro Fujimori, Toru Fujita, Jayson Goh, Makoto Ishii, Priya Iyer, Paul Lin, Harry Reddy, Hideo Uchida, Cathy Yum.

My special thanks are due also to Richard Gilman, the former publisher of the *Boston Globe* who read the manuscript and gave me most insightful comments; and Ira Alterman, who did a remarkable job in editing the full manuscript.

Once more, I have to express my utmost appreciation for my now life-long assistant, Deborah Cohen, who has given me more than 30 years of the most dedicated exceptional support. She has played an important role in every aspect of my professional life and certainly in this book.

Finally, my last words go to my family. My daughter, Nevita, and my grandson, Quin, as well as my son, Andrés his wife Verónica and my other grandson León, are at the core of my life, giving me continuous affection and support. From my wife, Neva, I have learned the true meaning of the word love, which as you will see, plays a very important role in the Delta Model. It has been my privilege to share my life with such a wonderful partner.

Cambridge, MA   A.C. Hax

Contents

Chapter 1
The Need for Reinventing Strategy

This book is about an innovative, new approach to business strategy that better reflects the realities of the global marketplace in a network economy. It was developed at MIT to help managers formulate, articulate, and implement more effective ways to achieve superior and sustainable financial performance and long-term profitability, providing a completely different perspective from the conventional strategic approaches used by most managers.

As you will see, our Delta Model (after the Greek letter delta, standing for transformation and change) encompasses a unique set of frameworks and methodologies that grew from our conviction that changes being experienced in the world of business were of such magnitude that existing managerial frameworks had become either invalid or incomplete. Moreover, the emergence of the Internet, with its previously unimagined potential for communication, and the incredible technologies surrounding e-business and e-commerce are enabling completely different business approaches than had ever been possible before.

The Dangers of the Conventional Definition of Strategy – Strategy as Rivalry

Until now, the prevailing view – shared by most practicing managers and academics – has been to define the goal of strategy as achieving sustainable competitive advantage. Most, if not all, of the most respected and popular frameworks that guide the strategy development process are anchored in this concept. This is a mindset likely to cause severe problems moving forward.

First, it puts our competitors at the center of our management process. Competitors become our driving force, our relevant benchmark. We look at strategy, and consequently at management, as rivalry. In order for us to succeed, we have to beat someone. Strategy is destructive; strategy is war. As recent history has confirmed, again, wars do not have victors. Wars only produce devastation and loss. Lord Wellington observed after defeating Napoleon at Waterloo, where tens of thousands of soldiers lay dead on the battlefield, "I can only imagine one thing worse

A.C. Hax, *The Delta Model*, DOI 10.1007/978-1-4419-1480-4_1,
© Springer Science+Business Media, LLC 2010

than winning a war and that is losing it." Not a very encouraging comment! Not a very promising strategy.

Second, and equally troublesome, using our competitors as a way to define our course of action basically anchors us in the past. On reflection, this is an approach that seems counterproductive in a time of revolutionary change, when we want to create discontinuities, not reaffirm old practices. Is this what we should be aiming at in today's turbulent environment, when change is virtually mandatory? We must challenge our previous state of business. We must have the ability to be creative and separate ourselves from the herd, to find a new and unique way of conducting business.

Often, companies seem obsessed with their competition, studying and watching it intensely to detect anything that could signal a way to operate more effectively. This might not be a very smart way to manage. I tell my students, "Study your competition deeply, but do not imitate them." I believe that strongly. It is a meaningful challenge. To separate ourselves from our competitors, we must offer our customers something that is truly unique and distinctive. How do we do that?

Third, the excessive concern about competitors can lead us, consciously or otherwise, into imitating their behavior. Our products begin to take on similar characteristics of those of the leaders. The development of our new products adheres to the prevailing standard of the industry, the channels of distribution that access our customer base are indistinguishable – in other words, the industry begins to converge into a well-established set of norms and standards. The result of this congruency leads toward the commoditization of our business, which is the worst possible outcome for all players.

Reject Commoditization – The Essence of Strategy Is to Achieve Customer Bonding

It is alarming to see how many firms are in a situation where a large percentage of their business has become commoditized.

The fundamental objective of any firm as a whole, as well as the individual businesses of the firm, is to achieve superior and sustainable financial performance as measured by long-term profitability. In order to achieve this outcome, we need to differentiate ourselves through leadership and a sense that our business is distinctive, which is exactly the opposite of a commodity. Commodities, by their nature, are ordinary and undifferentiated. It is not realistic to expect that a lackluster, commoditized business could generate any superior performance, let alone sustain it. The commoditization of an industry tends to erode everyone's profitability because it exacerbates the rivalry among competitors primarily by driving down prices for standardized products.

For superior financial performance to be sustainable, not only should the business aim at achieving a solid leadership position, but this position should be long-lasting, unassailable, and able to endure the inevitable changes that the environment will generate. This calls for flexible adaptation to new circumstances and the will and ability to transform the organization continuously. We should look forward, not backward. We should never be complacent. We should experiment and engage in a continuous learning process that propels us into uncharted territory. This will never happen if we are simply imitating or following in our competitors' footsteps. Using competitors as a benchmark leads to sameness, and sameness will never lead us to greatness.

The dangers of commoditization are real, and if you fall into it, the consequences are devastating. We believe that this is one of the greatest challenges companies face. The way to fight it is to abandon the mindset that accepts product standardization and industry convergence as an unavoidable reality. Instead, you must recognize that it is the customer who really matters, and that the customers are always different. It is a fatal mistake to commoditize them.

It is critical that you try to understand your customers' needs, to segment them so that you can recognize their differences, and to assess your competencies as a firm so that you can offer not just products, but also creative and unique solutions to each customer's pressing needs. Your own view of the enterprise must shift from that of an engine just developing, making, and distributing standardized goods or services to one possessing a bundle of competencies that can be packaged into a well-integrated portfolio of products and services that represent a unique value proposition to each customer.

This paradigm shift constitutes a big transformation that can produce a constructive, long-term relationship with the customer and culminate in *customer bonding*, a mutually beneficial engagement based upon unbreakable trust and transparency. Under this fundamentally different way of approaching the customer relationship, the essence of strategy becomes *not* to achieve sustainable competitive advantage with competitors as the benchmark – but to achieve customer bonding, with the customer as the driving force.

Managing in the Large and in the Small – The Extended Enterprise and the Individualized Customer

We come to what seems to be an inherent paradox: a desire to build an extended enterprise with individualized customers. In order to achieve this outcome, we need to simultaneously manage with the largest possible scope – to be able to offer up all of the capacities of all of the relevant players in our network – and to target each individual customer in the most granular way. This is only possible to a great extent due to the remarkable technological capabilities of the Internet. Let us be explicit.

Managing in the large means you cannot play the game alone. Regardless of how many resources you control, you will always need external support if you want to conduct your business intelligently. This calls for recognizing what we refer to as the *Extended Enterprise*, which includes you, your customers, your suppliers, and your complementors – meaning those organizations that provide products and services that complement and enhance your offers. Many great companies have understood this lesson well and have made it the cornerstone of their strategy. Think of Wal-Mart and Dell, two excellent companies that have adopted the concept of the extended enterprise as an extraordinary way of delivering remarkable value to their customers. Both of these companies have developed "virtual organizations" by linking themselves electronically to their customers and suppliers, obtaining a web of interactions that produces remarkable value. Wal-Mart knows, in real time, every transaction that takes place in every single one of its stores, communicating that information to all the relevant suppliers so that they know how to replenish their inventories optimally. Dell manufactures every computer according to customer specifications and delivers it by simultaneously executing the orders with all the relevant suppliers.

Managing in the small, on the other hand, means that, ideally, we should be treating each customer individually and providing a specific and singular solution to satisfy each customer need. Think of Amazon and iTunes. Whenever I log into their system, I am treated as a unique individual. The system knows my pattern of previous purchases and is able to recommend new purchases that are tailor-made to satisfy my demonstrated interests or needs.

Operating this way allows for customer bonding to become a reality, because you support the value proposition you offer to your customer based on the individualized knowledge that you acquire and through the support and assistance that you get from the full network of the extended enterprise.

This is a model that circumvents rivalry and competition as a basis for strategy and substitutes cooperation, close association, and customer intimacy instead.

The Selection of a Strategy and the Identification of the Required Competencies – A Preview of the Delta Model

One of the most distinctive aspects of the Delta Model is that it provides you with guidance on how to select the strategic positioning of your business and gives you the analytical tools to achieve it. This is a feature that is not available in any other business model, as far as we know.

How do you begin to develop a strategy based on a granular understanding of individual customer needs? As we have already asserted, the fundamental strategic objective is to obtain customer bonding – that is to attract, satisfy, and retain the customer. The Delta Model offers you three distinct options to reach that objective which can be applied, if you wish, one customer at a time. The three strategic options are presented in the triangle in Fig. 1.1.

In the **Best Product** option, the customer comes to you because of the superiority of your price offering – due to your low-cost infrastructure – or for some aspect related to the product functionality, brand, or appearance that differentiates itself from the competitive offers. In the **Total Customer Solutions** option, the customer is attracted because you are offering something beyond the product itself,

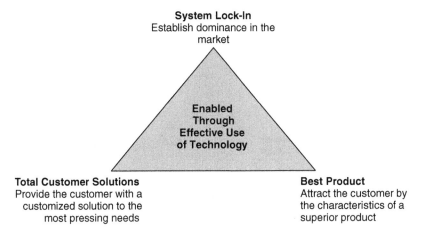

Fig. 1.1 The triangle – the three strategic options of the Delta Model

which implies transferring knowledge and services that address pressing needs the customer has. In the **System Lock-In** option, you have achieved such a strong dominance in the marketplace that the customer does not have options better than yours.

Figure 1.2 offers a highly summarized description of the characteristics of each of the three primary strategic options of the Delta Model and the necessary competencies that are required for their support. The resulting eight competencies that are part of the Delta Model framework are summarized in Fig. 1.3.

We will elaborate in later chapters the step-by-step process you must undertake in order to develop a customer bonding strategy tailored to your own organization. Our objective here is to introduce you to the idea that there are options other than the simple offering of a product – which is the dominant mindset of most executives – on which to base a successful business strategy. Moreover, the Delta Model framework assists you in examining the state of your existing competencies and – most importantly – in identifying the competencies you need to acquire to develop a truly winning strategy. We believe these two perspectives – strategic options and competencies – make the Delta Model an exceedingly useful device to guide your strategic thinking.

The Strategic Tasks of the Delta Model

The Delta Model, as we have argued in this introductory chapter, provides innovative new concepts and ideas that will make you see your business strategy from a fresh perspective, not anchored in the transitions of the past. It also provides you with a set of pragmatic tools to help you to carry on a rigorous, systematic, and

Best Product – The customer is attracted by the inherent characteristics of the product being offered. This is accomplished through a low cost – which allows offering the lowest price to the customer resulting from an efficient infrastructure – or by offering a differentiated product that the customer values and is willing to pay a premium for.

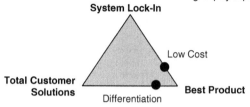

Total Customer Solutions – Customer bonding results from enhancing the capabilities of the customer by offering integrated solutions to address its critical needs. It is accomplished by a close proximity to the customer (Redefining the Customer Relationship), by transferring substantive capabilities and knowledge (Customer Integration), and by providing a full spectrum of products and services that satisfy most, if not all, of its needs (Horizontal Breadth).

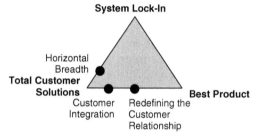

System Lock-In – The firm achieves a dominant position in the market that gives it uncontested leadership. This is accomplished through the development and ownership of the standards of the industry (Proprietary Standard), by becoming the interface between the customer and its suppliers (Dominant Exchange), or by becoming the sole source of the customer needs (Restricted Access).

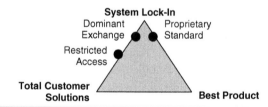

Fig. 1.2 The Delta Model – the three strategic options

thoughtful process of diagnosis and formulation of your own successful business strategy. Most of this book addresses that need.

After many years of working with numerous organizations around the world, we have learned that it is very important to keep the planning process as simple as possible, while retaining the ability to perform a careful, highly practical examination

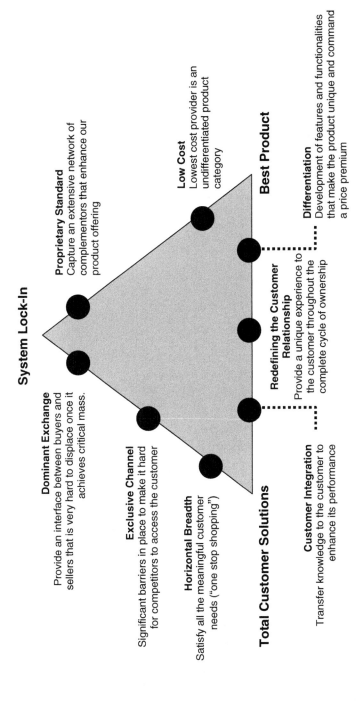

System Lock-In

Dominant Exchange
Provide an interface between buyers and sellers that is very hard to displace once it achieves critical mass.

Proprietary Standard
Capture an extensive network of complementors that enhance our product offering

Exclusive Channel
Significant barriers in place to make it hard for competitors to access the customer

Horizontal Breadth
Satisfy all the meaningful customer needs ("one stop shopping")

Low Cost
Lowest cost provider is an undifferentiated product category

Best Product

Differentiation
Development of features and functionalities that make the product unique and command a price premium

Redefining the Customer Relationship
Provide a unique experience to the customer throughout the complete cycle of ownership

Total Customer Solutions

Customer Integration
Transfer knowledge to the customer to enhance its performance

Fig. 1.3 Identifying the competencies of the business – the eight strategic positions as a guiding framework

of the complex environments and circumstances that surround your business. It is an enormously challenging and exciting task: to give purpose and direction to an organization and end up with an agenda that assures the proper implementation of a well-designed strategy. To that end, we have identified five broad tasks that will help you do this work, illustrated in Fig. 1.4. Throughout the book we will explain these tasks with considerable detail and provide real-life applications to illustrate how we have used them – and you can use them – in practice.

Fig. 1.4 The strategic tasks of the Delta Model

Task 1 Customer Segmentation and Customer Value Proposition (Chapter 3)

The first task we must undertake addresses the customer. We need to abandon our preconceptions and try to be as creative as possible in finding original ways to serve the customer. We begin by segmenting the customer base so that we can identify subsets of customers sharing similar needs, to which we will be providing distinct value propositions. We cannot overemphasize the importance of this task. It is the true foundation of a well laid out strategy. The Delta Model provides unique mechanisms to guide you through this process. The resulting customer value propositions should satisfy the following requirements:

- They must be unique – meaning that they truly differentiate us from what is ordinarily offered.
- They must be sustainable – meaning that their uniqueness cannot be easily imitated or substituted.
- They must provide a great deal of value to our customers and to us.
- They must create a significant amount of bonding among our customers and us.

Task 2 The Existing and Desired Competencies of the Firm (Chapter 4)

The previous task allows us to understand the demand side of our business in a creative way. This task forces us to deeply focus on the supply side, on our own capabilities. We perform it using another form of segmentation that is based on the eight strategic positions described briefly in Fig. 1.3. Every firm is a bundle of competencies. What are ours? These eight positions help us to assess our existing competencies and identify those that we must acquire in order to deliver the customer value propositions that we have identified in Task 1. The eight strategic competencies that are part of the Delta Model framework provide a powerful, concrete diagnosis of the capabilities we already possess, and the capabilities we need to develop to achieve a true position of leadership and excellence.

Task 3 The Mission of the Business (Chapter 5)

The previous two tasks – customer segmentation and customer value proposition; and existing and desired competencies – are the foundation of our overall diagnosis. What emerges is a clear understanding of where we are and what changes will be required to improve our existing circumstance. The true purpose of the mission statement is to capture and clearly articulate our intent. It is a critical task because it integrates the strategic tasks that we have conducted into a sole statement that defines the purpose of the organization and the challenges we face to move it in the desired direction. The mission is a fundamental vehicle to communicate our sense of direction, both inside and outside the organization.

Task 4 The Strategic Agenda (Chapter 6)

The strategic agenda attempts to identify and lay out in very pragmatic and concrete terms the specific tasks that we must undertake in order to serve our customers, define our new capabilities, and move the organization forward into the desired state of leadership. It should not only spell out the tasks but also identify who is accountable for their execution, as well as how to establish the necessary organization, information, and control mechanisms for its proper implementation.

Task 5 Monitoring the Strategy Execution (Chapter 7)

What happens after we have formulated what we hope is a winning strategy? The answer is obvious: we need to assure its proper implementation. In other words, we need to "manage by strategy" – so that strategy becomes the compass that directs the myriad tasks that are part of the routines of management.

Two important elements are required to assure proper implementation of the strategy, in addition to the unbounded attention that managers have to devote to its proper execution. The first is the development of an "**intelligent budget.**" The budget is crucial because it is what most organizations use as an implementation tool, and it commits a host of managers to delivering "the numbers" which, in turn, are part of the reward system. It is imperative to have a budget that is perfectly aligned with our strategic pursuits. To achieve that, the budget must pay equal attention to strategy and operations and effectively balance the short- and long-term implications of our actions. We will expand on the elusive concept of the intelligent budget in Chapter 7. We say elusive because we find that most organizations develop budgets that are exceedingly biased toward short-term results, a practice, and that would invalidate or obstruct our strategic commitments.

The second vehicle required to assure proper implementation is the use of the **Balanced Scorecard**, both at the business and individual customer tier. This allows us to continue to focus on how we deliver the differentiated value propositions for each individual customer group.

The Haxioms

The Delta Model challenges the conventional wisdom and the prevailing models of business strategy. As such, it is founded on a different set of principles, which jokingly I have come to call the "Haxioms." They constitute the basis for a philosophy of management, which might be useful for the reader to be aware of from the very beginning and are the underlying principles behind the Delta Model, gleaned from years of research and personal observation.

I pose these Haxioms in no particular order. Perhaps they will shed more light on the strategic philosophy, which I am so ardently championing.

1. **The center of strategy is the customer**
   This is the core of the Delta Model. It places the customer as the driving force of management, and if we accept this imperative, everything else follows. We need to understand the customer, and our challenge is how to provide our spectrum of customers the most creative, unique, and high value-added value proposition.
2. **You don't win by beating the competition; you win by achieving customer bonding**
   If the central focus of management is the customer, the essence of strategy is to achieve customer bonding. Bonding is realized when the relationships

characterizing our involvement with the customer are based on fairness and transparency, producing long-lasting, mutual benefits. Bonding goes beyond intimacy and proximity, it denotes trust and affection.

3. **Strategy is not war; it is love**

   By rejecting the notion that strategy is rivalry and its ultimate goal is to defeat your competitors, we open a much more constructive mindset. Instead of perceiving ourselves as in confrontation with our key constituencies, we should adopt the attitude of cooperation, understanding, and love. It sounds rather corny, but I really mean it. Imagine how much better the world would be if we all would assume this stance. I sincerely believe that this behavior constitutes a better and more effective way to manage. Caring about the customer with a high sense of integrity is the smartest way of doing business.

4. **A product-centric mentality is constraining; open your mindset to include the customers, the suppliers, and the complementors as your key constituencies**

   Don't play the game alone. The relevant entity is the *extended enterprise*. I don't care how many resources we might have access to. Given the complexities of global business, we will never be self-sufficient. We should accept that from the start and recognize how important it is to draw from all our natural partners to provide the elusive unique value proposition to our customers.

5. **Try to understand your customer deeply. Strategy is done one customer at a time**

   We have to focus our attention on the customer in a granular way, meaning that ideally we should consider each customer individually. We can accomplish this personally if the importance of the customer warrants it, or electronically if the personal contact is economically infeasible. The capabilities of the Internet are making possible something that was unimaginable in the past.

   Gone are the days that we define abstract business units, that we used to call the Strategic Business Units – or SBUs for short – as the focus of strategic analysis. This was a composite of products and markets aggregated in a form that obscured our capacity to provide tailor-made solutions to individual customers.

6. **Commodities only exist in the minds of the inept**

   The commoditization of a business results when we cannot claim any differentiation from what our competitors are offering. It is typically the consequence of paying excessive attention to the competition, which often leads to imitation and sameness. It is a prevailing situation in many businesses in the world. It is the most undesirable state to fall into because it deprives us of achieving any form of leadership, of gaining superior financial returns, of serving our customers uniquely, and of attracting top talent. The surprising fact is that commoditization should never happen if we are managing our business intelligently, simply because commodity businesses should not exist. A product can be a commodity – say, copper – but a business is not because every customer is different. Commodities occur when we commoditize the customer, which means that we do not try to understand deeply the customer's needs and just offer the same "me too" products to everyone. Take the case of copper. The way Siemens uses it for its power plants is quite different from the way Carrier uses it to make air-conditioning units, or the way General Motors uses it to build cars. If we do not understand this, we do not understand our business.

If we focus our attention granularly on the customer, commoditization can always be avoided. That is why I claim that "commodities only exist in the minds of the inept" – a strong statement to call our attention to an important issue.

7. **The foundations of strategy are two:**

   - **Customer Segmentation and Customer Value Proposition**
   - **The Firm as a Bundle of Competencies**
     We have to understand both the demand and the supply sides of the business.

     The customer represents the demand. Our first task is to segment the customer – so that we do not treat every customer in the same way – and to develop unique, sustainable, and high value-added propositions that create a great deal of bonding.

     The supply is represented by our firm's capabilities. The Delta Model provides a singular methodology to assess our existing and desired competencies according to our abilities to develop a full spectrum of strategic positions.

     The Delta Model gives us the conceptual understanding and the portfolio of tools that allow us to develop these two foundations of strategy.

8. **Reject the two truisms:**

   - "The customer is always right," and
   - "I know the customer needs and how to satisfy them."
     We are not selling standardized products; we are dealing with customer solutions.

     How could the customers be "right" if they do not have a clue as to what we can offer them; and how could we be right if we have not yet achieved a close relationship with the customers that allows us to understand their needs and what we can do together to develop a great value proposition?

     The identification and satisfaction of the customer solutions can only be done by working jointly with the customers.

9. **The strategic planning process is a dialog among the key executives of the firm – seeking consensus on the direction of the organization**
   The most important output of the strategic planning process is the process itself. My approach for a proper process is to engage all the key executives of the business in an open dialog, where ideas are candidly debated, that ultimately leads to consensus. What does consensus mean? I was once asked that question when I was helping Saturn – a company with one of the most participatory management styles that I have ever seen. My answer was – and still is – "Consensus is 70% agreement and 100% buy-in." This means that there is a time when you want to have every idea challenged through a constructive conflict, but then there is a time to come to a decision on where we want to go and how we are

going to get there. You cannot expect 100% agreement; this would probably lead to paralysis. Seventy percent is a sound and comfortable consensus, but with the understanding that everyone is now aligned with the final decisions.

If we have conducted the process effectively, there should be "sparks in the eyes" of the executives, meaning that we have reached a level of contagious enthusiasm that will assure that we have the energy and the commitment to implement the resulting strategic agenda.

10. **Metrics are essential; experimentation is crucial**

Metrics are essential to quantify the value we create for our customer and ourselves and to monitor the progress we make in the implementation of the proposed strategic agenda. The granularity requirement of the Delta Model demands that we develop a customer data bank, which contains information about the potential market available for each customer and the value created by our propositions.

Experimentation is crucial because the Delta Model often generates significant departure from existing practices. This means that we will be walking in untested territory – with the associated risks that are to be expected. Instead of implementing a full strategy under those conditions, it is wise to experiment first. We may want to conduct preliminary pilot programs, with select customers, to identify the best options to implement on a large scale.

These are the most significant principles that guide the Delta Model. Throughout the book you will learn about a variety of pragmatic tools to help you make these principles a reality in your organization.

Chapter 2
The Delta Model: Creating New Sources of Growth and Profitability in a Networked Economy

How to Achieve Customer Bonding: The Three Major Strategic Options in the Delta Model

Our fundamental premise is that the essence of strategy is to achieve customer bonding. At the core of bonding are the attraction, satisfaction, and retention of the customer. We have identified three very distinct strategic options for attaining this objective, as displayed in the triangle in Fig. 2.1. We have chosen the triangle to depict the different strategic options not simply because it is a visual icon that is easy to remember, but also because it represents the letter delta, which stands for transformation and change. The delta theme extends to the labeling of the business model in this book. We refer to the three strategic options for customer bonding as Best Product, Total Customer Solutions, and System Lock-In. Initially, we will introduce them as if they were completely different ways of positioning the business. Ultimately, you will see that a sophisticated strategy plays simultaneously in every corner of the triangle, depending on the way you choose to serve the heterogeneous diversity of your customers.

Best Product

Best Product positioning builds upon the classical form of competition. The customer is attracted by the inherent characteristics of the product itself – either through low cost, which provides a price advantage to the customer – or through differentiation, which introduces unique features that the customers value and for which they are willing to pay a premium. These are the two strategies proposed by Michael Porter many years ago. He claims that you have to select one or the other or you face the trap of being stuck in the middle (Fig. 2.2).

It is an inward-looking approach. Attention is centered on the product economics, the value chain, and the abilities to develop the capacities to deliver the best product. The major strategic driving forces are the development of an efficient supply chain, which guarantees a low-cost infrastructure; a proven internal capability for

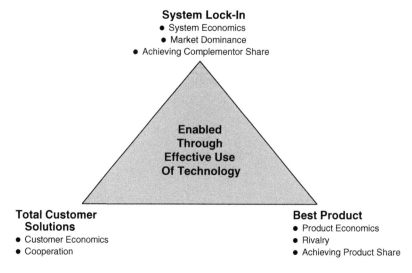

Fig. 2.1   The triangle: Opening the mindset to a new set of strategic options

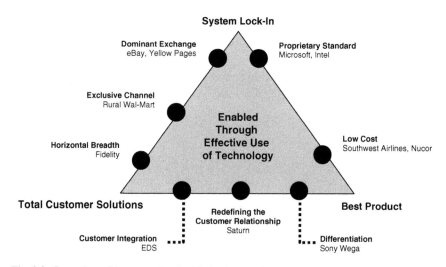

Fig. 2.2   Strategic positions associated with the three options

new product development, which assures the proper renewal of the existing product line; and the securing of distribution channels, which massively transfer the
products to the targeted market segments. The measure of success is product share,
which ultimately can fragment the business activities into a disconnected set of

product offerings. It develops a product-centric mentality guided by competitors as benchmarks. Strategy is defined as rivalry.

The products tend to be standardized and unbundled. The customer is generic, massive, and faceless and served through mass distribution channels, which contributes to the commoditization of the business. The central focus of attention is the competitor, which we are trying to equal or surpass. The drivers are the product economics and the internal supply chain, which provide the engine for efficient production. Innovation is centered on the internal product development process. In the best case, the firm has a common product platform that supports the rapid development of a stream of products enabling "first to market" positions and the establishment of the so-called dominant design.

The highest limitation of this approach is that it generates the minimum amount of customer bonding, hence making the incumbent firms most vulnerable to new entrants. Its obsessive concern with competitors often leads to imitation and price war, resulting in rivalry and convergence – the worst of all deals. In spite of the inherent limitations of this strategic position, it is by far the most widely adopted and the default position for those business firms that do not deliberately consider other strategic options.

Strategic Positions of the Best Product Option

Low Cost

The Low Cost position is based on attaining such an efficient cost infrastructure that it allows offering the most attractive price in the market. Everything being equal, the customer will choose the offer with the lowest price. The problem with this option is that it doesn't have any space. Obviously, there can be only one lowest cost producer in the industry. Therefore, this is a highly contested position that increases pressures for reduced margin. This is not to say that there are not great companies in this position, such as Southwest in the airline industry and Nucor in the steel industry. These exceptions, however, seem to justify the rule.

Differentiation

Differentiation, the other alternative, has also huge inherent limitations. It is an attempt to incorporate into the product some features or functionalities that make it different from the rest of the competitors' offerings and that the customer values enough to pay a premium for the resulting differentiated product. The problem becomes that as soon as the innovative product reaches the market, the competitors will recognize it and get ready to imitate it. Therefore, whatever advantages you generate will be short-lived, and you will be constantly chasing your tail.

For example, Sony Wega Television was a differentiated company (see Fig. 2.2) that combined distinctive features, initially unmatched by competitive products, by merging the technical prowess of Japanese Sony with the singular design of the

German Wega. This created the first flat television in the market, but as everybody knows, now every TV producer has a flat TV offering. Enough said for the long-term sustainability of differentiation.

Since it is only the product that attracts the customer, when a competitor emerges with a new and better product, which will no doubt be the case eventually, the customer should and will abandon you. To make things worse, many product-driven businesses are organized around products and reward their executives accordingly. This means that there will be strong internal barriers for a business to transform itself into a more customer-oriented entity.

In spite of the inherent limitations of this strategic option, it is by far the most widely adopted and it constitutes the default position for those business firms that do not deliberately consider other options.

Best Product: A Limited Option

Figure 2.3 provides brief definitions of Low Cost and Differentiation, the two strategic positions of the Best Product option, and gives a brief comment on the nature of the inherent limitations of those positions.

Strategic Position	Definition	Comments
Low Cost	Focus on being the lowest cost provider in an undifferentiated product category.	Since there is only one lowest cost producer, this strategy leaves very little space as a competitive position. It also tends to standardize the product offering, commoditize the customer, and intensify rivalry.
Differentiation	Focus on the development of features and functionalities that make the product unique and allow demanding a price premium from the customer.	As soon as the differentiated product emerges, competitors tend to imitate it. A competitive advantage is therefore non-sustainable.

Fig. 2.3 Strategic positions of the Best Product option

Business firms can certainly excel following a Best Product strategy. But it is a limited option. Although excellent companies can successfully overcome the challenges of playing in this arena, gains are inherently short-lived. We believe our aforementioned warnings are well founded and should not be ignored.

Towards a Stronger Bonding with the Customer

Having an efficient cost infrastructure and the ability to develop, make, and deliver a stream of innovative products – which are at the heart of the Best Product option – is central for a firm to achieve a significant competitive standing under any circumstance. In fact, these attributes are a solid foundation required from any company that aspires to succeed in the business world.

But customer bonding does not stop here. It starts here. Without abandoning the attributes based on a Best Product option, you need to embark on a transformation that will take you closer to the customer. If you attract, satisfy, and retain the customer based only on the product characteristics, your attention tends to stay focused on the product, not the potential future gain and long-term relationships that a customer bonding brings.

It is hard for us to imagine that a company will not benefit from understanding customers more deeply and seeking a closer relationship with them. Instead of providing an isolated product, a company can gain the mind and heart of their customers by presenting them an integrated solution with a unique value proposition composed of a coherent set of products and services exactly honed to answer their needs. This requires that you move along the triangle from the Best Product to the Total Customer Solution strategic option.

Total Customer Solution

Under Total Customer Solution, the focus of attention switches from the product to the customer. It represents a 180° change from the Best Product strategic option. The central concern is no longer product economics but customer economics, meaning that we strive to understand the drivers of customers' profitability and to develop new ways to help them improve their productivity and achievements. The relevant measure of performance is no longer product market share, but customer market share or share of wallet.

When addressing the customer, we reach beyond our own value chain toward the customer's value chain, expecting to find new ways to use our firm's competencies in order to enhance their performance. We also go further, pulling together the value chains of suppliers and complementors and acting as an Extended Enterprise. This is in fact the relevant domain to develop the best solutions for the customer.

The starting point in this strategic option is the proper segmentation of the customer base. We require a profound and intimate knowledge of the client's business and how it relates to our own business. Not all customers are alike nor do they have the same relative importance to our firm. Customers have different needs and priorities.

We have to discover the best way to leverage our resources and capabilities to help them. They also have to know us, learn from our history and background, and begin to respect and trust us to be able to advance into a mutually beneficial relationship. From the arms-length relationship of the Best Product strategy, we go all the way to a quite significant bonding with the customer.

The ultimate output of this strategy is an individual value proposition tailor-made for each customer and aimed at enhancing the customer's cost, revenue, or profit position. The resulting value added could be extremely high and the degree of bonding considerable.

When focusing on customers instead of the product, our relationship with them undergoes a profound transformation. If the Best Product strategic option prevails, we observe a *transaction* that typically results in a salesperson with a catalog of standardized products interacting with the purchasing person in the customer firm. The exchange is limited: I give you a product, and you give me money, and thank you very much.

If, on the contrary, the Total Customer Solutions strategy prevails, we aim at establishing a mutually beneficial *relationship*, an association that will lead to a long-term involvement that is hard to break; because it is unique, it has a high degree of value added, and both parties have made significant investments to support it. If things go right, this relationship ends up in a customer lock-in, the highest degree of bonding that can be attained. Total customer share is not only a relevant measure of performance for the firm, but a most telling indication of customer's satisfaction, whose needs we are attempting to satisfy in as comprehensive a way as possible.

A Total Customer Solution calls for three types of actions that have to be addressed simultaneously: Redefining the Customer Experience, Customer Integration, and Horizontal Breadth (Fig. 2.2).

Redefining the Customer Experience

This strategic position calls for captivating the customer from the point of acquisition through to the complete life cycle of ownership of the product. We have an opportunity to distinguish ourselves by departing from competitors' less-appreciated behaviors, thus altering the relationship with our customers in a way that embraces their full experience and fulfills their most cherished expectations.

This step is a true test for the creativity and uniqueness of the relationship we would like to create with the customer. In fact, the most successful strategy if we could ever achieve it, or if we could ever adopt it, is to produce such a novel value proposition that it breaks us away from the rest of the field. "Study your competitors not to imitate them."

When dealing with high-priority customers, we should abandon the practice of approaching them through the sales force. At the highest priority level, we want our CEO to interact with the CEO of the customer organization. In many cases, we need to bring a cross-functional team of executives, with backgrounds in finance, technology, manufacturing, and the like, to interact with their similar counterparts in the customer organization. The resulting dialog produces the kind of interaction that leads to customization and long-term bonding.

In other cases, it is simply the originality of the offer that might count. I was privileged to participate in defining the original strategy for Saturn. This was the first entry of an American-manufactured car into the small car segment. It is a crucial segment, because it usually involves the first car purchase decision an individual makes in his or her life. If you are young and just beginning to work, typically you cannot afford anything but a small car. If there is no American option offered in the market, American companies are liable to lose a customer for the rest of his or her life. The entry offers from foreign competitors such as the Toyota Corolla or the Honda Civic are extremely good. These two companies can take you from the first purchase to the end of your life cycle by offering you different models that match your needs and purchasing capabilities, as you grow older.

It is easy to see why GM decided to enter this car segment. What Saturn did was to break the mold, going as far from Detroit as possible, installing the plant in Spring Hill, Tennessee. It was hard, if not impossible, for Saturn to produce a better car than Toyota Corolla or Honda Civic. What it did instead was to produce as good a car as those two, but to bring in an extremely novel, constructive, and pleasant experience in the purchasing and owning of a car in America. This was exemplified by its commitment "Satisfaction guaranteed or your money back, no question asked." Saturn developed a kind of cult following among its car owners, because it demonstrated that it would deeply care. In this case, the product was not the one that makes the difference. The originality of the offer was the important factor.

Customer Integration

This is the second action we should take to consolidate a Total Customer Solution option. At one extreme, we find complete outsourcing, which implies an extensive substitution or leverage of the activities currently performed by the customer. This is the case of EDS and other IT firms when they fully run the information systems for a customer.

But we also find more subtle forms of integration when we establish a complex web of connections with the customer, thus enhancing their ability to do business with us, and to use our products. A telling example is the integration achieved by Dell and its corporate customers.

We should not limit the view of our company to a mere engine able to develop, manufacture, and deliver products. We should convey to our customers that we could help them in many different ways, because we have the capabilities and experience to do so. We should envision ourselves as a bundle of competencies and accumulated knowledge that can be transferred effectively to the customer to achieve its objectives.

For that we need a careful segmentation and granular knowledge of the customer to effectively understand its needs. An opportunity arises when the customer is unable to satisfy its requirements with its internal capabilities, and we have the qualifications to do so. The many channels of integration with our customers are a source of opportunities to respond effectively to the knowledge transfer challenge and to enhance our standing with them.

Horizontal Breadth

This is the third and final action that we should consider in seeking a Total Customer Solution option. We should make every effort to provide a complete set of products and services to our customers, in order to fulfill their entire set of needs. Bonding with the customers is the result of having a single point of contact, a single invoice, learning from their requirements, and most importantly, from the potential to customize our offer to their specific usages. Fidelity, in the financial services industry, is a company that thrives on doing this.

Horizontal Breadth goes beyond pure bundling, which is simply putting together a bunch of products that often makes the customer demand price discounts because only more volume is added without additional benefits. Horizontal Breadth is much more than simply volume discounts. It is integrating and customizing a related set of products and services to assist the customer better than would be done if each component were to be purchased and used separately. It culminates in the proverbial "one-stop shopping."

And if we alone don't have all the capabilities, we reach toward complementors. It may well happen that the range of the customer needs is of such a magnitude that it surpasses the offer we can provide. If this is the case, we simply extend ourselves with the help of external parties that enhance and enrich what we can do alone. Our capabilities reside not only internally in the firm, but also in the entire web of associated firms. The network of companies is a key strategic asset in bonding with the customer. Similar types of bonding should be developed with suppliers and complementors that are key members of our Extended Enterprise.

Toward a Customer Lock-In

Figure 2.4 provides brief definitions of Redefining the Customer Experience, Customer Integration, and Horizontal Breadth, the three strategic positions of the Total Customer Solutions option, and gives a brief comment on the nature of the inherent limitations of those positions.

We can see that there is much value to be created, over and beyond the Best Product option, when adopting a Total Customer Solution approach. A higher level of knowledge transfer and a richer relationship with the customer will invariably result in deeper bonding and higher profitability. This extra value should be documented and made transparently clear to all parties involved to allow for a fair appropriation of the economic gains generated.

In an ideal case, the joint benefits are high and sustainable. We gain because we establish with the customer a solid and enduring relationship. The customers also gain because they get a service they sorely need and greatly benefit from them. They are not thinking of deserting us or looking for alternative providers. In this way we achieve an individual customer lock-in and gain a profitable customer base that has unbreakable relationships with us. And it is a long-lasting relationship, because mutual learning and joint investments support it: A clear "win–win" situation.

But this ideal state is not always attainable. Not every customer can be dealt with this way. Often, customers that are treated at arm's length coexist with customers that are vastly served and deeply integrated with our company. The first group will limit their relationship with us to a simple transaction involving a product offering,

Strategic Position	Definition	Comments
Redefining the Customer Experience	The focus is placed on considering the full experience of the customer from the point of acquisition through to the complete lifecycle of ownership of the product.	This positioning is based upon an intimate knowledge of the customer, leading towards effective customer segmentation and a differentiated customer value proposition for each tier.
Customer Integration	This strategy seeks to provide full support to customers' activities by transferring knowledge to improve their performance. It involves a high degree of outsourcing, which develops a complex web of connections with customers that enhance their ability to do business and to use our product.	The firm is regarded as a bundle of competencies that will be brought to the customer to boost the customer economics.
Horizontal Breadth	The customer is provided with a customized solution involving a complete set of products and services: "One-stop shopping for a unique solution."	We are seeking a dominant position in "Share of the wallet of the customer."

Fig. 2.4 Strategic positions of the Total Customer Solution option

while the second will be the recipients of a deep knowledge transfer, becoming truly a part of the Total Customer Solutions option.

Paradoxically, large companies which are self-sufficient, and therefore don't need us except for access to our products, are going to be targeted as Best Products, while smaller, less self-sustained companies are candidates for a Total Customer Solutions strategic option.

There is, therefore, not only the coexistence of a variety of customers, but also the requirement for us to develop distinct sets of capabilities to respond to very different demands from customers.

System Lock-In

We used to think of the scope of strategy in rather narrow terms, most frequently using a definition of industry to frame the strategic thinking of the business. We expanded that in the previous section when indicating that the Extended Enterprise – the firm, the customers, the suppliers, and complementors – was a much more appropriate support mechanism for attracting and providing products and services to the customer. With System Lock-In, the strategic option with the widest scope, the full economic system gravitating around the firm goes beyond the Extended Enterprise. It includes the entire web of companies that are part of the firm's network.

To illustrate this distinction between Extended Enterprise and the entire system of companies, look again at the cases of Dell and Microsoft. Dell's strategic strength stems from an extraordinary close linkage between their suppliers and customers.

Dell is proud of what they refer to as a "virtual organization." But, there is nothing virtual about those relationships. Dell manages, and to a great degree controls, all of its connections. They are the force that makes Dell a most effective company, a true Dell Extended Enterprise.

A very different situation is present in the case of Microsoft, which is the epitome of a System Lock-In. It has over 90% market share in its industry, because to a great extent it commands 80% market share among complementors. They are not in any way managed by Microsoft, but they "have chosen" to work for it. And Microsoft reaps huge benefits from that decision, because consumers want to buy the computer with the largest number of applications, and those who write software applications or produce hardware support want to do it for the system with the largest installed base. We are witnessing the so-called network effects. It is not simply an Extended Enterprise. Nobody really manages the huge interactions that are taking place. They are simply dictated by the fact that Microsoft has achieved a System Lock-In.

There are three ways to get System Lock-In as illustrated in Fig. 2.2: Proprietary Standards, Dominant Exchange, and Restricted Access. Regardless of the option used, the result is always the same: market dominance. In any of these cases, the company has de facto monopolistic power which is characterized by a total market share of 70–75%.

Three Ways to Get System Lock-In

Proprietary Standards

Among the strategic positions you can strive for, Proprietary Standards is the epitome of the ultimate profit model. It brings the highest margins, the greatest market share, and the most enduring sustainability. Microsoft and Intel are the poster children for this position. In combination, they have what is commonly referred to as the Wintel standard. Customers are compelled to buy the Microsoft Windows operating system and the Intel microprocessor because they have the widest selection of available software applications. Over 100,000 applications are designed to work with the Wintel standard, whereas Apple's Macintosh Operating System has perhaps one quarter that number. If you want to use the latest or most esoteric software, you had better have Windows on your computer. Correspondingly, if you are a software company that wants to reach the most customers, you had better write your application to work first (or only) with Windows, because it is the operating system on the most computers. This creates a powerful positive self-reinforcing feedback loop – consumers choose Windows to gain access to the most applications, applications providers choose Windows to reach the most consumers. Once Wintel achieved a slight edge, it quickly became the overwhelming choice.

To achieve Proprietary Standard position, we certainly need as a first step to position our approach to the business as the natural choice and the crucial interface between all key participants in the overall system. Integrating disparate pieces in an open system requires adherence to a widely recognized standard. Our solution should become the natural selection to do so. This is by no means an easy task. But even this already difficult first step must be followed by an even harder second step if we want to reap the benefits of a Proprietary Standard. We need to achieve the full ownership of the standard to appropriate the major share of value created by its adoption. Not all standards are proprietary. Most, in fact, are non-proprietary and have no owner with the ability to appropriate system profits.

When the video recording industry emerged in the 1970s, Sony was first with the introduction of Betamax, followed by JVC, which introduced a competitive protocol, VHS. The battle had all the signs of competing standards. The companies couldn't do anything else. The complementors could. Their actions and decisions made the difference. JVC chose a strategy emphasizing alliances first in Japan, then in Europe, then finally in the United States – and concentrating on the video rental market. Sony chose to go it alone with an emphasis on the home recording market. Despite having a superior product and a first-to-market advantage, Sony lost the battle. But, it was a Pyrrhic victory for JVC. The standard they designed and fought for was not one JVC could appropriate. VHS is a non-proprietary standard that is used by all manufacturers today, including Sony, and it gives no special advantage to JVC.

Dominant Exchange

A business positioned as a Dominant Exchange provides an interface between buyers and sellers, or between parties that wish to exchange information or goods. Once this sort of business achieves a critical mass, it is very hard to displace.

This is the case of many companies. The most stellar case in the Internet economy is eBay. Sellers want to go to the site with the most buyers, and buyers want to go to the site with the most sellers. The Yellow Pages is also a prominent example. They are a venerable old institution that makes money the old fashion way – they print it, in a manner of speaking. In fact, they print books filled with advertisements paid for by local businesses and distribute them free to households. And for this public service they earn roughly a 50% margin on sales! After the deregulation of the telephone business in 1984, hoards of new competitors crowded the field aiming to show the regulation-bound, lethargic telcos a thing or two. In one case, the entire sales force of the incumbent Yellow Pages switched to a new competitor. This occurred because the Bell Operating Company had outsourced the sales function to another company, along with most other functions including the creative, printing, and distribution work. This company enviously eyed the margins of the Yellow Pages and thought they could easily replicate the product. Even if the margins fell in half, it would be a great business. So they hijacked the entire sales force. A vicious competition ensued. The analysts predicted a rapid loss of market share and declining margins. After the dust settled, the regional Bell Operating Companies held 85% of the market and retained their margins. Why? Because of System Lock-In.

In this case, local businesses want to advertise in the Yellow Pages book that gets used by the most consumers. Consumers, on the other hand, want to read the book with the most advertisements. As shown in Fig. 2.5, this constitutes a virtual

The Source of Profits for the *Yellow Pages*

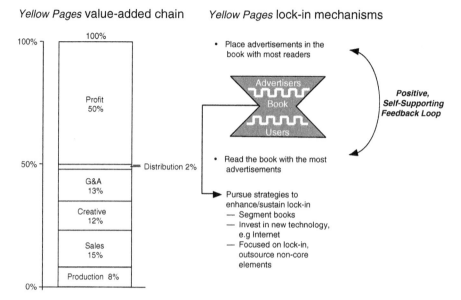

Fig. 2.5 The Yellow Pages have achieved unrivaled profitability by establishing a positive feedback loop between consumers and advertisers

feedback loop that is almost impossible for a competitor to break, whether with lower prices or with better features. When new companies entered the market, they could distribute books to every household, but they could not guarantee usage. Even with steep 50–70% discounts offered by new entrants, businesses could not afford to discontinue their advertisements in the incumbent book with proven usage. Despite the enhancements of color maps and coupons, the consumers found the new books with fewer and smaller advertisements to have more size than utility and threw them out. The virtual circle could not be broken, and the existing books sustained their market position.

Restricted Access

In the case of Restricted Access, the competitors are deprived of access to the customer because the channel has limited capacity to handle multiple vendors.

This is the situation of the Walls ice cream cabinets that Unilever has infiltrated throughout Europe, India, and the Middle East. Most small shops can store only one ice cream cabinet, and only a single company with high shop density can achieve economies of scale to deliver the product with the required frequency.

To achieve Restricted Access, we need to start with a full analysis of the overall delivery system to identify the most constrained points and bottlenecks and to position the business to dominate these points. If we accomplish this, we have a winning formula.

The meteoric rise of Wal-Mart from a small discount store to the most powerful retailer on earth is usually credited to the lock-out of competitors in the small cities and towns that were its cradle. Wal-Mart opened stores that would satisfy all the retailing needs of a rural area within a 15- to 20-mile radius. Also, it had to build a complete logistic system to satisfy the needs of its rising stores. Sam Walton had to overcome the bottleneck in distribution to rural communities and fill it so completely with a large-scale, low-cost channel that existing competitors could not afford to compete. As an added bonus, potential new entrants were preempted. Wal-Mart created a de facto monopoly for each rural location through Restricted Access.

System Lock-In: A Highly Desirable Strategic Option

Figure 2.6 provides brief definitions of Proprietary Standards, Dominant Exchange, and Restricted Access, the three strategic positions of the System Lock-In option, and gives a brief comment on the nature of the inherent limitations of those positions.

Strategic Position	Definition	Comments
Proprietary Standard	The customer is drawn to your product because of the extensive network of third party complementors that are designed to work with your product.	This option isn't available in most industries. If it can be achieved the rewards are enormous.
Dominant Exchange	With this strategy the company provides an interface between buyers and sellers that is very hard to displace once it achieves critical mass.	This is the most accessible of all of the systems lock-in options. The first mover advantage is critical.
Restricted Access	Significant barriers are in place that makes it difficult for competitors to even compete for the acquisition of customers.	This is a difficult position to achieve and to sustain. Regulatory practices tend to be deployed to prevent it, has to be accomplished one customer at a time.

Fig. 2.6 Strategic positions of the System Lock-In option

System Lock-In is the most desirable strategic option. But often it is not available as a feasible way of developing a strategy: (1) Not very many industries allow for standards to be developed, and if they are, for those to be appropriated by a single player; (2) few industries permit the consolidation of a single Dominant Exchange in the hands of one player; and (3) Restricted Access is even more carefully guarded, because its consolidation raises regulatory concerns.

This does not mean that System Lock-In is an irrelevant option for the majority of businesses. It may well be in the large, but not in the small. We should look not at the system as a whole, but at either individual customers or groups of them forming a segment as the focus of the lock-in. We benefit by thinking of System Lock-In simply as a series of barriers: Barriers for the customer to exit from you, and barriers for your competitors to gain entry to your customer. Raising those barriers sometimes is quite feasible, particularly when they are based in unique and sustainable value propositions that provide mutual benefits so strong that is unthinkable the bonding will be broken by either party.

System Lock-In Carries an Ethical Responsibility

It should be noted that System Lock-In confers to those who achieve it a de facto monopoly or something very close to it. It is a most powerful strategic position. In the developed world, monopolies do not have a good image and are looked at with suspicion. The expectation is that they will abuse the power they have, thus affecting the consumer adversely. Today, we have in place laws and regulations designed to curtail significantly their operations, in order to avoid the consolidation in a single company of excessive market power.

Interestingly, a System Lock-In is not the subject of concerns from consumers or the general public. There are social benefits that are reaped by them all. For example, are we better off or worse off by having a single standard in the PC system? We could certainly argue that it is a good thing to be able to communicate with one another without being constrained by the brand of equipment we are using. And although Microsoft and Intel have been obtaining generous profits, we cannot assert that they have been gauging prices to affect the consumer adversely. Similar positive assessments can be made for eBay and Yellow Pages. Even Wal-Mart, a company that has received some critical attention as of late, has been attributed a significant role in the containment of inflation that prevailed in the United States during a long period of time, as a result of its push for "Everyday Low Prices."

Certainly one wonders that if customers are not affected adversely, then who complains? The answer is obvious: Competitors do. It is extremely tough to face a company holding a System Lock-In.

But it is not only competitors. Even those who benefit from the situation may feel the discomfort associated with losing the ability to choose freely among alternative options. Customers, suppliers, and complementors resist and dislike being locked-in, even under a reasonable benefactor. This places on companies holding a System Lock-In a most serious obligation: To dispense that power in a way that is ethical and caring, eliminating even the slightest claim of abusive behavior. And this is for their own good. We know that, in the long run, the best way of conducting the business is by adhering to the higher standards of ethical behavior. Failing that, sooner or later, we will pay the price.

The Various Dimensions of the Triangle: A Summary

Figure 2.7 presents a profile of the three strategic options of the triangle. Many companies implicitly follow the practices of the Best Product option. In fact, these actions are often praised as "Best Practices" that should be applied by all

Descriptive Dimensions	Best Product	Total Customer Solutions	System Lock-In
Strategic Focus	Product The business, its industry and its competitors	The Extended Enterprise The firm, its customers, its suppliers, and complementors	The Network of Firms The interconnected web of companies that are part of the network
Driving Force	Competitors	Customers	Complementors
The Customer Value Proposition	Product focus Product economics	Customer focus Customer economics	System focus System economics
Product Offerings	Standardized products	Customized bundle of products and services	Portfolio of products and services extended by complementors
Relevant Supply Chain	Internal supply chain	Integrated supply chain: The firm, the suppliers, the customers, and complementors	System supply chain: The interlocking network of companies
Relevant Channels	Generic channels of mass distribution	Targeted direct channel	Massive direct channel
Impact on Brands	Product orientation Brand explosion	Brands harmonized around the customer Coherent portfolio of brands centered on the customer	Brands harmonized around the System Coherent portfolio of brands centered on the system
Innovation Focus	Internal product development	Joint product innovation with customer	Open architecture, complementors as key innovators
IT Role	Internal support e.g., SAP	Customer, supplier, and complementor support; e.g. e-business and e-commerce	Total network support e.g., e-system
Degree of Customer Bonding	Very small Depends exclusively on the product characteristics	Potentially high Reinforced by customization and mutual learning	Potentially the highest Reinforced by competitor lock-out and complementor lock-in

Fig. 2.7 Profiling the three strategic options of the triangle

companies. These include Total Quality Management, Business Re-engineering, Time-Based Competition, and Benchmarking. Best Practices are a by-product of a product-centric mentality.

We are not suggesting that a Best Product strategy cannot be the most appropriate one. In fact, there are excellent companies that are truly extraordinary in every conceivable dimension of performance which are in that vertex of the Triangle. What we want to warn against is the passive adoption of this strategy without considering other alternatives.

The danger of "functional silos" is well known. The fact of the matter is that functions rarely act as silos. By their very nature, they are obliged to exercise a high degree of synergy in an organization. If, in a functionally structured company, you are in charge of R&D, you are supposed to care for all of the innovation issues across all the products in your company, and it is hard to do otherwise-likewise if you are in charge of finance, human resources, manufacturing, and so forth. Product-centric business units are the prevalent silos in today's organizations. These often represent parochial territories that prevent a firm from intelligently using all of its capabilities to creatively serve the customer as effectively as it could.

If you look at Fig. 2.7 under the "Best Product" column, you can immediately visualize the narrow cascade of responses that are associated with this option. The strategic focus is the single product; the driving force is the competitors; the customer value proposition is dictated by the internal product economics; the product offering is standardized; the relevant supply chain is internal; the channels are generic and mass-driven; the product orientation leads to an explosion of disconnected brands; the innovation process is self-centered; the IT role, which is so critical for management today, deals with internal information. As a result, this brings only a feeble degree of customer bonding and a rather conventional view of the business, which might limit creativity. It is a fundamentally inwardly oriented strategy, with its outside view centered on competitors. With this perspective in mind, you can see how this is totally divorced from a network-based economy.

Contrast the Best Product option with the Total Customer Solutions option. You can envision the significant enrichment in scope and content that takes place. The strategic scope now looks across the Extended Enterprise, not just a single product or business; the driving force is the customer, not the competitors; the customer value proposition is dictated by the customer's economics, not just the product's internal economics; this value proposition is customized, rather than standardized; the relevant supply chain includes the customer, as well as the suppliers and complementors; the channels are targeted and direct, not wholesaled through mass channels; the customer solution orientation leads to a harmonization of brands; the innovation process emphasizes joint development with the customer, not just the typical stand-alone R&D center; the role of IT is to use the broadly available Internet infrastructure to inextricably link the customer to the firm, rather than to use proprietary internally oriented software. In the end, these actions create strong bonds with existing customers and generate assets and skills for the customer and the firm that are unique to that relationship. The firm benefits from the innovation by the customer as well as from their efforts. This is an outwardly oriented strategy, centered on the customer. In contrast with the Best Product option, this position is enabled by, if not dependent on, the network-based economy.

When we adopt the System Lock-In strategic option, we have to span even further. The strategic scope now covers the entire system, including the full web of firms that accompany, augment, and enhance our product, even though they might not be in the same "product" industry; the relevant benchmarks necessarily targets the complementors; the customer value proposition is focused on the system, not just what the product does on its own; the product offering entails the portfolio of applications extended by complementors; the relevant supply chain includes the overall system of companies; the channels to customers and complementors are massive, direct and indirect, because our share will dominate the system; the brand is harmonized around the system, a la "Intel inside" or "Microsoft compatibility"; the innovation process harnesses the creative juices of a multitude of complementors; the role of IT is to support the integration, efficiency, and compatibility of the complementors, and the entire system benefits from a common network interface. In the end, the system is bonded to the product. It attracts new customers to the product as well as adheres to existing customers. This strategy is centered on the system, particularly the complementors.

Chapter 3
Customer Segmentation and Customer Value Proposition: The First Critical Task of Strategy

Behind the Customer Segmentation Process

The Delta Model regards customer segmentation as the starting point for a creative strategy. If we are in a situation where we feel we need to consider a significant change in our strategy, this is our chance to rethink what we are doing and to redirect the organization toward a more constructive future. It is in here where our innovative capabilities are going to be tested. The final output of this process will clearly indicate whether we are going to depart from the inertia and momentum carried over from our past activities and will in fact determine a novel way of reconstructing the business.

All of us have been challenged to think "outside of the box," to break the mold of the conventional way of doing business. In the Delta Model, proper customer segmentation and the development of a rich value proposition for each resulting customer is the way to achieve that goal.

The Delta Model segmentation process groups selected customers that share some common attributes, leading toward distinct ways of serving them. This is actually the key. We want to segment customers to identify the best value proposition for each one of them. We cannot and should not treat every customer equally, because they are different. If we do not recognize this, we are making the fatal mistake of commoditizing customers, which ultimately leads toward the commoditization of the business. We have said, "Commodities only exist in the minds of the inept." This is basically true because there is no such thing as a commodity customer, which implies that there is no such a thing as a commodity business.

However, in most cases, we cannot deal from the outset with every customer as if it were a unique, singular entity. We need to find a comfortable middle ground. This is accomplished by a process of segmentation that identifies differences among the whole customer base but seeks some similarities in subgroups of customers that share similar requirements. We call these entities customer tiers. The art and science of customer segmentation – which is much more art than science – is to find proper criteria that will allow us to perform the segmentation in the most appropriate way. At the end of the process we arrive at a comfortable, manageable number of distinct tiers that will be subject to the definition of coherent value propositions.

A.C. Hax, *The Delta Model*, DOI 10.1007/978-1-4419-1480-4_3,
© Springer Science+Business Media, LLC 2010

Most of this chapter is devoted to understanding how this critical task is performed and to provide real-life examples that will make the process easy to grasp. But before doing that, let us first consider how to define the customer itself.

Who Is the Customer?

This is a very central question. The most obvious answer is that the customer is the one who pays. The relevance of this answer is evident, since it identifies who is directly responsible for generating our economic benefits. Therefore, we have to include the buyer as a critical element of our customer base. However, often we shouldn't stop there, because the customers of our customer, is either as important as, or even more important than, the buyer. We need to relate to that base for two reasons. First, we would like to help the customers to do a better job with their customers. Second, final consumers could be the most critical element in the economic chain. If they stop buying, everything stops. Think about the auto industry. There are two critical types of customers: dealers and consumers. We will see some examples of how to segment these two groups later in this chapter.

Moreover, if we regard the Extended Enterprise as the most relevant entity, we might expand the definition of the customer to include all of the remaining constituencies, meaning particularly suppliers and complementors. In the broadest sense, the relevant customer is everybody who should be the focus of a differentiated value proposition, because that is the foundation of a well-articulated strategy. Having said that, in most of what we write, the customer will be identified as either the buyer, or the consumer, or both.

Why Are Customers Different?

This is also a very critical question, because it will define the segmentation criteria that will be used in our analysis and that will lead to the development of the value proposition.

The conventional way of segmenting the customer is using demographic characteristics, such as age, levels of income, geographical locations, and the like. Another conventional way is to group them according to some generic business characteristics, such as size, vertical markets, levels of profitability, and others. We have found that, with very few exceptions, these criteria are not the most appropriate to characterize the differences across customers. They are useful in segmenting the "markets" but not the "customers," which is quite a different task. Remember that each resulting customer segment will be the subject of a distinct value proposition. Suppose that you choose to segment the customers by the size of the enterprise, say large, medium, and small, and even worse, either explicitly or implicitly assign priorities accordingly, meaning that large customers are better than medium-sized, and those in turn are better than small. Two fallacies result from this. One is that we will be treating all large customers the same. From a strategic point of view, that seldom makes sense. We are indiscriminately putting together customers that could have very different needs for support. Second, the priorities might be totally wrong. In fact, it is often the case that large customers are the least desirable ones, because they are totally self-sufficient and, therefore, they tend to commoditize us. On the contrary, medium and small companies can offer us great opportunities for the development of exciting value propositions based on the Total Customer Solution option. We address this point again in more detail in the remainder of this chapter.

The Generic Dimensions of Segmentation

We wish we could convey a neat theory about how to conduct the customer segmentation process in a way that would formulaically produce the optimal groupings every time. Unfortunately, we neither have the insights to do so, nor do we think it is feasible. As we have been stressing all along, each customer is essentially unique. Its proper definition is dependent upon the specific circumstances of its individual needs. Therefore, we do not think it is possible to offer a mechanistic way to arrive to the right answer.

This is not to say that we cannot help. Our approach is to offer five distinct criteria for conducting the customer segmentation task, with the hope that some of these options will both fit your needs and be comprehensive enough to cover most if not all businesses situations. We illustrate each of these five generic dimensions of segmentation with case examples developed during the course of our research and make general observations about circumstances in which they are most applicable.

The five generic dimensions are as follows:

- Customer attitudes and willingness to do business with us: Exemplified in the Castrol case
- Different degrees of value added: Exemplified in the Waste Management Company case
- Customer life cycle: Exemplified in the Investment Retail Company case
- The varying buying patterns: Exemplified in the Singapore Airlines case
- Alignment with distributor channels: Exemplified in the Unilever Food Service case

Segmentation According to Attitudes and the Willingness to Do Business with Us

The Case of Castrol

Castrol is one of the leading lubricant companies in the world. They realized that playing the Best Product strategy was not going anywhere, since the business was getting commoditized and differentiation through premium products was not generating a sustainable competitive advantage. Typically, 6 months after they would successfully introduce a new premium lubricant, competitors would launch a similar product. Selling lubricants by the gallon was not a very compelling proposition. After being exposed to the Delta Model, they decided to mobilize their efforts toward the pursuit of a Total Customer Solutions strategy.[1]

The foundations behind the strategy were twofold:

First, in the process of making lubricants, Castrol had accumulated a remarkable degree of knowledge about plant maintenance. This is not surprising, since the purpose of a lubricant is to improve the productivity of machinery and equipment of the plant. Rather than using this knowledge strictly for the development of new products, the idea that emerged was that it could be transferred to select customers with consequences that were far more important than merely delivering lubricants.

The second realization was that services were much more critical than products to fight a commoditization syndrome. Product can seldom, if ever, be massively customized; services, on the other hand, are inherently customizable. This led US to believe that a proper customer solution should be composed of a well-integrated set of products *and* services that fit the individual customer's needs.

Definition of Customers' Tiers

In order to develop an effective set of value propositions, Castrol undertook a careful customer segmentation project. Often, companies segment markets. Castrol certainly did that by identifying the major clusters of business applications: cement, sugar, pulp and paper, textile, food and beverage, wood, mining, and glass. But that was not enough. The brilliant next step for Castrol was to identify, within each market segment, which customers to target with varying degrees of priorities. They performed that task by recognizing the different attitudes the customers had about accepting a full Total Customer Solutions approach.

They considered three Tiers.

- *Primary Target Segment* – Productivity-Conscious Customers.
  These customers are eager to receive support that will enhance their productivity, reduce total costs, and promote higher sales.
- *Secondary Target Segment* – Cost-Conscious Customers.
  These customers are concerned about total costs but they believe new production does not necessarily yield higher sales or economies of scale.
- *The Least Desirable Segment* – Price-Conscious Customers.
  These customers are basically buying from the supplier that offers the lowest price.

Figure 3.1 illustrates the position in the Triangle of these three tiers.

Each of these positions is perfectly legitimate and reflects the different forms of beneficial relationships that exist among customers and suppliers, implicit in their attitudes and the corresponding needs and capabilities.

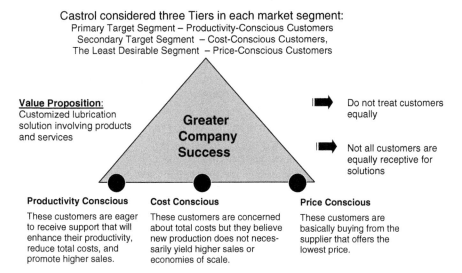

Fig. 3.1 Castrol – lubricants segmentation according to customer attitudes

Castrol summarizes this change in directions by issuing a statement that they call the Castrol Logic, which reads as follows:

A *customized* lubrication *solution* involving products and *services* that results in *documented* cost reductions and productivity improvements.

We have underlined in this statement the words *customized, solution, services*, and *documented*, because they truly capture the spirit of an offering that has nothing to do with a conventional commoditized lubrication product. Castrol, in fact, is selling documented ROI (return on investment) improvements. What a great way to go!

A completely different customer engagement process supports the delivery of this value proposition. Figure 3.2 tries to capture the essence of the process. As

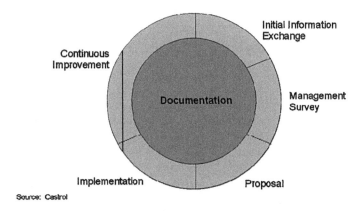

Fig. 3.2 Castrol's customer engagement process

we can see, at the heart of it is the documentation pre- and post-sales execution. By quantifying the expected results, their value proposition becomes objective and credible.

The process begins with a joint team of executives who exchange initial information and complete a management survey. A model of a generic plant is used as an initial platform from which to derive a customized version that will reflect the individual plant maintenance tasks to be completed. A proposal is drawn which results in a long-term contract which is properly implemented. Continuous improvement and learning produces the next stage of the cycle.

The lesson of Castrol is enormously impacting for a proper decommoditization of a product offering: do not treat each customer equally, sell solutions not products, document your value proposition, bring in the executive team to develop long-term relations based on learning, trust, and mutual benefits.

Reflections on Segmentation Based on Customer Attitudes

This is an appealing segmentation because of its enormous simplicity that cut to the heart of the differences in attitudes of the customer towards us. It is the simplest form of segmentation that can be used. It attempts to capture the diversity of the market we are serving by just three distinct tiers, which we call: Transaction, Support, and Relationship (Fig. 3.3). The message they convey is quite clear.

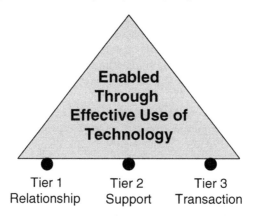

Fig. 3.3 Segmentation according to customer attitudes and willingness to do business with us

This segmentation is also very useful in helping to decommoditize the full business base. It recognizes that there are some legitimate customers, who fit in the transaction category, that only want a standard product at the lowest price from you. The reason behind that, most of the time, is that they are self-sufficient. The other two tiers offer opportunities for customization and uniqueness of delivery with different degrees of value added. The Support tier expects some help, normally in cost reduction. The Relationship tier seeks as full and complete assistance as it can be given, hoping that this will result in increases of revenues and profitability, as well as cost and productivity improvements.

Segmentation According to Different Degrees of Value Added

The Case of the Waste Management Company

In many respects, the experience of the Waste Management Company (WMC)[2] parallels very closely that of Castrol. Both companies were heavily anchored on a commoditized set of products, and they used the Delta Model as a way of reinventing themselves out of that undesirable position. In both cases, the thinking that led them to decommoditization was the recognition that they had accumulated a significant set of competencies that could be usefully passed to some of their customers. For Castrol, the expertise resided in plant maintenance. For WMC it was plant facilities management.

In the process of helping customers in the treatment and disposal of waste, WMC accumulated a huge amount of experience in logistics, on-site technical and field services, by-product management, R&D support, and facilities management in general. The major challenge was, therefore, how to structure a way to pass this experience in the most effective way to a selected group of customers. The answer to that question from the perspective of the Delta Model resides in the task of customer segmentation and value proposition.

Definition of Customers' Tiers

The selected customer segmentation that WMC adopted is presented in Fig. 3.4. The numbers of the tiers are labeled in decreasing order of value added. Tiers 4, 5,

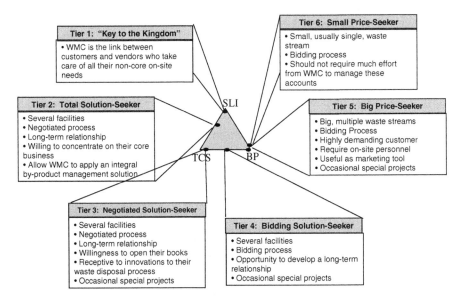

Fig. 3.4 WMC's customer segmentation and its main characteristics

and 6 have one thing in common. All of them request the supplier for the disposal of their waste go through a bidding process. This obviously conveys a clear message. The selected supplier of the winning bid will be most likely the one with the lowest price. That is why these tiers are placed in the Best Product position in the Triangle. What the customer wants is to assure that the waste is disposed in accordance to the Health, Safety, and Environmental Regulations. They perceive these tasks as an additional cost for their core businesses, a cost that is imposed by the regulatory practices that are in place.

Starting from the least attractive alternative, we have:

- Tier 6: Small Price-Seeker.
  They are comprised of a myriad of small companies that want a fairly standardized service of waste disposal. The margins are pretty low, but the total aggregated volume of business could be attractive to WMC.
- Tier 5: Big Price Seeker
  They are more demanding clients that require on-site personnel. But for WMC, having them as a customer is quite an achievement. This demonstrates that WMC has the stature, the competencies, and the credibility to deal successfully with major accounts. The favorable market implications of this are quite clear. In addition, there are real opportunities to engage in some special, more challenging projects that the company might provide to them, which are profitable activities.
- Tier 4: Bidding Solution Seeker
  This is the high end of those companies that still require a supplier bidding process. Although price is of paramount importance in the selection of the supplier, these customers require not just standardized services, but specific solutions to their individual needs. That is why Tier 4 is depicted in the middle of the base of the Triangle, implying that we are moving away from Best Product and getting closer to Total Customer Solution. These customers represent clear opportunities for the development of longer term relationship, and eventually they can move into a Tier 3 position.

  This bidding process is not at all uncommon as a business practice. It is often dictated to government companies that are mandated to be totally transparent in the selection of suppliers, which leads into the search for objectivity that results in the lowest bid. One could argue that this practice deprives the customer of a more meaningful solution to their specific needs, but that is an entirely different matter. Moreover, the degree of bonding among suppliers and customers could be extremely weak, simply because you have to reestablish your claim every time your bid is opened. Unless the previous experiences you have accumulated provide you with a significant advantage to regain the bid, the bonding is almost nonexisting. This is particularly true in Tiers 5 and 6.

  Tiers 1, 2, and 3 also share one thing in common: They select the customer through a negotiated as opposed to a bidding process. This opens up opportunities for WMC to bring to bear the full range of competencies they have and translate them into unique and creative value propositions that go beyond the mere disposal of waste.

- Tier 3: Negotiated Solution Seeker
  In this Tier we have one attribute, which is quite significant, and that is the customer's willingness to open their books to WMC and their receptiveness to innovations that could help them do a better job in their core business. This obviously could lead to a mutually beneficial long-term relationship and to a significant customer bonding. That is why we present this tier in the vertex of the Total Customer Solution in the Triangle.
- Tier 2: Total Solution Seeker
  This tier includes customers that are extremely comfortable with their relationship with WMC and depend strongly on that company for a full array of technical and business services. We represent them fairly close to the top vertex of the Triangle, to give an indication of the high degree of bonding that exists.
- Tier 1: Key to the Kingdom
  As its name implies, this tier is composed of customers in full alignment with WMC, establishing a long-term partnership. Under this alternative WMC provides the customer a total facilities management solution.

Identifying Incremental Solutions and Value-Delivery Mechanisms

As we have noted, the resulting six tiers require different degrees of knowledge to be transferred by WMC to customers. What are the different degrees of knowledge that will be imbedded in the solutions that WMC provides to the customers? Which are the delivery mechanisms that will be used to transfer that knowledge? The answers to these two questions are what we have attempted to capture in Fig. 3.4, which is quite specific in identifying the incremental knowledge that is the basis for the solution that WMC offers to the customer.

We start with the very basic: Compliance with environmental and safety regulations. This is the bread and butter of waste management, and results in delivering to the customer liability insurance, personnel training, and supplier certification process, as well as guaranteeing a constant review of the evolving regulations. If you look at this narrowly, this service results in an additional cost that the customer has to incur in order to properly dispense of the waste that is being accumulated.

The next two solutions that are presented in Fig. 3.5 produce a reduction in the total cost of by-products handling and better customer service and a reduction in administrative cost and headcount. These two solutions, far from adding an additional cost, represent significant cost savings to the customer. The figure reflects how WMC is transferring these services to the customer.

Finally, the remaining two solution elements are improved productivity and total facilities management. In these two cases, not only will customers benefit from cost reductions, but they will get cost enhancement and productivity improvements as well. Again, the figure shows the mechanisms that are used to deliver these solutions to the customer.

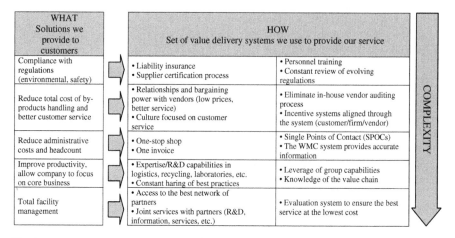

Fig. 3.5 The nature of WMC solutions and the delivery mechanisms

Definition of Customers' Value Propositions

The six tiers vary in terms of value added. Figure 3.6 shows the distinct nature of the value propositions to each tier and how the resulting benefits are partly passed on to the customer and partly retained by WMC. The evolution of these benefits becomes quite transparent. At the Best Product positioning, we are providing a service that generates a cost. As we move further and approach the full System Lock-in, the benefits increase both to the customer and WMC, leading toward cost reductions, productivity improvements, and higher profitability.

We have completed the full cycle of increasing value added. This is what makes the segmentation so transparent, easy to understand, and so useful if the conditions are such that these tiers capture the distinctiveness of the value proposition for each one of them. As we proceed from tiers 6 to 1, we have increased value added and knowledge transfer, enriched the complexity of the relationships, and generated higher margins and profitability, all of this resulting in greater bonding. This is one of our preferred criteria for segmentation.

Reflections on Segmentation Based on Different Degrees of Value Added

In our experience, this is perhaps the most effective way of segmenting the customer when the business conditions allow its use. It permits us to understand the customers' needs and capabilities and offer them the appropriate degree of value added. It normally covers the full range from the lowest end, which is totally arms length and product driven, to the high end, where we have the expectation of

Tier	Solutions we provide	Benefits for Customer	Benefits for WMC
Small Price Seeker	• Compliance with regulations • Lowest cost in by-product handling • Keep track of activities • *If profitable*, look for improvements	• Lowest cost available in the market	• Small margin gains in bided activities • One-time-events with potentially high margins
Big Price Seeker	• Handle multiple waste streams	• Better customer service • Expertise	• "Looks good in our resume" • Opportunity to learn best practices and new processes
Bidding Solution Seeker	• Reduce administrative costs and headcount	• Additional services & improvement projects if relationship develops	• Step-up of customer tier if able to develop relationship
Negotiated Solution Seeker	• Improve productivity, allow company to focus on core business	•Additional cost savings from non-waste processes	• Long term relationship • Higher margins
Total Solution Seeker	• Total facility management	• WMC as an on-site partner • Concentrate in core business	• Customer lock-in
Key to the Kingdom	• Total facility management	• One-stop solution	• System lock-in

Fig. 3.6 WMC value proposition and appropriability of benefits

establishing a long-term partnership with the customer, thus producing a high degree of bonding. As we discuss in the case of the WMC, some customers invite to a bidding process to identify their suppliers, which pushes them toward a Best Product positioning. This may be due to the competencies of the customer. They might not need any further assistance than a mere product.

Whatever the reasons, our challenge is to understand customers well and provide them with the most relevant value proposition.

The number of tiers could vary depending on the circumstances. In the Waste Management Company case, we selected six tiers. The generic example depicted in Fig. 3.7 shows just five tiers. This might be enough to cover the different degree of services and expected customer bonding in most cases.

In Chapter 8 (Putting it All Together), we present the case of DMK that uses a four-tier segmentation of value added. The point we are making is that this dimension allows some flexibility in this respect, but in any of its forms, it provides a segmentation in which we increase the value transferred to the customer, the complexities of the relationship, the size of the benefits to be appropriated, and the resulting bonding that will be established between the customer and us.

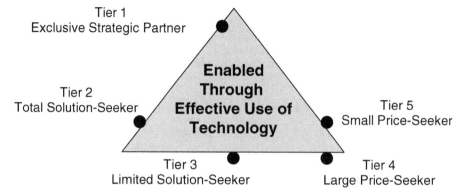

Fig. 3.7   Segmentation according to different degree of value added

Segmentation According to Customer Life Cycle

The Case of the Investment Retail Company (IRC)

Any institution that is part of the financial retail services industry[3] is faced with a huge number of customers seeking services that are critical for their wellbeing and which are of paramount importance at the end of the life cycle. Moreover, every transaction that is conducted is recorded, and every customer is quite distinct. These two attributes make the financial services industry ideal for the application of the Delta Model. Paradoxically, although the rhetoric used in the industry makes us feel that everybody is embracing the Total Customer Solution approach, the reality is often that customers face a bunch of commoditized products delivered with a rather arms-length attitude.

The traditional way in which the retail industry of financial services has segmented the customer is by the amount of the financial assets they have in place. An institution specializing in the high-end wealth management, for example, segmented its clients into four different tiers according to the amount of financial assets they own: (1) from $100,000 to $500,000; (2) from $500,000 to $5 millions; (3) from $5 millions to $50 millions; and (4) over $50 millions. The problem with this segmentation is that we get a snapshot that ignores the evolution of the customer. It could very well be that those who are in the low end today could evolve into the highest end in the future, but if we don't treat those customers appropriately, we might not be able to enjoy the benefits that a more visionary approach would have provided.

Definition of Customers' Tiers

One way of solving this problem would be to segment the customer according to the stages in their life cycle. This would allow us to identify the changing needs as they evolve from what traditionally is a very modest set of financial assets, when people are young, to the incremental accumulation of assets as they progress through life and become more successful. In this way, we will be able to capture these changing needs and produce value propositions that not only are meaningful for today's conditions, but also have long-term implications in mind. This could be properly grasped by segmenting customers according to the combination of three attributes: financial assets, trading behavior, and age. There is an underlying life cycle imbedded in this segmentation, which is complemented by the magnitudes of financial assets and the trading behaviors. The resulting customer tiers, in order of priorities, are:

- Tier 1: Family Office
- Tier 2: Wealthy Individual
- Tier 3: Mature Investor
- Tier 4: Accomplished Investor
- Tier 5: Basic Investor

Figure 3.8 displays the positions of the five tiers in the Triangle, and provide a brief description of each of them. Notice how the tiers span the continuum of bonding, from Best Product to System Lock-in. Also observe the mapping of the capabilities inherent to each of the strategic positions of the Triangle with the support that the customers tiers need.

Identification of Incremental Solutions, Value Delivery Mechanisms and Customer Value Propositions

The individual customer of an investment retail company is in search of assistance to manage as effectively as possible his or her portfolio of assets. With the exraordinary degree of complexity that exists in the current financial instruments, there are very few individuals that can address this important task without external help. Obviously the task becomes more complicated as the magnitude of the assets increases and the sophistication of the portfolio becomes more intense. It is imperative, therefore, to understand the knowledge that a financial firm can transfer to its clients, and the degree of value added that knowledge would generate. Also of utmost importance is the development of mutual trust beween the financial firms and its customers, based upon fairness and transparency in the relationships, which should create a strong customer bonding.

Figure 3.9 describes the kind of solutions that IRC is abe to provide to its customers and the mechanism to make those solutions available.

Figure 3.10 summarizes the basic benefits that will be accrued to the customer and IRC by each of the tiers. It illustrates what we have noted previously: that the benefits incrementally tend to increase from lowest to higher tiers, generating different degrees of profitability for each of the parties. However it is expected that the solution provided to each tier is the appropriate one for this stage and the customer would evolve as the accumulation of assets increase.

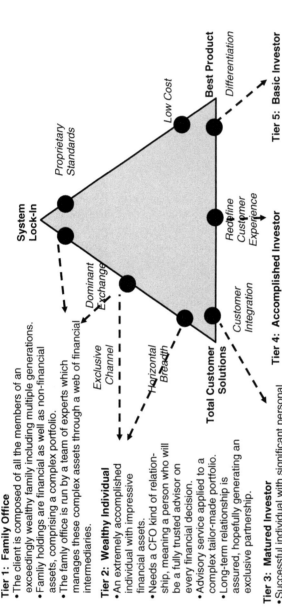

Tier 1: Family Office
- The client is composed of all the members of an exceedingly wealthy family including multiple generations.
- Family holdings are financial as well as non-financial assets, comprising a complex portfolio.
- The famly office is run by a team of experts which manages these complex assets through a web of financial intermediaries.

Tier 2: Wealthy Individual
- An extremely accomplished individual with impressive financial assets.
- Needs a CFO kind of relationship, meaning a person who will be a fully trusted advisor on every financial decision.
- Advisory service applied to a complex tailor-made portfolio.
- Long-term relationship is assured, hopefully generating an exclusive partnership.

Tier 3: Matured Investor
- Successful individual with significant personal holdings.
- Needs premium attention and customized services including complete estate planning, with emphasis on retirement assets.
- The creation of strong bonding based upon trust, transparency, and mutual benefits is established.

Tier 4: Accomplished Investor
- Typically a successful professional, at a middle career stage and promising future.
- Begins to accumulate some wealth.
- Requires advice on the selection of a more sophisticated financial portfolio, with clear understanding of risk/return tradeoffs.
- The seeds for a long-term relationship are planted, if value added can be demonstrated.

Tier 5: Basic Investor
- Typically a young person at the beginning of his/her professional career.
- Demands basic quality services with low-cost transactions.
- Needs guidance on simple investment choices.
- Potential for long-term relationship.

System Lock-In

Proprietary Standards

Low Cost

Best Product

Differentiation

Redefine Customer Experience

Dominant Exchange

Exclusive Channel

Horizontal Breadth

Total Customer Solutions

Customer Integration

Fig. 3.8 Investment retail company customer segmentation

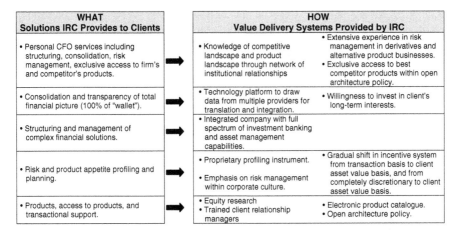

WHAT Solutions IRC Provides to Clients	HOW Value Delivery Systems Provided by IRC	
• Personal CFO services including structuring, consolidation, risk management, exclusive access to firm's and competitor's products.	• Knowledge of competitive landscape and product landscape through network of institutional relationships	• Extensive experience in risk management in derivatives and alternative product businesses. • Exclusive access to best competitor products within open architecture policy.
• Consolidation and transparency of total financial picture (100% of "wallet").	• Technology platform to draw data from multiple providers for translation and integration.	• Willingness to invest in client's long-term interests.
• Structuring and management of complex financial solutions.	• Integrated company with full spectrum of investment banking and asset management capabilities.	
• Risk and product appetite profiling and planning.	• Proprietary profiling instrument. • Emphasis on risk management within corporate culture.	• Gradual shift in incentive system from transaction basis to client asset value basis, and from completely discretionary to client asset value basis.
• Products, access to products, and transactional support.	• Equity research • Trained client relationship managers	• Electronic product catalogue. • Open architecture policy.

Fig. 3.9 Investment retail company (IRC) cusomer value proposition – what and how

Tier	Solutions IRC Provides	Benefits for Client	Benefits or IRC
(1) Family Office	• Outsourcing of Family Office management • Comprehensive CFO-type services (including structuring, consolidations, etc.)	• Comprehensive CFO services outsourced • Complete access to all FIC customized products and services	• System Lock-In possible through management of all financial intermediary relationships • Potential corporate investment banking relationship
(2) Wealthy Individual	• Some CFO-type services (e.g., risk management, exclusive products access) • Structuring and management of complex financial solutions • Consolidation of total financial picture	• Access to global and institutional/alternative products, and structuring of complex solutions • Long-term relationship • Potential for highly personalized CFO service	• High margin products • Cemented long-term relationship • Potential to maximize "share of wallet" • Potential next generation Family Office (dominant exchange and system lock-in)
(3) Matured Investor	• Consolidation of total financial picture • Some structuring and management of complex financial solutions • Risk and product appetite profiling	• Access to global and institutional/alternative products, and structuring of complex solutions • Long-term relationship	• High margin products • Cemented long-term relationship • Potential to increase "share of wallet" with IRC
(4) Accomplished Investor	• Some structuring and management of complex financial solutions • Risk and product appetite profiling • Products, access to products and transactional support	• Access to best-in-class products • Competitive pricing for wealth management services • Long-term relationship with access to additional resources	• Client beginning to develop taste for higher margin products • Potential to cement long-term relationship with more activist advisory services by CRM
(5) Basic Investor	• Risk and product appetite profiling • Products, access to products and transactional support	• Access to best-in-class products • Competitive pricing for wealth management services	• Potential to establish long-term relationship

Fig. 3.10 Investment retail company (IRC) – benefits created for the customers and IRC

Reflection on the Segmentation Based on Customer Life Cycle

When the needs of customers evolve through their life cycle, it is quite important to capture this transformation, not only to serve the customer as effectively as possible, but also to make sure that we develop, from the early stages, a relationship that will culminate in a strong bonding in the later stages of customer evolution.

This concept can also be applied to those situations where the ownership of the product through its life cycle is critical. The proper treatment of the customers in the first purchase is crucial. If we know how to treat them in every stage of ownership, they will generate repeated purchases in the future. A typical example of this is car ownership, and a simple segmentation that reflects on the life cycle of that industry is presented in Fig. 3.11.

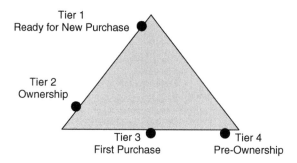

Fig. 3.11 Segmentation according to life cycle of ownership – the consumer in the car industry

We bring our attention to the customers prior to the purchase, to try to captivate them, and to persuade them to acquire our product. Then the first purchase comes. This is a critical moment to provide such an exciting experience that it will have the most favorable and long-lasting effects. Then we begin to take care of the customers through the process of ownership of the car, giving them a service experience that will be unparalleled. Finally, we guide the customers to dispose of their old car effectively and to replace it with an even better model that we produce. The customer retention in this industry is the only meaningful measure of customer bonding.

Another important industry in which the life cycle of the customer is quite significant is the healthcare industry. Often, the buyers are the medical doctors and, therefore, it is critical to establish not only a close relationship with them at a given point in time, but to accompany them as they progress in their careers. Figure 3.12 provides us with the segmentation relevant to a company in the healthcare business where the buyers are surgeons. The segmentation shows us the relative importance of doctors according to the role that they perform. We capture them at the beginning

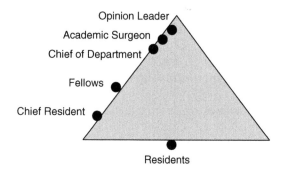

Fig. 3.12 Segmentation for a health care firm: surgeons as the key purchasing decision makers

of their careers, when they are residents, and then follow them as they move from that position to chief residents, fellows, chief of departments, academic surgeons, and opinion leaders. Perhaps the most critical tier in here is the fellows. We want to become an important contributor to the fellows' careers, providing them with professional support, grants, access to publications, continuous education enhancements, and the like. If we establish a proper bonding with them at that stage, we will enjoy the fruits that we have seeded when some of them reach the ultimate status of opinion leaders.

All these examples really show us how to decommoditize the customers by recognizing their changing needs through their life cycle.

We will continue developing the case in subsequent chapters to illustrate the full application of the Delta Model.

Segmentation According to Varying Buying Patterns

The Case of Singapore Airlines

How is it possible that an airline with no domestic market was able to, in the course of its short history, position itself to become one of the most respected and profitable companies in the world? Singapore Airlines (SA)[4] is indeed a remarkable success story.

Today, Singapore Airlines' route network reaches out to over 90 destinations in close to 40 countries, which is very similar to American Airlines, the largest airline in the world with about 8 times as many aircraft as SA. Singapore Airlines has consistently won awards and accolades from international travel magazines and peer industry reviews.

Definition of Customer Tiers and Customers' Value Proposition

Most people, including those who travel intensively for a living, might tend to regard all airlines to be quite similar. The prevailing sentiment is that we are facing a commoditized industry. Seldom do people have strong preferences for one airline vs. another, unless there are financial reasons that lead to individual discounts or the bonding from the frequent flyer bonus. Surprisingly, this is not the case with SA. Everyone who has enjoyed the experience of traveling with this airline has lived the difference. There is nothing about SA that breeds commodity. To understand that, it is useful to look at the way in which customers are segmented and the resulting value proposition provided to each tier. We start with a fairly simple characterization of four tiers:

- Tier 1, Business Professionals and Opinion Leaders
- Tier 2, Corporations, Companies, and Government

- Tier 3, Young High Potentials
- Tier 4, Mass Market

Tiers 1 and 2 constitute the high-end travel groups. Tier 3 is the future potential, and Tier 4 is the cost-conscious traveler. Understanding and clarifying the customer value proposition for each of the tiers provides great insight into what has made SA successful (Fig. 3.13).

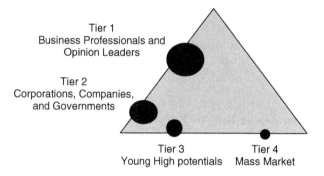

Fig. 3.13 Singapore Airlines customers' segmentation

Figures 3.14 and 3.15 provide descriptions of the value propositions for tiers 1 and 4, respectively, and serve to underline the high quality of service that SA is observing throughout its customer base.

SA strives to deliver air travel not as a commodity, as many airlines do, but as a complete experience from the moment that the customer checks in his or her bag at the airport counter to the point where he or she leaves the plane at the destination. Particularly in the case of Tiers 1 and 2, once the customers check in through the priority positions in the counters, they enter a "zone" where there is a complete suite of services available. Busy executives are able to eat from a superb buffet spread while working on their computers via wireless connections. The CEO or senior government official can relax or read to catch up with the day's news. The sports stars can watch a replay of their great plays on television or even play realistic computer games to sharpen their senses. It is interesting that while SA clearly pampers Tiers 1–3 customers, it does not compromise on the services to Tier 4. In fact, the airline recognizes that while it cannot afford every economy class passenger the same amount of attention, it maintains high service standards, and serves full and sumptuous meals. SA was also the first airline that offered free flow of champagne to the economy class, which in itself is a very strong but subtle statement that it values the business of the economy class passengers. This is a sensible strategy as some of these passengers are potential "upgraders" to Tiers 1–3, and it is a way of growing a base of loyal customers.

The common delivery system across all tiers is the Singapore Girl, for a very good reason. The Singapore Girl has been a powerful iconic symbol for SA since 1968 and has been the means through which SA has marketed and branded itself internationally. Whether it is making inaugural flights into a new city, announcing

	Value Proposition
Set of Experiences we will provide	• Provide them a level of service in the air and on the ground that is not only unmatched by any other airline, but also one that compares extremely favorably with the best in the food and hospitality industry. Attention to every detail and their travel needs. • Consistently provide new types of innovation and increased levels of service. Give them the sense that the next flight experience will always be better than the previous one. • 5-Star hotel in the air and on the ground. The experience begins the moment the customer steps into the SA lounge right until he leaves the aircraft.
Set of Value Delivery Systems needed to provide the experiences	• The iconic Singapore Girl as the key purveyor of in-flight services • Customer Relations Manager - Acquire feedback • Excellent selection of food and drinks • World-class in-flight entertainment systems with no peer. • 5-Star hotel standard comfort (seats, amenities, aircraft finishing). • Ease of travel changes (high frequency of flights and connectivity to major aviation hubs).

Value Appropriation	• Value gained by the customers:
	  - Arrive in comfort, well-rested and energized
	  - Feel pampered like a king/queen
	• Value gained by us:
	  - Loyalty
	  - Positive feedback to influential magazines, business surveys
	• Value shared by both:
	  - Productive partnership
	  - Establish long-term relationship

Fig. 3.14 Singapore Airlines value proposition for tier 1: business professionals and opinion leaders

the acquisition of new state-of-the-art aircraft, or the introduction of new business and first class seats, the Singapore Girl has been the iconic symbol gracing TV screens, billboards, or magazine and newspaper ads. Customers have been conditioned to perceive the Singapore Girl as the embodiment of all that SA stands for. For passengers, the Singapore Girl is the person that they will come into contact with for the longest duration of the journey. Through the interactions with the customer, she is also most likely to be the one who will receive instant feedback. Should there be a complaint, she can help to manage the situation and ensure that the customer's needs are addressed.

Reflections on Segmentation Based on Varying Buying Patterns

There are situations where the different purchasing patterns from the customer define the best way of selecting the proper value proposition.

	Value Proposition
Set of Experiences we will provide	• Provide them good quality service in the air and on the ground. • Consistently surprise them with increasing levels of service and innovation both on the ground and in the air. • Best economy class seats, service and amenities in the world. • Making them feel that they will arrive in style even if they are in economy class.
Set of Value Delivery Systems needed to provide the experiences	• The iconic Singapore Girl as the key purveyor of in-flight services • Customer Relations Manager to seek sporadic feedback • Great selection of food and drinks • World-class in-flight entertainment systems with no peer. • High standard comfort found in good class hotels (seats, amenities, aircraft finishing). • Free flow of champagne, alcohol, free toiletries • Ease of travel changes (high frequency of flights and connectivity to major aviation hubs).
Value Appropriation	• Value gained by the customers: - Arrive in comfort, well-rested and energized - Association with the best airline in the world • Value gained by us: - Loyalty - Consistent feedback • Value shared by both: - Establish long-term relationship

Fig. 3.15 Singapore Airlines value proposition for tier 4: mass market

The simplest way to address this task is to think in terms of the different degrees of affordability of the customer (Fig. 3.16).

It just shows four tiers according to the expectation of the quality of the products and services being received, and the different capacities of the customers to afford them. In Fig. 3.11, we show the segmentation of the car customer following the life

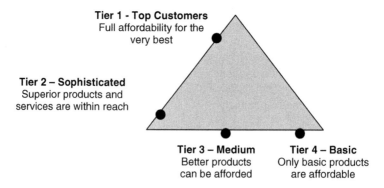

Fig. 3.16 Segmentation according to varying buying patterns – customer affordability

cycle. Now we can make a different kind of segmentation based upon the capacity of the customer to purchase a car. Let's say somebody is interested in buying a Toyota. Tier 4 would be a candidate to get a Corolla; Tier 3, a Camry; Tier 2, an Avalon; and Tier 1 a Lexus. Not only are the price, the quality, the comfort, the prestige, and the image of the cars different, but the services provided are also of a different sort.

Another dimension to capture the varying degrees of buying patterns is to think about the nature of the customer itself. Figure 3.17 helps us in understanding this approach. Under the life cycle segmentation criteria, we discuss the role of the surgeons in the healthcare industry. These segmentation criteria, although very critical, do not capture the whole complexity of the industry and the way to target the customer more effectively. Other determinant players that bring considerable weight in the purchasing decision are the hospitals. It is useful to segment them according to their individual nature, which cover teaching and nonteaching, suburban, rural, and government hospitals, as well as private surgery centers. The priorities are expressed from top to bottom in that list.

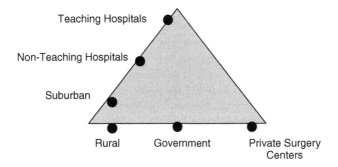

Fig. 3.17 Segmentation for a healthcare firm: purchasing pattern of different hospitals

Segmentation According to Alignment with the Distribution Channel

The Case of Unilever Food Services

The Channels Are Critical: They Own the Customer

Channels are essential in the development of a proper strategy. Whoever owns them, owns the customer. Therefore, if we are dependent upon generic channels to deliver our products to the final consumers, we have to exercise a high degree of care and attention to this issue. The channels can block us and, most importantly, can make us remote to the final consumer, impeding us in any effort to get a first-hand knowledge of market needs. This is a very vulnerable position to be in, since it makes us play the game blindly.

We use the case of Unilever Food Service to illustrate this issue. In the year 2000, Unilever acquired Bestfoods, a leading company in the food industry, in order to consolidate a strong position in food services, one of the few growing segments of the food sector. The food service industry is dedicated to providing consumers with solutions for meals consumed away from home. The industry expanded from $35 billion in 1977 to about $400 billion today. Due to the many pressures affecting society, meals prepared away from home are as much a necessity as a choice.

The newly created organization – Unilever Bestfoods North America (UBF) – enjoys a portfolio of extremely powerful brands, well known in most households: Lipton teas and soups, Ragu pasta sauce, Hellman's mayonnaise and dressings, WishBone salad dressings, Lawry's seasonings, Skippy peanut butter, Bertolli olive oil, I Can't Believe It's Not Butter margarine, and so on. In addition, Unilever global food division also produces Good Humor, Breyer and Ben & Jerry's ice creams, and SlimFast nutritional and health snack products. You might think that with this powerful product base, Unilever would be in an easy position to deploy a very successful business. Think again.

Figure 3.18 depicts the scope of the food service industry. UBF is one of the major suppliers of the industry. Its customers are the operators – restaurants that sell food to the final consumers. Food producers such as UBF do not have the capabilities to directly reach the thousands of restaurants that operate in the U.S. Besides UBF, there are a number of very strong food producers, which include among others Kraft Foods, Kellogg's, Nabisco Brands, Campbell Soup, Nestlé, and so on. They all depend on well-established distributors for the delivery of their products to their customers.

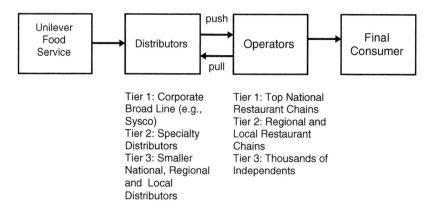

Fig. 3.18 The food service industry distribution system

The strongest distributors are those that represent a corporate broad line, which means that they carry a full array of products of all the major food producers. The most important broad line distributors are Sysco and U.S. Foodservice. Sysco is the industry leader with total sales of about $35 billion in 2007, operating in 177 locations, serving 400,000 customers with 51,000 associates throughout the US and Canada.

In the food service industry, Sysco carries a weight similar to Wal-Mart in the retailing business. The industry is extremely competitive and the margins are razor thin. The power of the distributors is enormous. They not only impose very tough terms on their suppliers, but also carry generic brands which they can sell at heavy discounts to the operators, since they do not have to incur significant marketing costs that are needed to support a brand. This represents a huge threat to UBF, since its primary strategy resides in the development of strong brands aimed at high consumer recognition and an indisputable guarantee of quality. That strategy does not seem to work in this setting because the operators do not exhibit the brand names of their ingredients. This is what the trade calls the "back-of-the-house" and the "front-of-the-house" brands.

Let us take the example of Hellman's mayonnaise, a very important back-of-the-house brand name. When it comes to, say, Applebee's, that brand is lost. The consumer will never know that the mayonnaise she or he is eating is Hellmann's. In other words, the front-of-the-house brand name has disappeared. Not only that, but the broad line distributor will pressure the operator to buy its generic brand name with a 20% discount over the branded mayonnaise, which for all intents and purposes are indistinguishable from each other as far as taste is concerned.

We have a ferociously intense rivalry confronting the food producers and the broad line distributors. The distributors are commoditizing the food manufacturing products and are attempting to displace them by pushing their generic products. This is the utmost of a commoditization game. How can UBF assert itself under these conditions? The answer is, as you would have expected, through proper segmentation and distinct and carefully drawn value propositions for each customer segment.

We start the segmentation with the operators, which are the real customer base for UBF. The fundamental concern is not to intensify an already conflicting rivalry, but make every effort to decommoditize the product offering. If the distributors will not push our products, we should make sure that our customers will have all of the incentives to pull them. How this can be accomplished differs greatly depending on how the customer fits in three very distinct tiers.

Definition of Customers' Tiers and Customers' Value Propositions

UBF chose to define three customer tiers with the following set of priorities:

- Customer Tier 1: Top National Restaurant Chains

Description

This segment is composed by about 100 national restaurant chains such as McDonald's, Burger King, Kentucky Fried Chicken (KFC), Applebee's, Taco

Bell, and TGI Friday's. They have enormous purchasing power, and it is quite tempting for them to use it in order to gain price discounts – additional pressure to commoditize UBF products.

Value Proposition

The way to gain close customer bonding and to guarantee a pull of UBF products through the distributors is to offer Tier 1 customers unique customized products, services, and delivery systems. This is possible due to the strong technical capabilities in food and flavor existing in UBF. For instance, we can offer a Bloody Mary mix to TGI Friday's that is unmatched by any alternative in the market and is exclusive to them; and we can supply a system to cook beans at KFC that assures an exquisite quality, with great consistency, to be perfectly prepared even by an unskilled labor force. Customization and system delivery is the central value proposition to this tier.

- Customer Tier 2: Regional and Local Restaurant Chains

Description

This customer tier includes about 1,500 smaller restaurant chains. They are important regional and local restaurants, but they do not have access to the superior managerial infrastructure that the top national chains have.

Value Proposition

Because of its internal competencies to provide customized services to this tier, a company such as UBF has a unique opportunity to help these small restaurant chains fundamentally enrich their business capabilities. The value proposition is to offer branded products – so as to regain the "front-of-the-house" branding image – supported by a set of customized services that provide product support and corporate management services. The combination of these two types of services is enormously impacting. Product support includes transferring culinary expertise, on-site marketing, improving consumer understanding, brand training, menu design, health and safety measures, merchandizing, diet nutrition, chef product preparation, and equipment utilization and training. Corporate management services transfer knowledge of IT linkages, EDI/Bar codes, logistics and material flow management, ABC costing, human resources training, and profit modeling capabilities. The combined effect of these two types of services has the power to produce a customer lock-in in this tier.

- Customer Tier 3: Thousands of Independents

Description

What remains are the tens of thousands of fragmented small restaurants spaced all over the country.

Value Proposition

A direct sales force of UBF serves customers in the two top tiers, and we certainly cannot offer to do that with this tier of customers. The challenge is to try to provide as many of the services outlined for Tier 2 customers as possible except that the delivery will be done through telemarketing and Internet services.

The positions of these three tiers are depicted in Fig. 3.19 of the Triangle. What seemed to be a problem impossible to resolve has been clarified by a careful segmentation that culminates in value propositions for each tier that breaks the commoditization of the initial offerings, and has all the potential for creating a high degree of bonding between UBF and each customer tier.

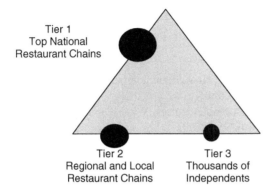

Fig. 3.19 UBF customer segmentation

The Segmentation of UBF Distributors

What remains to be done is to further segment the distribution channels to attempt to seek as much alignment as possible in this part of the system. This task was accomplished by defining the following three tiers (Fig. 3.20):

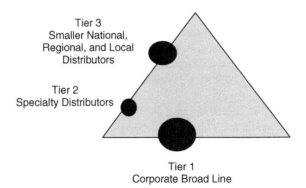

Fig. 3.20 UBF distributor segmentation

- Distributor Tier 1: Corporate Broad Line
  These are the large power bargaining and include Sysco and US Food Services. They are critical because of the reach of their coverage, but they are pursuing their own individual interests. Because of their importance, we have to develop satisfying relationships with them, but they may not be regarded as preferential partners.
- Distributor Tier 2: Specialty Distributors
  These channels provide an attractive focus for a particular segment and can act as an extension of our sales force.
- Distributor Tier 3: Smaller National, Regional, and Local Distributors
  Whenever the geography permits, this group becomes our preferred set of distributors, receiving the highest priority for business management attention and strategic alliance. UBF is ready to assist these distributors through training and technical services.

The intent is to create a close alignment between the distributors' objectives and UBF strategy, and to establish close collaboration with Tiers 2 and 3 distributors to make them legitimate complementors. What is intriguing about this case is that, at first sight, it seems to be an impossible puzzle to resolve. The powers of the distributors and operators seem too immense and disproportionate to overcome, and a company like UBF seems condemned to be commoditized. The moral of the story continues to be that we should never accept that fate. Ingenuity – matched with proper segmentation – can help you craft a creative solution. Remember: commodities only exist in the minds of the inept.

Reflections on Segmentation According to Alignment with Distribution Channel

If we are dependent upon a third party to reach our customer, it is a top priority to seek and obtain a full strategic alignment with the channel. This is because we lose direct contact with our final customer and we must rely instead on an intermediary who might or might not represent our interests in the way we wish. A channel conflict could be one of the most devastating problems that we could face.

To guide us in detecting the different kinds of loyalty and resulting bonding with the channels, we turn to the very simple distributors' segmentation presented in Fig. 3.21.

In essence, Tier 3 is commoditizing our offering, and it is not adding any significant value to the customer. This channel doesn't lend itself to providing any kind of unique value proposition to the customer. Unless we can change this attitude, we should avoid its use whenever possible, except for the delivery of a rather commoditized product offering. Tier 2 brings some solidarity and service support. The

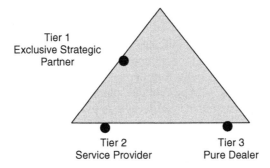

Fig. 3.21 Segmentation according to alignment with distributors' channels

situation is not as effective as we would hope, but there might be ways of construc-
tively operating with that channel. The ideal, of course, is Tier 1, where we have a
seamless extension of us to provide a complete solution to the customers' needs.

Sometimes we might want to address this alignment with the distributors in a
more direct way. This is the case when we assume an active role in training the distributors and providing them with as much value added as possible for them to be
able to offer the greater service to the final consumer. We have encountered this challenge in the car industry. Figure 3.22 illustrates a relevant distributor's segmentation
for that industry.

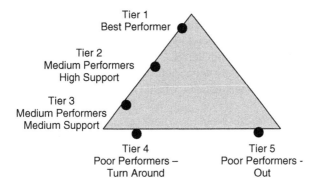

Fig. 3.22 The different degree of alignment with car dealers

In here, we are segmenting the dealers according the various levels of achieved
performance, and consequently the necessary support and attention that we should
give them in order to do a better job. So we go from Tier 1, the top performers, that
fundamentally should be left alone and require only the basic routine support; to
Tiers 2 and 3, which need different degrees of value added from us to improve their
act; and finally, Tiers 4 and 5, who are poor performers some of whom we may be
able to turn around, and others of whom we should actively disengage.

Some Pitfalls from Conventional Customer Segmentation

We indicated at the beginning of this chapter that the conventional criteria to perform customer segmentation – often based upon demographic attributes – are not effective enough to guide us in delivering the best value proposition. Remember also that one critical objective is to prevent the commoditization of the business, which implies that the segmentation should be able to grasp the unique characteristics of our customers in order to differentiate the way to serve them more effectively.

In this section, we provide examples that will help us to understand some of the traps that we can fall into and what we can learn from these pitfalls.

The Mobile Phone Business – The Case of Singapore Telecommunications (SingTel)

There is something paradoxical about the mobile phone industry. In principle, it has the ideal structure to offer in a most individualized way a meaningful value proposition for each of its customers. Every person has different communication needs, and the operators that provide mobile phone services record every transaction with their clients accumulating a wealth of knowledge that can be used to deliver an extreme case of mass customization.

Instead we encounter a completely different reality. The industry seems to present an extreme case of commoditization. Companies compete with cutthroat pricing using products that appear to be highly standardized. Customer switching costs seem to be negligible and customer bonding is nonexistent, which prevents the achievement of a long-term relationship that is so critical for industry profitability. To make things even worse, companies try to attract new customers by offering tempting discounts on new telephone devices, which contributes to an increase in customer churn rate.

One major cause of this problem, in our opinion, might be the practice that is used in segmenting the customers. Take the case of SingTel,[5] the leading operator of mobile telephones in Singapore. As presented in Fig. 3.23, customer segmentation is done according to trivial price plans that provide a limited range of dull options. The resulting narrow and meaningless plan is a sure recipe for commoditization, since it ignores the wealth of exciting possibilities imbedded in the diversity of needs and behaviors of the customers.

A more effective segmentation would be to recognize how the differences in requirements and affordability of the customers evolve as they travel through the various stages of their life cycle. This will allow us to detect changes in usage patterns, volume of use, and the needs for the suite of services that we could make available as the customer progresses with prosperity and age. The resulting value propositions can be supported by an intelligent customer database where we record the customer's transactions, learn their communication habits, and propose a continuously improved set of services.

	Free Incoming Video and Voice Calls All Day					Double Talk Time
	One SuperValue	One Plus	Two value	Two Plus	Three Plus	Classic
Monthly Subscription	$15.00	$25.68	$48.15	$82.93	$192.60	$29.96
FREE Local Calls	80 mins anytime (outgoing)	100 mins (anytime (outgoing)	300 mins anytime (outgoing)	700 mins anytime (outgoing)	2000 mins anytime (outgoing)	150 mins anytime 50 mins (off-peak)
FREE Local SMS	50	500	500	500	2000	360

Fig. 3.23 Singapore telecommunications – original segmentation by price

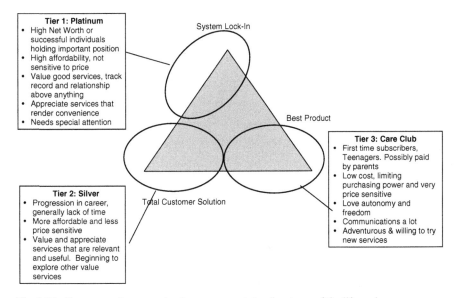

Fig. 3.24 Singapore telecommunications – segmentation by stages of the life cycle

Figure 3.24 presents a simple segmentation based on three tiers: Tier 1, Care Club; Tier 2, Silver Club; and Tier 3, Platinum Club. It attempts to capture three distinct stages in the customer life cycle. Figures 3.25, 3.26 and 3.27 give the details of the value propositions associated with each tier.

The central idea here is to understand that the mobile phone has become, particularly among young people, a central part of their lives and its use depends heavily on the circumstances surrounding each individual. The business is, therefore, as far removed from a commodity as one could imagine.

Tier 1 – Platinum Club

Business Scope for Tier 1 – Platinum Club	
Customer Dimension	Description
Products and Service Plan	• Highly customized services that fit into the lifestyle of these high net worth individuals or senior executives • Lifestyle-oriented services • Financial, mobile-commerce, information on demand services. Contextual, relevance and location-based services • Special customer service hotline that provides 24/7 exclusive and dedicated customer service
Customer Complementors	• High net worth individuals or senior executives with no concern over pricing • Visa, Mastercard, CNN, Merchants
Unique Competencies	• Deep knowledge of customer's lifestyle and development of "relevance" services to support their lifestyle • Highly customized suite of services around the lifestyle of customer to create bonding
Value Proposition for Tier 1 – Platinum Club	
Value Proposition	Description
Experiences	• Long-term relationship developed over time with deep understanding of individual's lifestyle
Value Delivery Systems	• IT system that constantly analyzes the lifestyle of customers • User of new technology like mobile-commerce platform, location-based service, advertising engine to integrate with database of customers to provide contextual and "relevance" services • Value-added by being a one-stop lifestyle center of customers

Value Appropriation	• Value gained by customer:
	     Convenience and needs met by press of a button
	• Value gained by SingTel:
	     Exclusive long-term relationship, higher margins, predictable revenue

Fig. 3.25 Customer segmentation of SingTel (Tier 1 – Platinum Club)

Tier 2 – Silver Club

Business Scope for Tier 2 – Silver Club	
Customer Dimension	Description
Products and Service Plan	• Highly customized services that fit into the busy lifestyle of this young professional • Focus on service that offers convenience to the customers. Data service, information, and entertainment services • Introduction of contextual, relevance, and location-based services
Customer Complementors	• Value Services at reasonable pricing • CNN, ESPN Sports, Visa and MasterCard
Unique Competencies	• Deep knowledge of customer's lifestyle and development of "relevance" services to support their lifestyle • Customize services around the lifestyle of customer to create attraction of the customers to adopt these services
Value Proposition for Tier 2 – Silver Club	
Value Proposition	Description
Experiences	• Medium-term relationship developed over time with relatively good understanding of individual's lifestyle
Value Delivery Systems	• IT system that constantly analyzes the changing lifestyle of the customers as they evolve from teenagers to young adults • Introduce new services through new technologies as customers evolve and become more affordable • Value-added by beginning to be a more lifestyle center of customers

Value Appropriation	• Value gained by customer:
	     Convenience and needs met by press of a button
	• Value gained by SingTel:
	     Continuation of relationship and opportunity to establish long-term relationship, reap decent margins, and predictable revenue

Fig. 3.26 Customer segmentation of SingTel (Tier 2 – Silver Club)

The Mobile Phone Business – The Case of Telefónica Móviles de Colombia

The case of SingTel concentrates exclusively on the consumer market of the mobile telephone business. Telefónica Móviles de Colombia[6] experienced frustration similar to that which we described in the SingTel case because of the intensity of rivalry

Tier 3 – Care Club

Business Scope for Tier 3 – Care Club	
Customer Dimension	Description
Products and Service Plan	• Competitive and low-cost service plan that meets the need of customers • Talk time and messaging service focus • Introduction of "fun services," e.g., ringtones
Customer	• Teenagers or dependents • Price conscious but willing to adopt new services
Complementors	• ESPN Sports, Games providers and other "fun" content providers
Unique Competencies	• Knowledge of customer's usage pattern and development of specific plans that meet their usage, as well as their limited financial affordability • Highly customize price plan to meet their needs and maintain competitiveness
Value Proposition for Tier 3 - Care Club	
Value Proposition	Description
Experiences	• Accumulated knowledge to devise a service plan that will be optimal to meet the needs of "fresh" subscribers
Value Delivery Systems	• IT system that constantly analyzes the changing usage pattern changes • Introduce new and fun services as they become available • Value-added by constantly optimizing the service plan for the new customers

Value Appropriation	• Value gained by customer:
	   Both lifestyle to talk with friends and financial needs are met through optimization
	• Value gained by SingTel:
	   Gain a customer, a step into the house and opportunity to establish a long-term relationship as this "young" customer evolves

Fig. 3.27 Customer segmentation of SingTel (Tier 3 – Care Club)

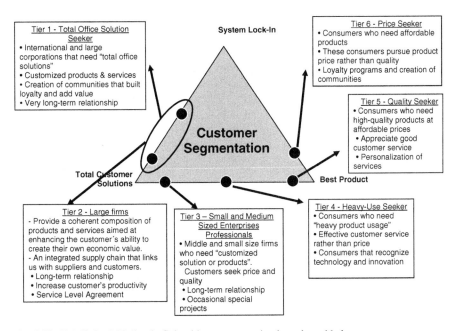

Fig. 3.28 Telefónica Móviles de Colombia – segmentation by value added

in a market that had become fully commoditized. In this case, however, Telefónica was attempting to address not only the consumer market but the business and professional markets as well. This led to a customer segmentation based upon six tiers, as presented in Fig. 3.28.

The three tiers that we clustered around the Best Product positioning in the triangle are part of the mass consumer market. The segmentation captures the predominant concern for prices, with some subtle different emphasis: For Tier 6 Price Seekers, the primary concern is affordability; Tier 5 Quality Seekers have a requirement for better quality products; and Tier 4 Heavy-User Seekers need more demanding services.

The remaining three tiers addressed the professional and business needs. Tier 3 provides customized solutions to small- and medium-sized enterprises as well as single professionals. Tiers 1 and 2 target Large Corporations where the mobile phone is a central part of a communication and management system that supports critical decisions in those firms.

We hope these two mobile telephone industry cases clearly illustrate the message that commoditization often is due to poor practices on the part of the participating firms and ignoring the market differences in needs and affordability within their client base. Sound customer segmentation with creative value propositions is often the proper remedy to change this situation.

Corporate Banking – The Case of Bank of Tokyo-Mitsubishi

Another form of segmentation that might not be very appropriate for the development of a sound strategy is segmentation by size. This is what the Corporate Banking Business of the Bank of Tokyo-Mitsubishi[7] used to categorize its corporate customers, as is displayed in Fig. 3.29, where the segmentation is based on the level of sales. One can argue that the size of the client company is a relevant criterion to recognize distinct needs across the customer base. However, this often does not turn out to be the case when trying to define an appropriate and effective value proposition. Not all large, medium, and small companies are alike. They do

	Main Customer Needs	Credit Risk	Comments
Global and large Japanese and Non-Japanese companies Annual sales more than $1B	• Global and domestic syndicated loan • Global cash management service • Global and domestic M&A advisory and Management Buy Out and Leveraged Buy Out loan • Investment service • Bond and equity underwriting • Derivatives and foreign exchange and settlement service	Very low	• Do business globally • Most of them are listed and can raise money from market (CP, bond, etc.) • Needs sophisticated "Total customer solution service" beyond finance
Medium to large Japanese companies Annual sales between $30M and $1B	• Low loan interest rate • Derivatives and foreign exchange and settlement service • Domestic M&A advisory and Management Buy Out and Leveraged Buy Out loan • Support in IPO • Support in starting international business	Low to middle	• Do business mainly in Japan • Need developed loan • Look toward listing
Small and medium Japanese companies Annual sales less than $30M	• Easy application process and quick loan approval • Accessibility even in a bad credit situation • Business succession	High	• Some of them are "papa and mama" companies • Needs simple loan as quickly as possible if necessary

Fig. 3.29 Conventional customer segmentation by size

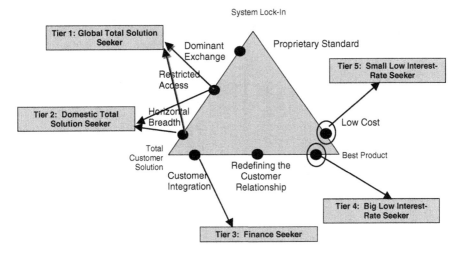

Fig. 3.30 Customer segmentation according to value added

not have the same needs or the same attitudes toward the bank. Often it is better to resort to a different driving force, such as the value added that can be provided to each customer tier, without regard to size.

Figure 3.30 suggests a segmentation based on five tiers, with increasing degrees of value added. The corresponding value propositions are presented in Fig. 3.31. Although size might still be a relevant determinant for identifying the membership of each tier, we are now looking through a different lens – the needs of our customers and our ability to solidify them appropriately – that could lead to a better expression of value proposition.

The Steel Business – The Case of Termium

Ternium is one of the leading steel companies in Latin America.[8] It manufactures a broad array of products through integrated processes that involve the extraction of iron ore from its own mines.

Like most mining companies, Ternium regarded its products merely as commodities. Customers were segmented into two large groups: domestic and export markets. Within these groups, customers were differentiated by the kind of products they bought and the kind of industry they belong to. Figures 3.32 and 3.33 give us the broad segmentation according to the products and industry.

It is not uncommon to find situations where managers use product- or industry-driven market segmentation. Notice that we are using the term "market segmentation" as opposed to "customer segmentation," which is what concerns us. We have to understand our customer needs to be able to provide creative value propositions. If we look at the customers strictly from a product lens, we will tend to commoditize

	Solutions We Provide	Our Financial Service	Benefits for Customers	Benefits for MUFG & MTMU
Tier 5 Small low interest-rate seeker	• Provide easy & quick examination process but high interest rate loan	• High interest rate quick loan using our credit scoring model	• Get quick & easy loan availability	• Reduce cost of loan application & examination process
Tier 4 Big low interest-rate seeker	• Provide low interest loan • Help their business succession	• Low interest rate prime loan • Business succession advisory	• Get low interest loan. This helps them reduce interest payment in a short-term	• Win loan deals to good borrowers in tough competition
Tier 3 Finance solution seeker	• Provide developed loan with derivatives • Support in IPO • Foreign exchange service	• Market-interest-based loan, IPO • Derivatives, foreign exchange service and settlement	• Get "best finance solution". This helps them get stronger financially in a long-term	• Build long relationship with customers through customized service though the customization is partial
Tier 2 Domestic total solution seeker	• Financing (beyond loans_, inc. IPO • Help their cash management • Help their growth through M&A deals of their international business start-up • Help their management of surplus funds	• Syndicated loan, IPO, bond & equity underwriting • Cash management, foreign exchange, settlement & A/R securitization • M&A advisory & loan • Support in starting international business • Investment service	• Get "best solution" beyond finance & "one stop service" in both commercial & investment banking. This helps them growth further	• Build long relationship with customers through customized service • "System Lock-In" (this would be great progress in the market in which transactions have been basically on deal by deal basis).
Tier 1 Global total solution seeker	• Global financing (beyond loans) • Help their cash management globally • Help their growth through global LM&A deals • Help their management of surplus funds	• Global & domestic syndicated loan, bond & equity underwriting • Global cash management service foreign exchange, settlement & A/R securitization • Global & domestic M&A advisory & loan • Investment service	• Get "best solution" beyond finance & "one stop service" in both commercial & investment banking, & both globally & domestically. This helps them growth further.	• Build long relationship with customers through customized service • "System Lock-In" (this would be great progress in the market in which transactions have been basically on deal by deal basis.

Fig. 3.31 Value proposition for each customer tier

- Raw Materials
- Semi-Finished Steel
- Flat Rolled Products
- Long Products
- Welded Tubes
- Beams
- Roll-Formed Products

Fig. 3.32 Ternium original segmentation by product

- Steel Makers
- Metal Mechanics
- Constructors
- Automotives
- Packing and food canning industrials
- Tubers
- Roll-Formed Product Users

Fig. 3.33 Ternium original segmentation by industry of users

the offer because most likely we will end up giving them undifferentiated products. Likewise, if we catalog customers according to the industry they belong to, we lose our capacity to differentiate them. Are we going to treat every customer in the automotive industry equally? That does not make much sense. Therefore, we need to rethink the segmentation criteria and offer a dimension different from products or industries.

Again, a better answer to the segmentation question seems to be to differentiate the customers according to the various degrees of value added that we can provide to them. This is presented in Fig. 3.34. The corresponding value proposition for each tier is given in Fig. 3.35.

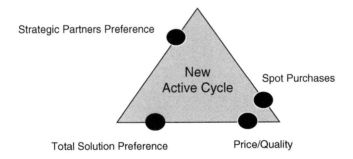

Fig. 3.34 Ternium original segmentation by value added

The Test of the Quality of the Customer Value Proposition

Having completed the customer segmentation and developed corresponding value propositions for each tier, it is proper to ask how powerful those value propositions are. We have indicated all along that companies typically face a broad array of

Tier 1	Strategic Partner Preference: Customers who provide a lock-in relationship with their supplier. Ternium contributes with its full experience and network to help to develop and improve the customer performance. Services include management training, relationships between the customer and their customers, sharing best management techniques, transferring best processing and production practices, and supporting strategic evaluation and implementation of future businesses.
Tier 2	Total Solution Preference: Customers that lack adequate structure to solve problems related to processing the material. Normally they are not able to overcome difficulties when the material has little variation in their specifications or when they need new product development.
Tier 3	Price/Quality Preference: Customers buy products with a regular frequency with preference for high quality at convenient price. Normally these clients do not need additional services except when they find quality problems
Tier 4	Spot Purchases Preference: The customers prefer to buy products at low price with relative quality. Usually they are spread around the world and make spot purchases.

Fig. 3.35 Description of customer tiers

customers that are treated according to their needs and capabilities. We have shown that the resulting tiers often lie across the full spectrum of positions in the Triangle. Therefore, we could expect to have a fairly heterogeneous set of distinct offers, some being extremely novel with a high value added content, and some getting close to a commodity offering.

Figure 3.36 describes the four tests that we run: Uniqueness, Sustainability, Value Added, and Bonding.

Tests for the Quality of a Customer Segmentation Value Proposition
Degree of Differentiation: How unique is the value proposition for each tier – meaning how distinct is it from the state-of-the-art offerings of a relevant competitor?
Difficulty of Imitation: If the value proposition is truly unique, how difficult is it to imitate or counteract it by the competitors – in other words how sustainable and long lasting is the differentiating quality of the value proposition?
Amount of Value-Added: How much value-added to the customer is implicit in the proposition – meaning what is the size of the benefits that the customer will be receiving?
Size of Bonding: What is the resulting degree of bonding between us and the customer – meaning what is the size of the switching cost and how much loyalty from the customer is the value proposition creating for us?

	UNIQUENESS Degree of Differentiation	SUSTAINABILITY Difficulty of Imitation	VALUE ADDED Amount of Value Added	BONDING Size of Bonding
Tier 1				
Tier 2				
Tier 3				
Tier 4				
Tier 5				
Tier 6				

Key: H = High, M = Medium, L = Low

Fig. 3.36 The test for the quality of the customer value proposition

To illustrate the application of these tests to a specific situation, we will use the Waste Management Company case that we discussed earlier in this chapter. Figure 3.37 reproduces the six tiers that WMC uses to segment its customers and

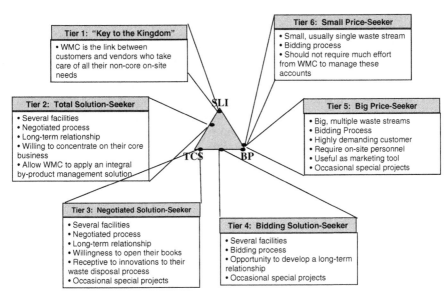

Fig. 3.37 Waste Management Company customer segmentation and its main characteristics

illustrates their positioning in the Triangle, which reveals the nature of their expected uniqueness, sustainability, value added and bonding.

The result of these four tests for the WMC tiers is presented in Fig. 3.38.

What the figure uncovers is not at all unusual.

Tiers 1 and 2, which are the premium options, contain an enormous amount of originality, value added and bonding, which is extraordinarily hard to imitate. The resulting value propositions are based on a deep proximity to the customers and jointly developed with them. It is not surprising, therefore, that we place them near a System Lock-in due to the very intense nature of the relationship.

	UNIQUENESS Degree of Differentiation	SUSTAINABILITY Difficulty of Imitation	VALUE ADDED Amount of Value Added	BONDING Size of Bonding
Tier 1	H	H	H	H
Tier 2	H	H	H	H
Tier 3	H	M	M	M
Tier 4	M	M	M	M
Tier 5	L	M	M	L
Tier 6	L	L	L	L

Key: H = High, M = Medium, L = Low

Fig. 3.38 The test for the quality of the customer value proposition applied to the WMC

Tiers 3 and 4 bring well-integrated solutions, which add significant value to the customer. But once they emerge, the top competitors most likely have the capabilities to imitate that offer, which makes the degree of bonding with the customer somewhat weaker.

At the end of the spectrum, Tiers 5 and 6 are inherently based on products that are not highly differentiated. The attributes of Uniqueness, Sustainability, Value Added, and Bonding begin to resemble those of a commodity product. Unless we ignore the less attractive markets, our portfolio of value propositions will cover the wide range of System Lock-in, Total Customer Solutions, and Best Product. That is one of the lessons of the Delta Model. Important companies play everywhere in the Triangle.

Who Is the Most Attractive Customer?

The test of the value proposition that we have just completed provides the basis to address the question, "Who is the most attractive customer?"
It is:

- The one who has the greatest gap between its needs and capabilities, and we are in a best position to close that gap
- The one who receives the highest value added
- The one who has the most positive attitudes towards us
- The one with whom we can jointly define a unique sustainable high value-added value proposition leading towards an unbreakable bonding.

If these conditions are met, these customers should also be the most profitable.

The Need for a Customer Database

It is clear by now that the Delta Model is based upon obtaining a deep and comprehensive knowledge of the customer. We can only define a proper customer value proposition if we understand thoroughly the customer needs and are able to propose customized solutions to them. Although the customer segments help us in bringing some order and uniformity to the ways in which we are going to be treating customers sharing some common attributes – which is the essence of the customer tiers – ultimately, we should deliver the value proposition in a granular way: One customer at a time.

This calls for the need to design, develop, and maintain one very important asset: A Customer Database. We should be careful in defining its content. At a minimum we should record the existing sales for each customer and its total available market to determine the amount that is unserved by us. This will allow us to determine the so-called white spaces, which are the additional sales opportunities that are available to us. This information is critical to developing a bottom-up estimate of potential sales. Rather than forecasting demand, which typically involves an extrapolation of the past into the future, this bottom-up approach of estimating the potentially available market gives us a preferred way of assessing opportunities for growth.

The customer database should also allow us to identify our profitability by individual customers. Often customer profitability is a steep nonlinear function, where a small percentage of customers concentrate a large portion of our profits, while a significant number generate losses. This information is extremely critical to possess.

Finally, the customer database should provide us with the basis to quantify our value proposition, namely what are the benefits to be received by the customer, and what are those that we will appropriate. Each customer should be mapped to only one customer tier, which identifies the best way to serve its needs. The database allows us to have a granular representation of each individual customer, the nature of our relationship, and expected degree of value added and the resulting bonding.

The Need for Experimentation

The application of the Delta Model, particularly if we do it the first time, invariably requires some fundamental changes to take place in the management of our business. Typically, we go from some existing customers that are served by the Best Product option to the definition of value propositions that will be anchored on the Total Customer Solution option. Ultimately, if at all possible, we will continue our search for System Lock-in opportunities.

All of this will lead to very challenging changes. The resulting mandate pushes us into an unknown territory. Often we may have intuitions and hypotheses about the nature of the changes we are recommending, but given that we have never tried them, their achievement is far from easy to realize. It is also extremely risky. We are abandoning our well-established practice, where we feel comfortable, to penetrate into a highly unpredictable arena. How are we going to do this?

Figure 3.39 is a good way to convey the enormous complexity of change. If we try to grasp the options to change in terms of size and speed, two central characteristics of this effort indicated in the figure, we can easily conclude that change is impossible! Small change executed slowly is irrelevant in this extremely fast world; large change implemented slowly is equally unacceptable; large scale change executed rapidly is way too risky; and finally, small change conducted too fast lead us into an excessive incrementalism that is incompatible with the demanding conditions of the business world.

What can we conclude from this? That change is impossible? We hope that this is not the case. The answer to this riddle is experimentation, as illustrated in Fig. 3.40.

Before embarking on a massive implementation of change, bringing most if not all the organization in that direction, we need to acquire the confidence that the value propositions that we have designed are correct, and that we can deliver what we are promising. To achieve that state of knowledge, we resort to experimentation. We should embark on a "pilot" effort (which involves a small scale project that we can execute rapidly). Take two or three special customers per tier, not necessarily

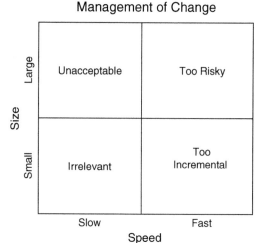

Fig. 3.39   The options and the obstacles to change

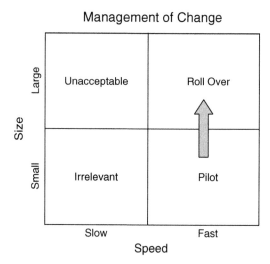

Fig. 3.40   Breaking the paradox of change – the need for experimentation

the most important ones, but those who are closer to us, to whom we can honestly admit that we would like to engage them in a pilot study that will culminate into the confirmation or the modification of our intended value propositions for those tiers. Once the pilots are completed, we will learn a great deal, and we will be able to roll over to the entire customer base the solutions that we have tested. Invariably, experimentation is a crucial part of the Delta Model.

Notes

1. We want to acknowledge the contribution of Brian Shaw in the definition of this segmentation dimension.
2. The company that is the subject to our analysis is being called The Waste Management Company, although this is not its real name. For reasons of confidentiality, we are not revealing the actual name. We would like to acknowledge the contribution of former MIT Sloan students Enrique Perez and Nicolas Droguett who undertook this assignment.
3. The Investment Retail Company is a fictitious entity that we are using to illustrate the strategic issues that confront institutions in financial retailing, particularly those in the Wealth Management Services industry. We would like to acknowledge the contribution of former MIT Sloan Fellow Todd Gershkowitz who provided invaluable assistance in this analysis..
4. This presentation is based upon the work of former Sloan Fellow Kelvin (Choon Koong) Chia, 2006, as part of the requirements of the MIT Sloan School Strategic Management course. It does not intend to represent the views of Singapore Airlines on how to manage its customer base.
5. This presentation is based upon the work of former Sloan Fellow Hai Thoo Cheong, 2008, as part of the requirements of the MIT Sloan School Strategic Management course. It does not intend to represent the views of Singapore Telecommunications on how to manage its customer base.
6. This case is from a lecture at MIT Sloan School, presented by Sergio Regueros, "MOVISTAR: The Delta Model in Action," December 5, 2006.
7. This presentation is based upon the work of former Sloan Fellow Toru Fujita, 2008, as part of the requirements of the MIT Sloan School Strategic Management course. It does not intend to represent the views of The Bank of Tokyo-Mitsubishi on how to manage its customer base.
8. This presentation is based upon the work of former Sloan Fellow Carlos Brovarone, 2008, as part of the requirements of the MIT Sloan School Strategic Management course. It does not intend to represent the views of Ternium on how to manage its customer base.

Chapter 4
The Firm as a Bundle of Competencies: Understanding the Depth and the Breadth of Our Capabilities

There are two very different tasks that we have to address to perform the strategic analysis required in the Delta Model. The first one is to look into the demand side of the business, which leads to Customer Segmentation and Customer Value Proposition, the subject that we covered in the previous chapter. The essence of that analysis is to break the total marketplace into elements that allow us to target the individual needs of the customers in the most effective way.

The second task required by the Delta Model is to do a strategic analysis that is of a very different nature. Now, our attention turns to the supply side of the business. Instead of decomposing the whole into relevant pieces, we must focus in an integral way and with the largest possible scope on the full set of competencies of our own organization.

Whether it is a corporation that contains a portfolio of businesses or a single business entity, it is important to examine the firm as a whole, because we would like to bring all of our capabilities to bear in order to develop the most effective value proposition. In fact, we might even look beyond our own organization and include all of the key participants of the Extended Enterprise.

To guide us in this effort, we use the eight strategic positions of the Delta Model that we introduced in Chapter 2 (illustrated in Fig. 4.1) to make a catalog of the existing and desired competencies of the firm. We already utilized them in Chapter 3 to discern the role they play in serving each specific customer tier.

We do not want to create a trivial list of things that we do well – the so-called "strengths" of the more conventional analysis. We are not looking for a recital of "things that we do well." Rather, we want to identify our legitimate claims for leadership. It is a serious attempt to capture those competencies in which we are second to none in each of the eight critical dimensions in the Triangle. Keep the following in mind with respect to determining the firm's underlying competencies of each of the eight strategic positions:

Best Product

- Low Cost: Identify the capabilities that allow us to get significant advantages in our cost infrastructure relative to our competitors.

A.C. Hax, *The Delta Model*, DOI 10.1007/978-1-4419-1480-4_4,
© Springer Science+Business Media, LLC 2010

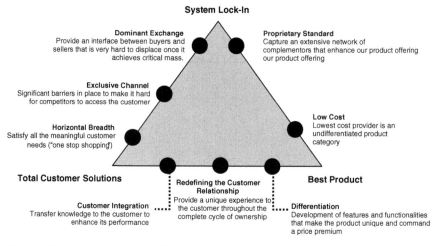

Fig. 4.1 Identifying the competencies of the business – the eight strategic positions as a guiding framework

- Differentiation: Examine the superior attributes that we possess and that allow us to develop and deliver a stream of products with characteristics distinct from the rest of the pack.

Total Customer Solutions

- Redefining the Customer Relationship: Analyze the advantages we might have surfaced from a deep understanding of our customers and the way we attract, satisfy, and retain them.
- Customer Integration: Assess the nature of our unique knowledge base and develop a firm understanding of how it can be transferred to our customers for enriching the solutions to their most critical problems, thus enhancing their profitability.
- Horizontal Breadth: Review and catalog the fullness of the portfolio of products and services that we can provide to our customers either alone or with the support of our Extended Enterprise.

System Lock-In

- Restricted Access: Look at the existence of possible barriers to entry that impede our competitors from reaching into our customer base, and the barriers to exit that hold our customers in our orbit.
- Dominant Exchange: Examine our capacity to transfer to our customers systems that we own and are critical to the conduct of their business.
- Proprietary Standards: Detect our capacity to generate important and impacting intellectual value that attracts complementors and produces a strong network that, to a great extent, we are able to control.

These brief descriptions are sufficient to convey the central importance that each of these dimensions can have in consolidating the capabilities of the firm. Each one of them carries a unique form of competitive value.

Identifying the Bundle of Competencies in Practice

We started this book by affirming that the essence of strategy should not be viewed as achieving competitive advantage but rather as a way of gaining customer bonding. We also warned against the use of competitors as benchmarks, because this could lead to imitation, congruency, and, eventually, commoditization.

These warnings are first addressed in the strategic task that we labeled Customer Segmentation and Customer Value Proposition. The proper execution of that task is an extremely effective way to distance us from our competitors. However, we need to go beyond that into the analysis of the firm's competencies. In this case, we compare ourselves against the leading competitors, not to imitate them, but to assess our capabilities to deliver to our customers value propositions that are unequivocally unique.

The Value Propositions are future oriented. It is not what we are doing, but what we wish and intend to do that defines their content. Therefore, when addressing the firm's competencies, we begin by examining what our existing capabilities are and then focus on the future competencies that we must develop to meet the challenges implicit in the Value Proposition.

Cataloging the existing and desired competencies of the company is not nearly as difficult as the demanding job of segmenting the customer and defining the value proposition. The tasks associated with the identification of capabilities for the Best Product option are quite concrete and tangible. Analyzing the Total Customer Solution could be more taxing, particularly if the firm starts from a position of being either totally or significantly product-centric. But revealing the necessary competencies to accomplish this task is vital, because going from Best Product to Total Customer Solution is a mandatory transformation.

What is most surprising is the way companies respond when asked to identify System Lock-In competencies. So many companies are mute when asked to perform this exercise that one might assume that this is a rare and demanding position. On the contrary, our experience indicates that invariably executives are able to uncover not one but several claims that might link them to System Lock-In strategic positioning in the future. This is very encouraging, even if the output may be a bit unrealistic. There is nothing wrong in engaging in the pursuit of a hard-to-achieve ideal. This seems to indicate that when executives are challenged to take on extraordinarily high levels of excellence, they match the task. One wonders how much potential is not properly reached, simply because of a mindset that is anchored in goals that are easy to accomplish.

Investment Retail Company as a Bundle of Competencies

In the previous chapter we provided an introduction of the Investment Retail Company (IRC) and analyzed its customer segmentation. Here, we detail the

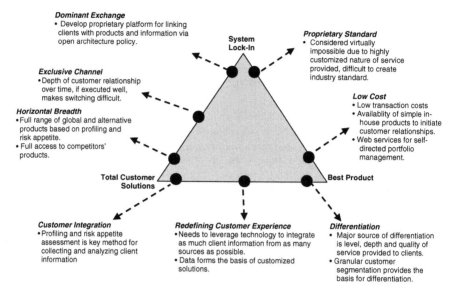

Fig. 4.2 Investment retail company (IRC) – bundle of competencies analysis

competencies of this business according to the eight strategic positions of the Triangle (see Fig. 4.2).

The cataloging of the competencies of IRC allows us to understand what constitutes the basis for a successful strategy and how broad the strategy could be. By examining the capabilities of IRC, as described in Figure 4.2, we conclude that the firm is in a very strong position to serve the quite demanding set of customers that we identify in Chapter 3, covering the three major options which are spelled out by the Delta Model: Best Product, Total Customer Solutions, and System Lock-In. Let us review each option.

● Best Product

Undoubtedly, wealth management is not a low-cost business, particularly when dealing with the high-end customer tiers. That does not imply, however, that IRC should not be making significant efforts to achieve a very effective platform that will support low-cost transactions. This, together with the availability of an in-house set of simple products, will permit IRC to attract the Basic Investor, which is critical for the development of a robust client base in the future. Also the availability of a sound web site is essential for those customers who want to have access to information that facilitate a self-directed management of their investment portfolio.

Differentiation capabilities are also of vital importance in the financial service industry, where so often the products tend to be commoditized. The major source of differentiation resides in the quality, depth, and personalization of the services offered to the customers. This is accomplished by a well-trained group of managers, supported by a granular customer database and compensated with the proper incentives that seek alignment between the interests of the customers and those of IRC managers.

• Total Customer Solutions

We strongly believe that financial service institutions can particularly benefit from adopting the Total Customer Solutions option that is part of the Delta Model.

This is so because every customer transaction is recorded, which provides the basis to satisfy the individual needs of each one of them. Because financial services are often being commoditized, recognizing this opportunity could allow a firm to develop strategies with high degree of uniqueness and great value added to the customer. In other words it will allow the financial company to be extremely successful in this industry.

In Fig. 4.2 we identified the competencies that would permit IRC to develop a sound customer solutions strategy. Redefining Customer Experience means to offer the kind of uniqueness we refer to; it has to be supported by leveraging technology to permit the building of granular databases and the integration of the client information from as many sources as possible. The Customer Integration is achieved through the development of careful profiling of each customer that allows understanding their willingness to assume risks by acquiring financial instruments with high-return potentials. Horizontal Breadth is the availability of a complete range of products and services including those available through competitors.

• System Lock-In

Out of all the options to achieve System Lock-In only two are available in this industry: Exclusive Channel and Dominant Exchange. We think it is fair to rule out the development of Proprietary Standards due to the highly customized nature of services provided, particularly to the high-end customers.

Exclusive Channel is obtained one customer at a time through the creation of such an in-depth relationship that will make both undesirable and infeasible for the customers to switch to a competitor. Dominant Exchange is obtained through the development of proprietary platform that allows giving the customer a richness of information that is not available elsewhere.

The collectiveness of all of these capabilities will allow IRC to serve each of its customers in a way that is suitable for the individual needs in every stage of the life cycle. The lesson here is to be fully aware of the dynamics of the evolution as the customer begins to mature and most likely acquire larger financial assets. We should travel with this customer through his or her life being a loyal counselor for the important decisions that represent wealth management.

Singapore Airlines as a Bundle of Competencies

Back in the late 1960s and early 1970s, when Singapore was struggling to build a nation, the odds of an airline company surviving without a domestic market were slim. From a domestic traveler's point of view, there was no need to have a national airline.

Many of the competitive advantages that SA enjoys today arise from decisions made by the Singapore government over the last four decades. It is important to highlight three of the most significant competitive advantages and discuss how SA has leveraged them to get to where it is today.

In the 1960s and 1970s, both SA and the Singapore government recognized the strategic role that a premium airline would play not only in promoting the Singapore brand name overseas, but also in developing the advantage of Singapore's strategic geographical location. At the crossroads of flights from Europe to Australia, South Asia to Northeast Asia, and America to South Asia, and with Singapore as its home base, SA is a key node in international air travel between these major geographical regions.

A second competitive advantage was the excellent airport infrastructure that helped to enhance Singapore's position as a key strategic hub. The efficiency of a world-class airport in the early 1980s to meet the increased demands of international air travel, and the continuous expansion and upgrading of the airport well into the 1990s and even to this day facilitated the expansion of SA.

A third competitive advantage accrues from the adoption of an "open skies" policy by Singapore and a number of free-trade agreements. These have allowed SA to make entry into new markets.

There are five cornerstones of SA competencies: total service delivery and service excellence; service and product innovation; strong branding; training; and sound management practices.

- Total Service Delivery and Service Excellence
  Many airlines view air travel merely as a commodity sold to the customer to enable him or her to move from Point A to B at the lowest cost. Unlike them, SA strives to deliver a total experience that makes the journey enjoyable. It goes all out to pamper the customer, and deliver a high and consistent level of service that is unmatched anywhere else. Today, SA does not only benchmark itself with other leading airlines, namely Cathay Pacific, Qantas, and British Airways, it seeks to emulate the best practices of the hotel and service industries to provide more unique experiences. For example, many of the exclusive SA lounges are like 5-star hotel lounges with equivalent level of service. Again, the key role played by the Singapore Girl must be highlighted. SA has found no better way to communicate the airline's commitment to service than through the Singapore Girl providing stellar service and the delicate touch of Asian service and hospitality to all passengers.

  Service excellence is continuously honed through constant service improvement. Customer feedback, whether compliments or complaints, serves as a great tool to refine the customer experience. Staff feedback at all levels is also encouraged to enable everyone to contribute to service enhancement. There is a quarterly Service Performance Index that is used as a barometer to measure the airline's performance and to highlight which areas need improvement.

For SA, the commitment to customer retention is defined as

$$\text{Service Delivery} = \text{Zero Defects},$$

and

$$\text{Service Recovery} = \text{Zero Defections}.$$

This is based on SA's statistics, which reveal that customers who experienced bad service complain, on average, to 11 people, while those who experience good service only tell 6 people. They also find that it is 5 times more expensive to attract a new customer than it is to retain one.

- Service and Product Innovation
  One of the pleasures of flying SA is that it is always adding new services and products to its already impressive portfolio. Besides keeping an eye on its competitors, SA is constantly studying other industries for trends in related service industries, such as the restaurant, hotel, and credit card businesses, to understand changing customer tastes and needs. SA is recognized as the global market leader in redefining air travel.

  SA has a reputation for many firsts. In the 1980s, it had the first A300 Superbus, the B747-300 Big Top, the B757, and the A310-200. It was also the first airline in the world to operate an international commercial flight across the Pacific Ocean with the 747-400 Megatop. In the 1990s, Singapore Airlines revolutionized in-flight communications and entertainment through the KrisFone – the first global sky telephone service – and KrisWorld offerings. More recently, it became the first to introduce fully reclining seats in business class. A glance of the news and press releases through the website will reveal that this is a company that is in constant motion, and constantly innovating.

- Strong Branding
  The Singapore Girl icon has survived more than 30 years. It is a testament to the deliberate and focused efforts of clever branding and marketing. Using the Singapore Girl is a wonderful way of selling the company as it is not an abstract concept that is hard for the common person on the street to grasp. The Singapore Girl is the epitome of service to SA's customers and somebody with whom you can interact and identify easily.

  The SA brand is further bolstered by other factors such as having one of the youngest fleets in the world and being the foremost reference for the quality of service provided to the customer in the large passenger aircraft category.

- Training
  Recognizing that the business is service-oriented, customer-centric, and that customer tastes and needs are constantly evolving, SA invests heavily in training the front-line staff, particularly the stewards and stewardesses, counter staff, and customer relations, as they represent the primary customer–company interface. Staff are taught how to deal with the stress and demands of handling customers' high expectations. A recent initiative is Transforming Customer Service (TCS), which involves five groups – cabin crew, engineering, ground services, flight operations,

and sales support. This is to ensure that there is full integration across the five groups to provide an even higher quality of customer service.

- Sound Management Practices
  SA is the world's most profitable airline not by chance but as a consequence of very sound management practices that have been instituted over the years. SA has excellent financials and a strong cash flow position. This serves as a strategic buffer against shocks such as economic downturns and oil price hikes. The strong cash position also allows the company to invest in strategic growth areas as well as to engage in oil hedging positions to minimize risks to the company's bottom line. The decision to maintain a very young fleet is also a strategic management decision not only to preserve the premium brand but also because of the fuel savings that would accrue.

Figure 4.3 follows the Delta Model Framework to catalog the competencies of Singapore Airlines according to the relevant strategic positions in the Triangle. Notice that none is offered in the categories of Low Cost, Restricted Access, and Proprietary Standards, because they are not relevant to explain the level of excellence achieved by this airline.

Delta Model and Competitiveness: A New Approach to Competitor Analysis

In the previous sections we have discussed the ways in which the eight strategic positions of the Delta Model can be used in guiding the descriptions of the competences of the firm, and we have given illustrations to help in clarifying these concepts.

There is another use of the eight competitive positions that we have found quite intriguing. This is to use them to conduct a competitor analysis. We have hinted at it when introducing the definition of the firms' competencies. We stated that this exercise forces us into a comparison with the leading competitors. If we claim to possess uniqueness and leadership in some capacities, implicitly we are asserting that we are superior to our competitors in them.

To illustrate how to perform a competitor analysis we will now compare the capabilities that Sony and Polycom[1] bring to capture the video conferencing market. We will examine first Sony's competencies in this business, and then we will contrast them against Polycom's competencies, the leading company in that industry.

Sony Video Conferencing: An Analysis of Its Competencies

In 1987, Sony started developing video conferencing products to enhance conference room productivity for global businesses, using them to conduct meetings, training, and consultation between various locations across the world. Today, high-quality visual communication systems are widely used for international board meetings, large exhibitions, and international conferences.

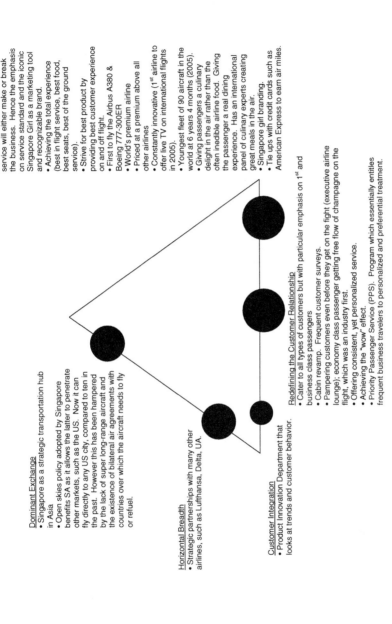

Differentiation
- Understanding that the airline industry is by nature a service industry, and that the quality of service will either make or break the business. Hence the emphasis on service standard and the iconic Singapore Girl as a marketing tool and recognizable brand.
- Achieving the total experience (best in flight service, best food, best seats, best of the ground service).
- Strive for best product by providing best customer experience on and off flight.
- First to fly the Airbus A380 & Boeing 777-300ER
- World's premium airline
- Priced at a premium above all other airlines
- Constantly innovative (1st airline to offer five TV on international flights in 2005).
- Youngest fleet of 90 aircraft in the world at 6 years 4 months (2005).
- Giving passengers a culinary delight in the air rather than the often inedible airline food. Giving the passenger a real dining experience. Has an international panel of culinary experts creating great meals in the air.
- Singapore girl branding.
- Tie ups with credit cards such as American Express to earn air miles.

Dominant Exchange
- Singapore as a strategic transportation hub in Asia
- Open skies policy adopted by Singapore benefits SA as it allows the latter to penetrate other markets, such as the US. Now it can fly directly to any US city, compared to ten in the past. However this has been hampered by the lack of super long-range aircraft and the existence of bilateral air agreements with countries over which the aircraft needs to fly or refuel.

Horizontal Breadth
- Strategic partnerships with many other airlines, such as Lufthansa, Delta, UA.

Customer Integration
- Product Innovation Department that looks at trends and customer behavior.

Redefining the Customer Relationship
- Cater to all types of customers but with particular emphasis on 1st and business class passengers
- Cabin revamp. Frequent customer surveys.
- Pampering customers even before they get on the flight (executive airline lounge); economy class passenger getting free flow of champagne on the flight, which was an industry first.
- Offering consistent, yet personalized service.
- Achieving the "wow" effect.
- Priority Passenger Service (PPS). Program which essentially entitles frequent business travelers to personalized and preferential treatment.

Fig. 4.3 Competencies of Singapore Airlines

Sony possesses a broad line of equipments and systems for the office environment, including visual communication products (VC), LCD projections, plasma panels, networking storage players, and other consumer products.

Figure 4.4 describes the competencies that Sony has acquired in the video conferencing business. A close examination leads us to conclude that Sony has quite an outstanding set of capabilities, spanning literally all of the positions in the Triangle. We can imagine Sony executives feeling very comfortable with this impressive foundation for their business. The surprising story, however, is that Sony is only the number three player in that market.

It is natural, therefore, to turn our attention to Polycom in order to explain why Sony's performance is lagging significantly the leader.

A Comparison of Polycom and Sony Video Conferencing: A Contrast of Competencies

Polycom enjoys 45% market share and the No. 1 position for many years in the VC market. It earns over $300 million annually, which is 3 to 4 times Sony's annual revenues. Its reputation in the industry has been remarkably high. The word "Polycom" is as strongly identified with visual communication products as the word "Walkman" is with small cassette recorders.

Figure 4.5 describes Polycom's competencies according to the eight strategic positions in the Triangle. (Note that the size of the circles represents the magnitude of the competencies in each of the strategic positions possessed by Polycom. Key: black = competencies equally shared by Sony and Polycom and therefore neutralize each other; gray = competencies that only Sony has and therefore gives a competitive advantage with regard to Polycom; gray Italic = competencies that only Polycom has and therefore give a competitive advantage with regard to Polycom.) This figure also serves to contrast Polycom's and Sony's capabilities by distinguishing three categories: (1) competencies that Sony has and Polycom doesn't have, (2) competencies shared by both Sony and Polycom (they are on the same foot on these qualifications), and (3) competencies that Polycom has and Sony does not.

To assess the relative strength of Sony and Polycom's competencies in each one of the eight positions in the triangle, we have added the circles in Figs. 4.4 and 4.5. The size of the circles in Fig. 4.4 represents the capabilities that Sony has in each strategic position. It is apparent that Sony has great capabilities in Best Product, less significant ones in Total Customer Solution, and extremely embryonic in System Lock-In. Figure 4.5 reflects a completely different story for Polycom. We can see that the size of the circles are much better balanced, demonstrating that Polycom is an equal effective player in both Best Product and Total Customer Solutions, and claim strong qualifications in System Lock-In.

This requires a further analysis. At the position of Low Cost, Sony seems to have slightly more advantages than Polycom, but the differences are not so significant. When it comes to Differentiation, Polycom has outstanding capabilities for long-term video conferencing and audio conferencing technologies, emerging from

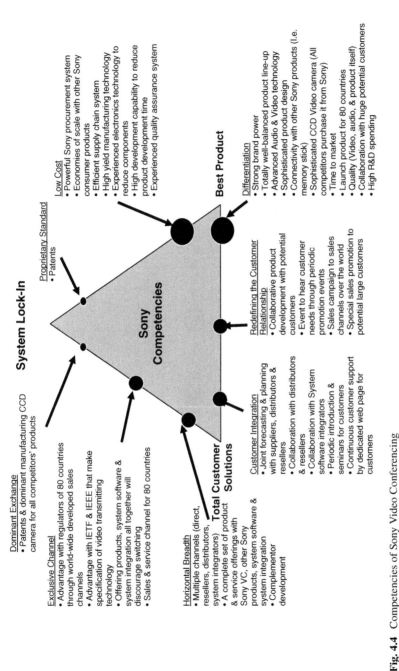

Fig. 4.4 Competencies of Sony Video Conferencing

Note: The size of the circles represents the magnitude of the competencies in each of the strategic positions possessed by Sony.

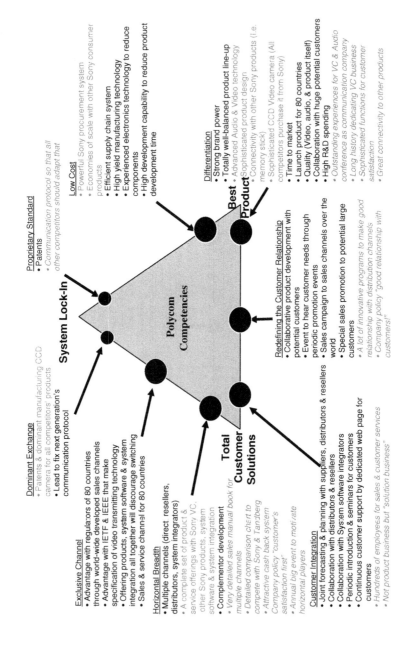

Fig. 4.5 Polycom vs. Sony Video Conferencing: a contrast of competencies

a long history dedicated to the VC business, sophisticated patents, and great connectivity of Polycom products with other vendors' products. This is particularly true for its echo-canceling technology, which is crucial for smooth remote conversations and is much superior to all competitors' products, including Sony.

Regarding Customer Integration, Polycom has several hundred employees dedicated to sales and customer services, compared to around 50 for Sony. In addition, Polycom's top management believe that VC is not a "hardware business" but a "solution business," and act accordingly. In the Customer Engagement position, Polycom has been promoting innovative programs to assure good relationships with channels. With regard to Horizontal Breadth, Polycom provides very detailed sales manuals to the distribution channels, including product comparisons. It also offers attractive cash-back systems and organizes a big annual event for all its distributors. All of these efforts produce a highly motivated distribution force.

Concerning the "System Lock-In" position, Polycom focuses on the development of important technical standards, such as the next-generation communication protocols, video and audio codec, and other crucial technologies, attracting complementors to lock-in to the Polycom platform.

Now we understand much better the superior qualifications of Polycom vs. Sony and the challenges that it implies for this firm. What could Sony do to respond? Certainly, Sony has to devote a substantial effort to counteract its limitations in this area. At this stage, we can suggest at least two things.

First, we have to go back to Customer Segmentation. We have to make sure that we can offer our existing and new clients superior and sustainable value propositions that will add considerable value to them and will lead to closer bonding.

Then we reflect on the Existing Competencies and decide what new capabilities we should add to narrow the gap with Polycom, but most importantly to help in the creation of a superior customer offering.

The initial process to accomplish these two tasks is presented in Fig. 4.6, where we propose a new customer segmentation for the Sony Video Conferencing business and also match the competencies required to support each corresponding value proposition.

Using the Delta Model to Assess the Merits of Possible Mergers and Acquisitions – The Case of Cognos and IBM

Often the reason that drives a firm to acquire or merge with another company is to strengthen its strategic capabilities. When the two firms have assets and competencies that complement each other, the potential rewards of this acquisition could be quite significant.

The methodology that we have developed with the Delta Model framework to assess the competencies of a firm can be very useful to assess the merits of such an acquisition. We illustrate this point using a case involving the acquisition of Cognos by IBM[2] that took place in November 2007, a $5 billion investment that constituted

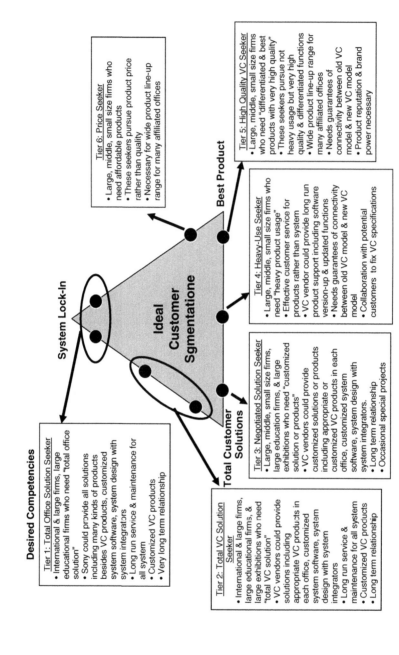

Fig. 4.6 Proposed customer segmentation for Sony Video Conference business – matching the new and desired competencies

the largest acquisition in IBM's history at that time. Cognos is an Ottawa-based Canadian software company. Its area of expertise resides in business intelligence, which is an umbrella term used to describe a market that has its roots in executive information systems that extract and leverage data to enable monitoring and supporting decision making. One of its breakthrough products is ReportNet, a completely web-based enterprise reporting solution to address all the organization's reporting requirements.

Typically, in analyzing the impact of an acquisition, we would first describe the competencies of the acquired and acquiring companies and then assess the resulting capabilities of the combined entity. In this case, given the size, complexities, and diversified nature of IBM, we will limit ourselves to assessing the existing competencies of Cognos prior to this acquisition – which is presented in Fig. 4.7 – and the resulting competencies of Cognos after the acquisition – which is illustrated in Fig. 4.8. The conclusions are fairly straightforward. Let us examine what has been enhanced in each strategic position:

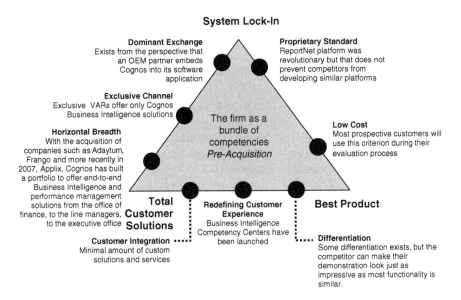

Fig. 4.7 Competencies of Cognos pre-acquisition by IBM

- *Lost Cost*: This is not a business where a lowest cost structure provides significant competitive advantage. Although this position is enhanced by the acquisition it is not a very productive area in which to concentrate our efforts.
- *Differentiation*: Significantly strengthened by the enormous weight of the IBM brand.
- *Customer Integration*: Huge amounts of relevant knowledge and practices that can be of productive use to customize offers and then provide integrated solutions to the customers.

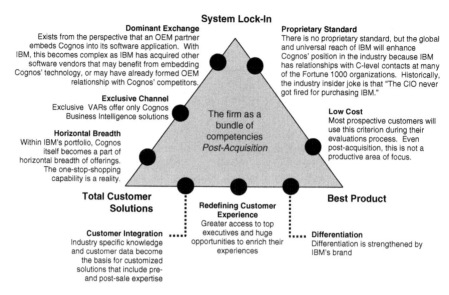

Fig. 4.8 Competencies of Cognos post-acquisition by IBM

- *Redefining the Customer Experience*: IBM's relationships with the executives and its depth of business knowledge allow for the development of unique experiences.
- *Horizontal Breadth*: Cognos is now able to extend its breadth of products and services to provide a genuine one-stop-shopping opportunity.
- *Exclusive Channel*: There are many Value Added Resellers (VAR) who offer exclusively Cognos systems with Business Intelligence solutions. This is enhanced by IBM extension of businesses.
- *Dominant Exchange*: This position is affected both favorably and unfavorably with the acquisition, since IBM can both promote OEM relationships that imbed Cognos in their offering – which is a plus – but also had acquired competitors of Cognos that have established a relationship with some OEM that exclude Cognos.
- *Proprietary Standard*: Although Cognos software is a revolutionary platform, it does not constitute a standard for the industry that cannot be developed in similar platforms. However, the enormous presence of IBM in the industry could easily help Cognos to become the preferred Business Intelligence system.

The final conclusion is that, indeed, there is a significant enhancement of the competitiveness of Cognos after the acquisition by IBM. As with every merger, however, this comes with both opportunities and challenges. Integrating into an organization is never easy, particularly when dealing with a company of such complexity as IBM. Cognos had a payroll of about 4,000 employees at the time of the acquisition, about one-hundredth of IBM's. Not the least of the challenges will be for Cognos to retain its culture and identity once it becomes part of such a strong organization as IBM.

We have limited our discussion to understand how Cognos gains in terms of its strategic competencies. Further analysis can be done to address the task of the changes that Cognos will introduce to their customers' value propositions and to examine the benefits of enhancing its extended enterprise – two topics that also can be properly studied with the help of the Delta Model.

Lessons from the Delta Model

Think of your firm as a bundle of competencies, not merely as an engine for developing, making and distributing products.

This is a major switch in mindset. So many firms are frustrated, particularly with the low returns that they get from their technology investments, because they tend to apply that technology strictly to the development of new products or to making them more efficient. Because of the pervasive nature of technology, it can seldom be the source of singular competitive advantage. However, if we use our knowledge base to provide solutions for our customers, it is most likely that we will produce singular answers.

Understand deeply your customer needs. Segment the customer base to differentiate meaningful value propositions to each customer tier.

This is another task that sometimes is neglected in the business world. Companies tend to give much more attention to their competitors than to their customers. It is much easier to search for sources of growth and profitability once you understand in a granular way your customer base.

The key to exploit opportunities for growth and profitability is to match your competencies with your customer needs. Try to be creative, bold, and fast.

The two tasks that we have addressed in Chapters 3 and 4 are the genuine foundations of a proper strategy. Understanding your competencies and your customers and matching your capabilities with your customers' needs is of the essence.

The great companies play simultaneously in the three vertices of the Triangle

- Best Products: All of them enjoy outstanding operational effectiveness which produces a low-cost infrastructure and a differentiated stream of products of great quality.
- Total Customer Solutions: All of them have a deep understanding of their customers, who receive creative and unique value propositions.
- System Lock-In: All of them have at least one legitimate leadership claim to achieve some form of System Lock-in. This is normally achieved through admirable innovation and effective use of information technology.

Notes

1. This presentation is based upon the work of former Sloan Fellow Makoto Ishii, 2006, as part of the requirements of the MIT Sloan School Strategic Management course. It does not intend to represent the views of Sony or Polycom on how to manage its customer base.
2. This presentation is based upon the work of former Sloan Fellow Cathy Yum, 2008, as part of the requirements of the MIT Sloan School Strategic Management course. It does not intend to represent the views of Cognos or IBM on how to manage its customer base.

Chapter 5
The Mission of the Business: Capturing the Strategic Transformation

The mission of the business integrates the diagnostic tasks of the previous two chapters – developing our customer segmentation strategy on the demand side and identifying the firm's bundle of competencies on the supply side of the business – so we can capture and articulate the nature of the transformation we intend to pursue.

Together, both tasks provide us with an innovative diagnosis of our strategic situation and guide us into a more productive redefinition of our business strategy. They produce important insights into the way we should change the current focus of the business.

What we mean by the "mission statement" is not a set of polished and cosmetic-driven pronouncements that we read in annual reports. Rather, what we want to generate at this stage of the planning process is a redefinition of our business strategy, an objective assessment of where we are and where we want to go. This acknowledgment of the challenges facing our organization is essential to the development of the strategic agenda – the pragmatic action programs that will allow us to execute the transformation we intend to undertake.

Strategy Means Change

It would be a pleasant state of affairs if we were so pleased with our current strategic situation that no change were needed in the way we ran our business. Alas, this is rarely the case. Strategy means change in direction, and the mission is the construct that allows us to meaningfully define and communicate the nature of that change both inside and outside of the of the organization.

We can't possibly over overemphasize this point. A strategy that is not well communicated is meaningless, and it will never become an effective reality. That is why the mission is crucial in the strategy formation process. It aggregates and describes the strategic change we intend to conduct, captures the challenges implicit to that change, and helps us to communicate them effectively to all relevant parties.

A.C. Hax, *The Delta Model*, DOI 10.1007/978-1-4419-1480-4_5,

The Mission of the Business

Three elements need to be addressed to fully define the mission of the business. They are the selection of a planning horizon, the description of changes in the business scope, and the statement of the mission. Let us examine each of these three elements.

Planning Horizon

In order to describe the existing and future state of the business, we need to develop a planning horizon that defines how far into the future we plan to look to capture the transformation we desire. In this highly turbulent environment, a planning horizon of 3–5 years may be optimal. There are obvious exceptions, such as the case of an extraordinarily changing business environment, where you should shorten the horizon to 1 or 2 years; or if you are in an industry with a slower clock speed, such as mining or energy, which needs extensive time horizons to deploy net assets. In these instances, 10–15 years may be a more appropriate timeline.

The Description of the Changes in the Business Scope

Defining the changes in the business scope is an activity that should capture the existing, the future, and the otherwise desired state of the business you seek. We want to be concrete, objective, and specific in this description. To accomplish this task we employ eight dimensions required to give as full and yet succinct a description of the business as possible. These eight dimensions are listed in the working format we use for this purpose and are presented in Fig. 5.1. They represent the key strategic descriptors of the nature of the business. In their description we do not want to provide a detailed listing of the components of each dimension, but rather give a summary of the intended transformation of the business.

The eight dimensions include:

1. **Product Scope:** Articulate all critical changes we feel are central for our product portfolio to reinforce our strategy.
2. **Service Scope:** Service is the central pieces needed to transfer relevant knowledge to the customer and to launch a powerful approach toward total customer solutions. We need to recognize which new initiatives are required to consolidate this deliverable.
3. **Customer Scope:** Having completed the customer segmentation, assigned the proper priorities to the resulting customer tiers, and developed the respective value propositions, we need to summarize the expected changes that we plan to implement in our customer base.
4. **End-User Scope:** In many businesses we need to recognize the end-user as a separate market entity. This is typically the final consumer or the customer of

Mission Statement

Changes in Business Scope
Product Scope From: To:
Service Scope From: To:
Customer Scope From: To:
End-User Scope From: To:
Channel Scope From: To:
Complementor Scope From: To:
Geographical Scope From: To:
Unique Competencies Scope From: To:

Fig. 5.1 The format to describe the mission statement and the changes in the business scope

our customer, who needs to be properly addressed in our value propositions. Indicate the changes that we expect to make to target this constituency.

5. **Channel Scope:** Channels are very central to a sound strategy, because they are the mechanisms we use to reach our customers. What changes in the scope of the channels or distributors do you plan to include in the mission?

6. **Complementor Scope:** The complementors are an important part of our extended enterprise. They need to be included and given the recognition they deserve. What plans do we have to transform our relationships with them?

7. **Geographical Scope:** Extending the geographical reach of the business is a dimension of critical importance, in particular, when it involves penetration in a wide array of countries in the pursuit of a global strategy. Where do your opportunities lie?

8. **Unique Competencies Scope:** This issue should be the subject of deep reflection when assessing the existing and desired competencies of the business. Summarize your conclusions and stress the changes necessary to carry them out in the future.

Each of these dimensions carries critical strategic importance. A composite of the full set allows us to present a fairly comprehensive description of our strategic intent.

The Mission Statement

The last key component left to produce is a compelling, dynamic, and well-reasoned mission statement. It should be a brief declaration of what we intend the business to become and clearly communicate our expectations for leadership, for the way we will serve our key constituencies, and for the future performance of the organization.

Such a document often is written by the CEO, conveying his or her core beliefs, and is used broadly in and out of the business organization to communicate the essence of what we are.

Strategic Transformation: What Others Have Done

The Case of the Chemical Coatings Company

To understand better the central issues of this firm and properly appreciate the definition of its mission statement, we briefly introduce the company and give a sense of its customer segmentation.

Chemical Coatings[1] belongs to one of the major chemical corporations in the USA. Its primary activity is to sell a host of products, including solvents, resins, additives, and colorants to paint and coating manufacturers. Sales are made directly or through major distributors. The final end-users are companies in a wide variety of fields, such as architecture, automotive, industrial maintenance, building products, appliances, and metal office furniture. Figure 5.2 identifies the key players in the industry.

The company's link to the Delta Model originated with the newly appointed CEO, who had been exposed to the Model as a student at the Sloan School. He called one day for advice. "The Delta Model doesn't work," he said. When asked to explain the problem, his answer was "Because all of my customers just want me to sell them a commodity product at the lowest possible price." We knew immediately that something was wrong because it was very unlikely that all of his customers were behaving in identical ways. Our suspicions were confirmed in a subsequent meeting. The problem was that the CEO was treating every customer equally, in effect, commoditizing his entire customer base. We worked together to create a proper

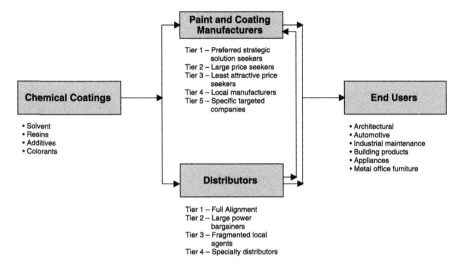

Fig. 5.2 The paint and coating industry: key players

customer segmentation, to see if there was any way we could apply the Delta Model to his company. The result was a five-tier segmentation shown in the triangle in Fig. 5.3.

- Tier 1: Preferred Strategic Solution Seekers
  Position in the Triangle: Total Customer Solution

Contrary to what had been stated, there were a large number of important companies that would greatly benefit from the technological knowledge that Chemical Coatings

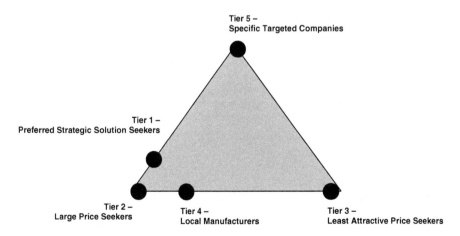

Fig. 5.3 The Chemical Coatings Company's customer segmentation

had. We identified those companies and proceeded to target them, in order to define a completely different way of serving them.

- Tier 2: Large Price Seekers
  Position in the Triangle: Temporarily as a Total Customer Solution

This position is a "parking lot." In here, we find large companies that we wish to move into Tier 1, but we are not sure that we could accomplish that. If after making a substantial effort to elevate them into that position we do not succeed, we would transfer them to Tier 3.

- Tier 3: Least Attractive Price Seekers
  Position in the Triangle: Best Product

Companies in this position indeed want nothing but a commodity product. They are large, self-sufficient companies that rightly or wrongly believe they don't need any additional support, and what they expect is highly standardized products and prices as low as possible.

- Tier 4: Local Manufacturers
  Position in the Triangle: Approaching Total Customer Solution, but not quite there yet

These are thousands of relatively small companies around the world to whom we could not afford to give the services that we are providing to Tier 1. Therefore, we are transferring to them as much knowledge as possible, by resorting to e-Business and Telemarketing Technologies.

- Tier 5: Specific Targeted Companies
  Position in the Triangle: System Lock-In

These are fairly small companies that excel in some pioneering technology that offer exciting new solutions, particularly in the area of ecology, which is very critical for paints. Our intent is to study them to familiarize our sales force with them, and then, if convinced that they might bring something special, we might proceed to acquire them.

Mission Statement of the Chemical Coatings Company

It is clear by now that the Chemical Coatings Company was leaning excessively toward the commoditization of its customer base. Therefore, the primary concern was to decommoditize, if not all, most of it.

The mission statement and the transformation that supports it are a reflection of this objective. A complete description of all the components of the mission statement is provided below.

The Mission Statement

Chemical Coatings will become the recognized leading product and service supplier to the paint and coatings industry.

We will accomplish this by developing a forceful strategy that will make us the preferred total customer solutions provider to the paint and coating manufacturers. We will seek alignment through a careful segmentation process to develop a distinct set of relationships with our customers, distributors, end-users, and complementors.

We will have a coherent global strategy that maintains our strong business base in the United States and Western Europe while seeking geographical expansion in selected developed and emerging economies in the world. We will implement this transformation through the addition of a significant set of new competencies. As a result of this effort, we are confident that we will reach exciting levels of growth and profitability, gain superior customer loyalty and bonding, and generate a working climate characterized by "*A Spirit of Success.*"

Statement of Products Scope and Services Scope

From:

A portfolio of products characterized by significant breadth covering oxygenated solvents, resins, coating additives, curatives, and colorants. This portfolio is composed by 20% of flagship products – specialty solvents, coalescents, cellulose esters, and colorants. The majority of the remaining products have low margins and are being perceived primarily as commodities. This product portfolio is supported by a variety of IT, technology, and supply chain services. The resulting products and services offering is rather fragmented and is not focused on providing an integrated, customized set of solutions to our targeted customers.

To:

Our product and service portfolio will consist of a properly packaged set of integrated solutions to our primary customers, the paint and coating manufacturers. The resulting value proposition that will emerge will be directed to properly segmented and selected customers, which will constitute the essence of our leadership in the paint and coatings industry.

Statement of Customer Scope

From:

Covering a large set of global, multi-regional, regional, and local paint and coatings manufacturing customers without a well-defined targeted strategy.

To:

A focused segmentation with the differentiated strategies to satisfy, in the most effective way, the distinct needs for products and services of five tiers of paint manufacturers.

- *Tier 1*: Preferred Strategic Solution Seekers
  These are strategic solution seekers that will be the recipient of total customer solutions provided by a team approach. We will target these preferred companies by offering solutions intended to increase productivity and performance, reduce

supply chain costs, provide e-business solutions, and develop jointly unique products and a variety of other value-added services. It is mandatory that the customer value propositions will result in quantified and well-documented cost reductions, performance and productivity improvements for our clients, improving our customers and our shareholders profitability.

- *Tier 2*: Large Price Seekers
  Composed of large price seeker paint and coatings manufacturers, which may not be as responsive to receive the total customer solutions approach of tier 1 customers. Our intent is to make every effort to move these accounts toward a closer collaboration, seeking a true partnership for value added.
- *Tier 3*: Least Attractive Price Seekers
  These are the least attractive price seekers that have nonexistent switching barriers to select a supplier. These are primarily transactional customers who will receive minimal services.
- *Tier 4*: Local Manufacturers
  These are composed of a large number of local paint and coatings manufacturers, who, because of their collective volume, provide attractive opportunities for us, but who cannot be targeted in the manner of tier 1 and 2 customers. We will utilize e-business and telesales technology to address and satisfy their needs.
- *Tier 5*: Specific Targeted Companies
  Composed of targeted companies that, although small in size, deserve special attention because they are either highly innovative or address unique environmental concerns.

Statement of End-User Scope

From:

Currently, our relationships are rather remote, lacking deep understanding of their business. They are classified in a rather conventional way into the following market segments: architectural, automotive, industrial maintenance, marine, building products, general industrial (machinery, equipment), appliance, metal office furniture.

To:

To have a thorough understanding of the end-user's product and service needs so that we can assist the paint and coatings manufacturers in providing solutions to their customers. We will understand the value system as a whole, so that we will identify where the major opportunity resides. Once again, the major objective is to increase the profitability of our customers and our shareholders, and quantify, document, and communicate cost reductions, performance, and productivity improvements.

Statement of Distributor Scope

From:

A loosely defined set of relationships with large numbers of national (US), regional independent, specialty distributors, and local agents.

To:

The classification of distributors according to the four tiers signaling different kinds of relationships with Chemical Coatings with respect to the degree of strategic alignment existing between us and the distributors group.

- *Tier 1*: Full Alignment with Chemical Coating
  This group becomes our preferred set of distributors, receiving the highest priority for business management attention and strategic alignment (training, tech service).
- *Tier 2*: Large Power Bargainers
  This group is formed by large distributors who are power bargainers pursuing their own individual interests. Because of their importance, we have to develop satisfying relationships with them, but they may not be regarded as preferential partners.
- *Tier 3*: Fragmented Local Agents
  Provide customer relationships and transactional capabilities with no real long-term strategic solutions
- *Tier 4*: Specialty Distributors
  These distributors provide an attractive focus for a particular segment and can act as an extension of our sales force

Statement of Complementor Scope

From:

A lack of an integrated approach in the use of complementors

To:

The concerted effort to add value to our customer solutions by a comprehensive use of partnership of both internal and external partners.

Statement of Geographical Scope

From:

Being primarily an North America and Europe-centric organization.

To:

Extend significantly our business presence in selected areas in the world. Our intent is to provide global support to our preferred paint and coating manufacturers, wherever it provides mutual value. We will continue our commitment to the US and Western Europe and the countries where we have an established business presence, such as Central and South East Europe, Korea, Canada, Australia, Japan. Additionally, we will provide new emphasis in emerging economies such as Greater China, Mexico, and Brazil.

Statement of Unique Competencies Scope

From:

Chemical Coatings is a leading company in its industry. Among our most salient competencies we can cite: our global coatings portal, our open business environment, our unique breadth of technological capabilities, our ability to manage large integrated manufacturing sites, our excellence in the supply chain.

To:

In order to achieve our desired customer solutions strategic position, we need to incorporate a set of new critical competencies. The primary ones are activity-based costing and business system; TQM; the achievement of positive net flow of talent; technology programs focused on customer, market, and business needs; highly leveraged procurement; efficient operation of small-scale batch processes; small site management capabilities; deep domain knowledge along the value system; tier-driven sales process; develop partnering skills; establish a total customer solutions engagement process; and customer-driven services.

We want to emphasize that this is not the kind of public-relation-driven and cosmetic statement that we see in annual reports. It is an attempt to capture the power of the transformation that we are conducting in the organization.

The first component of the mission attempts to summarize what we stand for. Then it addresses the transformation associated with each of the eight dimensions. We should be prepared to make this document available widely in and out the firm.

We believe that the Chemical Coatings Company provides a very good illustration for the development of a mission using the Delta Model methodology.

The Case of Singapore Airlines

We have used Singapore Airlines as a case to illustrate the two initial tasks of the Delta Model: customer segmentation and customer value proposition; and the firm as a bundle of competencies. We will carry this case to completion with all of the subsequent tasks, and will use it briefly here to describe how the mission statement is formulated in accordance with the Delta Model:

The Mission Statement

Singapore Airlines is a world-class company dedicated to provide air travel services of the highest quality to our global customers. We are committed to set the pace and standards for global air travel, and will achieve this through continuous innovation and the forging of new strategic alliances. We will continue to extend our global network to provide greater reach and connectivity for our customers, and to maximize returns for the benefit of our shareholders and employees.

This mission is underpinned by the following core values:

- **Pursuit of Excellence:** We strive for the highest professional standards in our work and aim to be the best in everything we do.
- **Safety:** We regard safety as an essential part of all our operations. We maintain and adopt practices that promote the safety of our customers and staff.
- **Customer First:** Our customers are foremost in our minds all the time. We go the extra mile to exceed their expectations.
- **Concern for Staff:** We value our staff and care for their well-being. We treat them with respect and dignity and seek to provide them with appropriate training and development so that they can lead fulfilling careers.
- **Integrity:** We strive for fairness in all our business and working relationships.
- **Teamwork:** We work with pride as a worldwide team to achieve success together.

Statement of Product Scope

From:

Air transportation services. Extensive tie-ups with travel-related companies.

To:

Air transportation services. Further product and service tie-ups with other premium travel-related services and companies.

Statement of Services Scope

From:

Offers comprehensive travel experience of world-class standards.

To:

Comprehensive travel experience of world-class standards. Customizing flights to various customer segments in terms of design. Thematic interior design, for example, for flights between India and Singapore.

Statement of Customer Scope

From:

Global. Caters to broad range of customers from the mass market to niche customers.

To:

Global. Further segmentation of customers into specific groups.

Statement of Complementor Scope

From:

Hotels, travel companies, credit card companies, other airlines providing connections within the network.

To:

Further extension of the network of hotels, travel companies, credit card companies, and other airlines providing connections.

Statement of Geographical Scope

From:

Global, but with limited reach in certain countries.

To:

Global with extensive links to the most dynamic regions throughout the world. A truly global airline with significant presence in high growth regions.

Statement of Unique Competencies

From:

Singapore Girl for global branding. World-class standards of service in the airline industry

To:

Singapore Girl remains as the key iconic symbol for global branding. Be a leader in services and service innovation not only in the airline industry but also in other related service industries.

As we have indicated, the mission allows us to make a summarized statement of all of the issues that we have uncovered in the strategic analysis preceding it and shows clear directions of the transformation that the organization is intending to carry.

The **mission statement** of Singapore Airlines underlines the commitment toward the highest-valued global customers and squarely positions the airline within the global network. The mission also includes a statement of core values, which represent an affirmation of the principles that they stand for. There is, therefore, a dual purpose that is achieved: Communicate the essence of what the firm is, and express the uncompromising commitment to excel on principles that should guide everybody's behavior.

The statement of changes in each of the relevant dimensions of the mission reinforces the conclusions that have emerged in the strategic analysis that we have described, namely

The **product scope and service scope** calls for maintaining the highest quality in global airline travel, but puts a special emphasis on premium travelers.

The **customer scope** calls for emphasizing the need for segmentation and the treatment of every tier in a differentiated way.

The **complementor scope** reinforces the notion that Singapore Airlines gives the highest priority to a host of complementors, such as hotels, travel agents, credit cards organizations, and other airlines in the network that contribute to make the SA travel experience the most unique one.

The **geographical scope** underlines the need to emphasize the high-growth regions in the world.

And finally, the **unique competencies scope** show SA's search for leadership in services not only in airlines, but also in related industries.

Notes

1. The name of this company has been disguised for confidentiality purposes.

Chapter 6
The Development of the Strategic Agenda: A Call to Action

The three tasks that have been the basis for our analysis so far – customer segmentation and customer value proposition; the bundle of competencies; and the mission statement – have only one purpose, and that is to develop a strategic agenda. This is the end result of the strategic planning process. In the end, all of the diagnosis that we have conducted has to converge into the definition of a clearly defined strategic agenda that identifies the actions that we will take to lead the organization into the desired transformation.

The Identification of the Strategic Thrusts

We call strategic thrusts as the elements that comprise the strategic agenda. Thrust is a very powerful word, because it suggests a propulsive force, as in a rocket. This is not a bad analogy, since we intend the strategic thrusts to forcefully move the organization into the new state we have laid out in the mission statement.

Strategic thrusts are the primary *action-oriented* issues the firm has to address in order to achieve a desirable strategic position. The collective of strategic thrusts constitute the strategic agenda. By their nature, strategic thrusts are broad issues. We do not want the strategic agenda to be a laundry list recital of the many things we would like to do. Instead, we envision it to be the depository of the most critical strategic initiatives, a call to action. We are often asked what the proper number of strategic thrusts should be. Although obviously the answer to this question varies with the specific circumstances of the business, our belief is that a typical number should be about 10 to 15. This number should be sufficient to capture the essential issues facing the organization, signifying a robust, well-considered strategic agenda.

The strategic thrusts should invoke action and not be merely expressions of desire. For instance, "increase market share," "reduce costs," "improve profitability" are not strategic thrusts, because they define ultimate objectives without giving a clue on how to reach them. For example, if we indeed want to reduce costs, we should indicate the actions we would take to make that happen.

Another common mistake that should be avoided is to include action programs that are part of the routine managerial activities of the company in the strategic

A.C. Hax, *The Delta Model*, DOI 10.1007/978-1-4419-1480-4_6,

agenda. Every executive has a well-established set of responsibilities that is part of his or her duties. The strategic agenda should not include a simple reminder of obvious assignments that need to be performed. For instance, "attract and develop talent," in our view, is not a strategic thrust. Do we need to remind ourselves that this is at the essence of every manager's job? In fact, the only time these routine issues emerge in the strategic agenda is when we find ourselves in a crisis for having ignored some obvious requirements of overall managerial performance, such as not having the necessary talent to do our work. We are not disregarding the importance of having talented people in our organization. On the contrary, the issue is so central for a well-managed business that it is intrinsically part of operational executive duties.

Think of the strategic agenda as the collection of strategic commitments that top executives have in their business. Every organization has something like a "Top Executive Council." The strategic agenda provides a charter for the CEO to monitor the progress that these top executives are making in managing the change that they would like to instill in their organization. In the face of daily routines that put excessive pressure on the operational side of the business; the strategic agenda should help us to better balance our strategic concerns. Where do you begin to create a strategic agenda? What is the path other successful companies have followed?

The Components of the Strategic Agenda

We propose a simple framework to assist us in the development of the strategic agenda, whose primary components are presented in Fig. 6.1. This will guide us to understand how this document is constructed, how the resulting responsibilities are assigned within the existing organizational structure, and how the managerial indicators of performance are designed to properly monitor its execution. All these components are intrinsically intertwined and, as the figure indicates, there is no beginning or end, because they represent a cycle. The only time when there is a

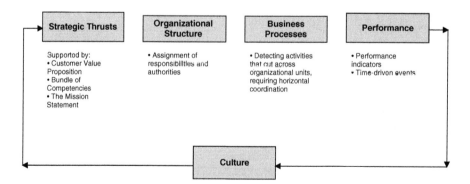

Fig. 6.1 The components of the strategic agenda

chronological issue surrounding their development is when we do it for the first time, in which case we adhere to the following sequence:

Strategic Thrusts

The customer segmentation and value proposition, the bundle of competencies, and the mission statement support the identification of strategic thrusts. When completed, each one of these tasks allows us to uncover many suggestions for strategic actions that could become part of a preliminary list of strategic thrusts. Later, you will learn how to assign priorities to this list and consolidate the final agenda.

You will also learn a set of tests you can use to make sure that the resulting strategic agenda is of the highest quality and relevance.

Organizational Structure

Once we complete the set of strategic thrusts, we need to identify those who will be responsible for their execution. This is done by matching each thrust with the existing responsibilities inherent in the current organizational structure of the company. The process of allocating these responsibilities is fairly straightforward. What is not that simple is how to resolve a possible mismatch that might exist between the new strategic agenda and the existing organizational structure.

How might this mismatch happen? As we know, strategy is an act of segmentation, particularly when it comes to defining the proper value proposition for each customer tier. The Delta Model puts a significant emphasis on the customer as a driving force of the strategic thinking process.

On the other hand, the organizational structure is also an act of segmentation. We start with the CEO and segment the tasks among a coherent set of people that report to him or her, continuing this process until we reach the lower echelons. There are various criteria that companies can use in doing this segmentation, including functions, products, markets, geographies, and the like. However, what we observe in practice is that most often the companies are product centric, which implies they have a well-developed back end, which is how we segment products and technologies. Unfortunately, this also means that companies have a much more embryonic front end, which is how we segment customers and markets. We will examine how to detect possible mismatches and what to do about it.

Business Processes

Regardless how the company decides on its organizational structure, most likely the strategic thrusts will generate business processes. A business process is a set of activities that cut across organizational units, because it cannot be delegated to just one single entity in the organization. Because of the extensive nature and the broadness of the strategic thrusts, they typically involve several organizational units in their execution. We have to be alert to recognize these processes, to understand their nature, and to put into place the necessary coordinating mechanisms that are needed for their proper execution. This is because the hierarchy doesn't function in the management of processes, since they involve lateral as opposed to vertical interactions. This is another issue to bear in mind.

Performance

The final component of the strategic agenda is imbedded in the metrics that we are going to use to evaluate the performance of each strategic thrust. We need two kinds of metrics. The first one is what we call performance indicators that describe the expected output that will be generated. It could be "improvements in revenues," "reductions in cost," "increases in market share for specific market segments," etc. For each strategic thrust, we should understand the expected impact that they will produce in the organization and how to measure it.

The second element of performance is what we call "time-driven events." Strategic thrusts might take a long while being fully implemented. It is important that you pay attention to the way in which each thrust is deployed. We recommend you initiate a chronological monitoring schedule for every thrust. That will allow you to track the progress being made in every quarter. You must identify a triggering event that initiates your performance metrics (such as a presentation to the board, a completion of a feasibility study, the opening of a store, etc.) and the date on which that event is supposed to happen, then make sure that you follow and assess the progress of each strategic thrust on a fixed, periodic basis.

The performance metrics allow you to determine appropriate rewards for everyone engaged in the execution of the strategic agenda. Moreover, these monitoring capacities constitute an important element of an executive information system that will enable you to target the top managers of the company who are ultimately responsible for the agenda's execution.

Culture

Strategic thrusts, organizational structure, business processes, and performance are the four critical components of the strategic agenda. But the culture of the organization is also a key underlying factor in determining the outcome of any major change initiative. Culture is what captures the values adhered to by the organization and dictates the rules of individual and collective behavior. It is the main determinant of the character of the organization, and as with individuals, firms are all different, and this difference stems primarily from their cultural values.

There are two considerations that we need to make with regard to the role of culture and the strategic agenda.

The first is how deeply performance metrics and reward systems affect the organizational behavior. That is why we sequence performance right before culture, to signify the influence that performance has in shaping behavior. This is relatively obvious, because people by and large want to succeed, and success is interpreted by the way we measure and reward individuals.

Second, we have positioned culture right before strategy, which also signifies the important influence that the values and behavior have on our ability to redirect the firm. If we engage in a countercultural strategy, we will be facing an enormously difficult challenge with great associated risks. This is not an easy or recommendable course of action to take, except under very extreme circumstances.

The Strategic Agenda as the Integrator of Strategy, Structure, Process, Performance – The Case of Chemical Coatings Company

We developed a very simple way to integrate these central components of the strategic agenda – strategy, structure, processes, and performance – while seeking a proper alignment and congruency across these four dimensions.

Figure 6.2 shows a chart that allows us to do this integration. In order not to address this question in a vacuum, we will be using the case of the Chemical Coatings Company that we introduced in the previous chapter. This will allow us to make comments that help us point out some of the subtleties of this chart.

The first column lists all the strategic thrusts of the organization in order of priority. We tell you later how to develop these priority assignments. But what is important here is to recognize that the first column of this chart provides a full sequential overview of the actions that the organization must undertake, from the most significant ones through to the end of the agenda, in order to implement the Delta Model customer bonding strategy.

The case of the Chemical Coatings Company is useful because it serves to illustrate a typical agenda for a company that starts from a highly commoditized environment and uses the Delta Model for the first time as a framework to achieve a Total Customer Solution position. The agenda is a compilation of the critical tasks that are needed, starting from the requirement to identify the value propositions and the delivery mechanisms for customers and distributors, and ending with a call for the attraction of proper complementors.

The agenda is forceful in revealing the significant amount of knowledge regarding customers, processes, and value systems that the company needs to grasp and acquire to be able to develop the proper infrastructure needed for the application of the Delta Model.

The second part of Fig. 6.2 shows the existing organizational structure of the Chemical Coating Company. Once the role of the key individuals is identified in the

STRATEGIC THRUSTS	ORGANIZATIONAL UNITS											BUSINESS PROCESSES	METRICS
	CEO	COO	CFO	SALES	STRATEGY	DISTRIBUTION	MARKETING	R&D	HR	OPERATIONS	INTERNATIONAL		
Value proposition development & delivery mechanism for paint manufacturers Tier 1, 2, 5 Tier 3 Tier 4	1	1	2	1	1	1	1	2			2	CT	Completion of Assignment
Value proposition development & delivery mechanism for distributors Tier 1, 4 Tier 2 Tier 3	1	1	2	1	1	1		2		2	2	CT	Completion of Assignment
Develop domain knowledge of customers & end users			2	1	1	1	1	2		2	2	CT	Progress Report
Total Customer Solutions Engagement Process	2	2	2	1	1	2	1	2	2	2	2	CT	Termination of Pilot Study
Alignment of structure, processes, measurements & rewards to our total customer solutions strategic position Organizational structure, processes & teams Measurement & rewards Communications & image	1	1	1		1	2	2	2	1	2	1	B	Presentation of proposal
Operational effectiveness both internally & customer driven			2	2	2	2	1	2	2	1	2	OE	Submittal of Proposal
Value system analysis (from supplier to end user)			1	1	1	1	1	2	2	1	2	OE	Submittal of Proposal
Entry into emerging markets	1	1	1	2	2	2	1	2	2	2	1	CT	Submittal of Proposal
Business Innovation program focused on customer & market needs				2	1	2	1	1	2	2	2	I	Submittal of Proposal
Complementor partnerships to enhance customer solutions	1	1	1	2	2	2	1	1	2	2	1	CT	Identification of Network

1 – Key role in formulation and implementation   2 – Important role of support and concurrence   1 (Shaded box) "Champion," "Leadership role in execution of Strategic Thrust
B – Business Model   CT – Customer Targeting   OE – Operational effectiveness   I – Innovation

Fig. 6.2 Strategic agenda: an illustration of the Chemicals Coating Company

structure, we proceed to assign responsibilities to those in charge of formulating and implementing the strategic thrusts. A "1" denotes a key role, a "2", an important support. The resulting chart should be a blueprint for understanding the interface between strategy and structure. The following points are quite evident:

- The Density of the Matrix
  By just looking at the concentration of 1's and 2's in the whole of the organizational structure, one could make inferences about the flexibility, the agility, and the interdependencies that exist among the key players. It is obvious in the case of the Chemical Coatings Company that the functional nature of its structure forces a great deal of interconnectivity and coordination among all of its executives. Incidentally, this is not such a novel thing. In the complex, interdependent world of today, this is the rule rather than the exception. That is why teams are beginning to replace the hierarchy as the most relevant way of conducting business.

- The Nature of Strategic Thrusts
  We must look at each strategic thrust at a time. The mapping of the thrust into the organizational structure tells us specifically who is involved and in what capacity. We demand that there should be only one "champion" in each thrust, meaning that there is no ambiguity with regard to who carries the ultimate responsibility for the thrust implementation. This means that if there is more that one 1 – meaning more than one individual playing a key role in the thrust – we should decide who would become the champion. We have indicated that role with a shaded area in the figure.

- The Nature of the Responsibilities of Each Individual Executive
  We now can look at the columns of the chart in Fig. 6.2 to identify clearly the responsibilities that reside in each of the executives represented in each column. It makes patently clear the roles a person has in implementing the strategic agenda, how primary or secondary each role is, and most importantly, how the "champion" responsibilities are spread out. In the case of the Chemical Coatings Company, it is quite obvious that there is a very well-balanced allocation of duties, and that is a fairly desirable state of affairs. It reflects an organization in which a number of key people are sharing the conduct of business strategy.

- The Nature of the Business Processes
  The penultimate column in Fig. 6.2 records the nature of the business process that each thrust generates. As we have indicated before, each strategic thrust represents a process, because it requires that several people participate in its execution. This is quite apparent from just looking at the large number of 1's and 2's associated with every strategic thrust. What remains is to understand the nature of this process. We recognize four such processes:

  - Operational Effectiveness (OE). This process is responsible for the delivery of products and services to the customer, and as such, defines the cost infrastructure of the business. This process is central to the support of the Best Product option.

- Customer Targeting (CT). This process encompasses the activities intended to attract, satisfy, and retain the customer and insures that the customer relationships are managed effectively. It is responsible for enhancing our revenue infrastructure of the business, and it is of central concern to the Total Customer Solution option.
- Innovation (I). This process insures a continuous stream of new products and services to maintain the future viability of the business. It mobilizes the creative resources of the firm, including its technical, production, and marketing capabilities to develop an innovative infrastructure for the business. This process is of central importance for the achievement of the System Lock-in.
- Business (B). This process has to do with the reinforcement of the managerial infrastructure of the business. It primarily encompasses the processes that are of general management concern, not relevant to the previous three processes.
  In Fig. 6.2, we can see that the great majority of the strategic thrusts are of a customer targeting nature. This is not a great surprise, because, as we have indicated previously, the fundamental focus of the strategy of the Chemical Coatings Company is the decommoditization of its businesses by aggressively pursuing its transformation from the Best Product to the Total Customer Solution option.

- The Making of an Executive Information System
  The last column of Fig. 6.2 describes the metrics associated with each strategic thrust. Collectively, therefore, they can be regarded as the basis for the executive information system that should guide the deliberations of the company's top management. This metric allows the monitoring of the programs that are part of the strategic agenda, as well as providing an aggregate of indicators of performance that constitutes a relevant strategic scorecard in its own right.

As we can see in Fig. 6.2, the nature of the strategic agenda of the Chemical Coatings Company is just to deploy the necessary infrastructure for the implementation of the Delta Model. It is not surprising then, that all of them are merely projects and their performance metrics simply record the culmination of these efforts.

These brief descriptions should make clear how this methodology, to define the strategic agenda, captures the interrelationships that exists among strategy, structure, processes, and performance, which demand a high degree of congruency and alignment.

Identifying the Priorities of the Strategic Thrusts

The strategic thrusts are listed in the strategic agenda represented in Fig. 6.2 in their order of priority. The methodology that we use to reach a consensus in determining priority is depicted in Fig. 6.3.

In short, a brainstorming session is conducted in which we record suggested strategic thrusts simply in the order in which they emerge in our discussion. This

	A	B	C	WEIGHT (3*A+2*B+1*C)	FINAL RANKING
Alignment of structure, processes, measurements & rewards to our total customer solutions strategic position Organizational structure, processes & teams Measurement & rewards Communications & image	8	10	7	51	5
Business Innovation program focused on customer & market need	0	18	7	43	9
Value proposition development & delivery mechanism for paint manufacturers Tier 1, 2, 5 Tier 3 Tier 4	24	1	0	74	1
Complementor partnerships to enhance customer solutions	0	3	22	28	10
Develop domain knowledge of customers & end users	15	3	7	58	3
Total Customer Solutions Engagement Process	10	8	7	53	4
Operational effectiveness both internally & customer driven	8	9	8	50	6
Value proposition development & delivery mechanism for distributors Tier 1, 4 Tier 2 Tier 3	20	3	2	68	2
Value system analysis (from supplier to end user)	8	9	8	50	6
Entry into emerging markets	7	11	7	50	8

(25 people voting)

A - Absolute first priority (postponement will hurt strategic position significantly).
B - Highly desirable (postponement will affect strategic position adversely).
C - Desirable (if funds were available, strategic position could be enhanced).

Fig. 6.3 Assignments of priorities to strategic thrusts

is represented in the first column in Fig. 6.3. When the process of generating the strategic thrusts is over, we count them up (in our example we got 10) and attach a label to each in the following way:

A – Absolute first priority (postponement will hurt strategic position significantly)
B – Highly desirable (postponement will affect strategic position adversely)
C – Desirable (if funds were available, strategic position could be enhanced).

The process of generating and evaluating thrusts is conducted by a group of executives who are the architects of the ultimate agenda. We would like each one of them to assign an A, B, or C priority to these thrusts. In order to make this allocation of priorities meaningful, we try to evenly divide the number of thrusts by three, and we determine the number of As, Bs, and Cs that each participant has noted. Since in this case 10 is not a number divisible by 3, we have to do some rounding up. This means that they have to assign 4 As, 3 Bs, and 3 Cs to the full set of thrusts. In fact, the task is even simpler: Select what you think are the top 4 thrusts (the As), and the bottom three (the Cs). The remaining three, of course, should be the Bs. We assign three points to each A, two points to each B, and 1 point to each C. We collect the votes for each participant, and the results are registered as illustrated in Fig. 6.3. In this particular example, there are a total of 25 people voting. The weights are collected in the penultimate column. The last column gives the final ranking, which is passed on to the Strategic Agenda in Fig. 6.2. Sounds cumbersome, but it is very simple and can be a lot of fun. People seem to enjoy this exercise.

Test for the Quality of the Strategic Agenda

To conclude the process of the development of the strategic agenda, we submitted to five tests, to get a sense of how effective it is.

1. Comprehensiveness

   • Have we included every single critical issue that the business is facing?
   • If not, have we left aside some crucial action programs because we need to postpone them at this stage?
   • How comfortable are we that we have completed the task we have put in front of us?

2. Stretch

   • Is the agenda challenging enough?
   • Are we putting the bar so high that it will discourage most people, because they are condemned to fail in the pursuit of this strategy?

- Or, on the contrary, are we putting the bar so low that we know that most of the things that we are addressing are already under way, and there is very little that represents a true, demanding challenge?

3. Ease of Implementation

- Do we have all of the necessary resources – financial, managerial, technical, human, and all the rest of the capabilities – that are necessary to put the strategy in place?
- Do we have the necessary systems, control mechanisms, and rewards that are central to a proper implementation?
- Are there any significant, additional barriers to facilitating the strategy implementation that we should be aware of?

4. The Quality of the Working Climate

- Is the strategic agenda inspirational enough to create a contagious enthusiasm among all of those involved?
- Does the agenda produce a sense of excitement that will satisfy the individual needs of employees to feel that they are making significant contributions to society?
- Is the working environment that we are creating characterized by a "spirit of success"?

5. Vulnerability

- What can possibly go wrong?
- Are there threats that might originate from the external environment that invalidate our basic assumptions and that would require us to reconsider the courses of action under a different scenario?
- Most importantly, are there internal vulnerabilities resulting from forces that emerge from our own organization that we should be aware of and be ready to confront creatively?

It is vital that the executives engaged in the definition of the strategic agenda reflect on these tests and take corrective actions where needed. Hopefully, they should end up with an enthusiastic consensus on the quality and power of the final strategy.

The Case of Singapore Airlines

We have already used the case of Singapore Airlines to illustrate the previous three tasks that we have discussed:

- Customer Segmentation and Customer Value Proposition in Chapter 3
- The Bundle of Competencies in Chapter 4, and
- The Mission in Chapter 5.

For continuity, we turn to Singapore Airlines again to illustrate the task of developing the strategic agenda.

Strategic Challenges and Opportunities

SA will continue to face a very challenging business environment in the next few years. The era of budget airlines in Asia has already taken off, modeling the successes of budget airlines in the US and Europe. Tier 4 customers have been the first to flock to these low-cost carriers. At the same time, long-time competitors such as British Air, Cathay Pacific, and Qantas are getting better at the game. If SA is not careful, it will also erode market share in the Tiers 1–3 markets. Fuel costs will remain a key expenditure item for SA, and it is critical for the firm to make long-term hedges to ensure price stability. The development of the super long-range jumbo aircraft is a double-edged sword for SA. While it allows SA to expand capacity on existing routes without having to increase flight frequencies and bypass transit points, Qantas is also buying these long-range aircraft so that its aircraft do not have to transit in Singapore.

Meanwhile, many opportunities abound. The volume of international travel is expected to grow at phenomenal rates for the next decade as the Chinese and Indians start traveling. They will provide a steady stream of customers for the next decade and create a critical new market for SA to tap into. What this means too is that it is necessary to tailor the SA experience to suit new customer profiles and tastes. What has worked in the past might not necessarily work in the future and it is critical that SA have a finger on the pulse of shifting consumer trends, tastes, and travel preferences.

At the end of the day, the airline industry is ultimately a service-oriented industry. Getting it right in the service arena is one of the critical factors to success. In considering its strategic thrusts, SA must continue to ensure that service excellence initiatives to deliver exceptional service to the customer remain top priority. Without the distinctive service excellence that SA is well known for, it will become any other airline. This is the fundamental competitive advantage that SA has to maintain and strengthen.

SA cannot and should not compete on costs. It has wisely decided to create a new budget airline subsidiary called Tiger Airways, which will enable it to compete head on with other budget airlines, without diluting the SA branding. SA has to continue to focus on preserving the Tiers 1–3 markets.

The overall Strategic Agenda of SA is presented in Fig. 6.4.

Conclusion

SA is a world-class airline that provides the highest standards of travel service in the air and on the ground. It is profitable, continues to grow yearly, and has few peers in its industry. SA has been successful because of the way it has segmented the market

Corporate Strategic Thrusts	Organizational Units					Business Processes	Performance Metrics
	Senior Mgt.	Corporate / Customer Services	Strategic/Global Sourcing Department	Aircrew	Supporting Ground Staff		
Tiers 1,2, 3 – Customer Development Programme	1	1		1	2	CT	Performance scorecard, customer feedback
Global Marketing/ Branding	1	1	2			CT	Reviews on travel and industry magazines
Global sourcing for best products and services	2	2	1			OE	Rate of implementation of new products and services
Global Operations	1	1	1		1	OE	Revenue growth
Fleet Management & Acquisitions	1					B	Financials, balance sheets, cash flow statements
Business Development	1	1	1			B	Revenues from new businesses
Customer Response Group		1				CT	Customer feedback
Human Resource Development	1	1				B	Recruitment and retention rates
Global sourcing for alliances	1		1			B	Quantity and quality of product and service enhancements
Expansion of air rights, routes	1		1			OE	Rate of growth of flight routes
Service Development and Training				1		CT	Customer feedback, performance scorecard
Financial Hedging (for e.g. Fuel Costs)	1		1			OE	Fuel expenditure

Fig. 6.4 The strategic agenda of Singapore Airlines

and focused on the high-payoff customer tiers. It also has a suite of strategic advantages and core competencies, which it has continued to maintain. However, the firm is also feeling tremendous pressure from global shifts in the airline industry. There are many new players on board, and it is absolutely critical that while it preserves its core competencies, new competencies must be nurtured and global alliances forged to ensure that SA remains a great way to fly.

Chapter 7
Monitoring the Strategy Execution

Strategy formulation concluded with the development of the strategic agenda discussed in the previous chapter. The next task we face is paving the way for implementation of the strategy we have chosen. There are two key steps we must take.

First, we have to evaluate the economic merits of our strategy and translate our strategic and operational commitments into financial statements. We will accomplish this through the development of an *Intelligent Budget*.

Second, we must design managerial indicators that will allow us to achieve our goals in all the relevant dimensions of the business, then create a set of performance measurements that support our efforts to monitor the process of strategy execution. We will accomplish this using the *Balanced Scorecard*.

The Intelligent Budget – A Requirement for Proper Strategic Execution

Budgets represent projections of revenues and costs normally covering one or more years. The budget is a critical document in most firms because it constitutes the commitment for implementation. Executives are compelled to meet the budget figures. Their rewards and promotions are normally linked to their ability to deliver the "numbers." It is therefore of greatest importance that the strategic planning process produces what we call "an intelligent budget," which is not a mere extrapolation of the past into the future, but a statement that contains both strategic and operational commitments. Strategic commitments pursue the development of new opportunities, which introduce significant changes in existing business conditions. Operational commitments, on the other hand, are aimed at the effective maintenance of the current business base.

A way to break this dichotomy within the budget is to make use of both strategic funds and operational funds to distinguish the role that those financial resources will have. *Strategic funds* are expense items required for the implementation of strategic action programs whose benefits are expected to occur in the long run, beyond the current budget period. *Operational funds* are those expense items required to maintain the business in its present position.

A.C. Hax, *The Delta Model*, DOI 10.1007/978-1-4419-1480-4_7,

There are three major components of strategic funds:

1. *Investment* in tangible assets, such as new production capacity, new machinery and tools, new vehicles for distribution, new office space, new warehouse space, and new acquisitions.
2. *Increases (or decreases) in working capital* generated from strategic commitments, such as the impact of increases in inventories and receivables resulting from an increase in sales; the need to accumulate larger inventories to provide better services; increasing receivables resulting from a change in the policy of loans to customers, and so on.
3. *Developmental expenses* that are over and above the needs of existing business, such as advertising to introduce a new product or to reposition an existing one; R&D expenses of new products; major cost reduction programs for existing products; introductory discounts, sales promotions, and free samples to stimulate first purchases; development of management systems such as planning, control, and compensation; certain engineering studies, and so on.

The budget should recognize these three forms of strategic funds. Although all of them contribute to the same purposes, namely the improvement of future capabilities of the firm, financial accounting rules treat these three items quite differently. Investment is shown as an increase in net assets in the balance sheet and as annual expenses through depreciation in the profit and loss statement. Increases in working capital also enlarge the net assets of the firm, but they have no annual cost repercussion because they are not amortized. Developmental expenses are charged as expenses in the current year income statement and have no impact on the balance sheet. Since there might not be immediate profitability results derived from these strategic funds, it is important to make a manager accountable for the proper and timely allocation of those expenditures using performance measurements related to the inherent characteristics of the action programs they are attempting to support.

Let us use a very simple example to make the strongest possible argument for splitting strategic and operational funds. Assume we are employing a conventional budget statement – that is, no separation between the two kinds of funds – to make a manager accountable for his or her divisional performance. The first column of Fig. 7.1 provides such an illustration.

The manager is supposed to generate 100 of sales, to spend 30 in variable manufacturing cost, 20 in depreciation, and 10 on the fixed manufacturing cost, which leaves 40 for divisional gross margin. From that we subtract 15 in marketing expenses, 10 in administrative expenses, and 5 in research and development. The final bottom line is 10 of divisional margin. That is what the executive is intended to do and his/her career will be strongly dependent on fulfilling this commitment. Assume that sales drop to 90, from its intended 100. Can the manager still give us 10 of divisional margin? Obviously yes! There are many options to cut expenses that will assure the requested performance. Of course, there could be strongly negative long-term implications from these actions, but in the short term nobody will detect them.

	Conventional Statement	Operational Expenses	Strategic Expenses*
Net Sales	100	100	-
Less:			
Variable mfg. costs	30	30	-
Depreciation	20	20	-
Other fixed mfg. costs	<u>10</u>	<u>5</u>	<u>5</u>
Gross margin	40	45	-
Less:			
Marketing expenses	15	5	10
Admin. Expenses	10	5	5
Research Expenses	<u>5</u>	<u>0</u>	<u>5</u>
Division margin	10		
Operating margin		35	
Total strategic expenses			25

* Also called Development Expenses

Fig. 7.1 Splitting the Profit and Loss Statement of a division in terms of operational and strategic expenses

Consider the option of splitting the funds. Now we should look at the second and third columns of Fig. 7.1. The operational expenses column tells us a different story. Now the manager is giving us 45 in gross margin, since only 5 of the "other fixed manufacturing expenses" are operational expenses and 5 are to be assigned to the expansion of production capacity associated with one of our strategic programs.

Similarly, only 5 of the 15 marketing expenses are operational, the remaining 10 are to develop a new product launching. Only 5 of the administrative expenses are operational, the other 5 are to be dedicated to the development of an MIS system.

Finally, all research and development expenses are strategic in character. What we now have is a very different assignment for the divisional manager. He or she should deliver 35 in divisional margin coming from the existing business base, and efficiently allocate 25 in strategic expenses that will lead the future of the business in its intended direction. We hope this simple example conveys this important message of the accountability of performance in two modes: operational and strategic.

Figure 7.2 gives us an illustration of a budget that contains the splitting of operational and strategic funding. The numbers attached to the figure are totally artificial; they merely represent an example. What is important, however, is to emphasize

| | History | | | | | Current Year | Projections | | | |
	2003	2004	2005	2006	2007	2008 Budget	2009	2010	2011	2012
Total Market	4032.0	4994.0	5822.0	6722.0	7820.0	9266.0	11120.0	13123.0	15012.0	19312.0
Market Share (%)	52.0	51.0	52.0	49.0	49.0	49.0	50.0	50.0	51.0	52.0
Company Sales	2083.0	2568.0	3002.0	3316.0	3799.0	4502.0	5522.0	6577.0	8123.0	9966.0
• Operating cost of Goods Sold	1789.0	2138.0	2499.0	2771.0	3165.0	3760.0	4612.0	5492.0	6789.0	8336.0
Gross Operating Margin	294.0	430.0	503.0	545.0	634.0	742.0	910.0	1085.0	1334.0	1630.0
• Operating SG&A	62.0	103.0	110.0	121.0	138.0	162.0	199.0	241.0	295.0	366.0
Operating Margin	232.0	327.0	393.0	424.0	496.0	580.0	711.0	844.0	1039.0	1264.0
• Strategic Expenses	130.0	165.0	204.0	213.0	251.0	321.0	396.0	497.0	626.0	789.0
SBU Margin	102.0	162.0	189.0	211.0	245.0	259.0	315.0	347.0	413.0	475.0
• Taxes	5.0	18.0	23.0	27.0	32.0	35.0	43.0	56.0	70.0	93.0
SBU Net Income	97.0	144.0	166.0	184.0	213.0	224.0	272.0	291.0	343.0	382.0
• Depreciation	18.0	21.0	26.0	32.0	38.0	46.0	56.0	67.0	82.0	100.0
• Capital Investments	32.0	57.0	87.0	128.0	115.0	150.0	195.0	169.0	202.0	183.0
• Increases in Working Capital	0.0	0.0	0.0	0.0	0.0	0.0	0.0	0.0	0.0	0.0
Contribution/Request of Funds to the Corporation	83.0	108.0	105.0	88.0	136.0	120.0	133.0	189.0	223.0	299.0

Fig. 7.2 Strategic funds programming and operational budgets – an illustration

some of the key conceptual differences that this type of budget has compared with a conventional one.

The budget presents both a history and a future projection. This is helpful for understanding the evolution of the financial results and the extent of drastic departures from expected to past performance. The budget starts with figures measuring the Total Market of the industry where the business resides. This will allow us to see immediately the market share position of the business and the evolution of the industry life cycle. The relationship between the Total Market and the Company Sales determine the Market Share of the business.

From the Company Sales we subtract the Operating Cost of Goods Sold and the Operating SG&A (Sales, General, and Administrative Expenses). The key word here is "operating." Namely we are not allocating any overhead or expenses that have strategic purposes. This allows us to obtain an Operating Margin of the business. From that we subtract Strategic Expenses, Capital Investments, and Increases in Working Capital – the three components of the Strategic Funds of the business. By separating the operating from the strategic expenses, we can track the financial performance of the business in these two different modes. One derives from the existing activities of the business; the other comes from its future potential.

The bottom line measures what is usually defined as the "free cash" generated by the business. This is cash coming from operations after the deductions of interest, taxes, and all the strategic funds committed, and the addition of depreciation.

The flow of free cash is what has to be discounted to obtain the Net Present Value of the business, which measures the wealth created for shareholders. It is this figure that captures the economic value created by the business. We will not expand on this subject because we assume the reader is knowledgeable about this matter.

The Balanced Scorecard

The Balanced Scorecard[1] was a brilliant idea that originated during the 1990s and set the business world on fire. Its great success resided primarily in its simplicity, its pragmatism, and its relevancy. It started by making the claim that financial measures alone are incomplete and do not provide a full understanding of the performance of a business. Although their importance is unquestionable, since they deal with the heart of what a business intends to generate – economic value to its shareholders – these measures only deliver an historical evaluation of how the business has performed in the past. It seldom captures the way the business is prepared to face the future challenges. Financial metrics are critical, but need to be complemented by three other important dimensions of performance that are

- The Customer Perspective – How do we look to our customers?
- The Business Perspective – What business processes are the value drivers?
- The Organizational Learning Perspective – Are we able to sustain innovation, change, and improvement?

The composite of these four perspectives, if we include the financial perspective – provides a well-balanced picture of the overall performance of the business, which explains the name of this attractive concept.

Figure 7.3 illustrates the typical representation that is used to depict the components of the Balanced Scorecard and to explain the intention of each perspective. We will discuss its use within the context of the Delta Model, but prior to doing so we want to make some comments about the use of the Balanced Scorecard in practice.

Source: "The Balanced Scorecard – Measures That Drive Performance," Robert S. Kaplan and David P Norton, Harvard Business Review, January-February 1992.

Fig. 7.3 The Balanced Scorecard

Strategy at the Center of the Balanced Scorecard

As Fig. 7.3 has properly captured, strategy should be at the center of the Balanced Scorecard. This means that after we have determined the strategic direction we would like to give to the business, and after we have set up the corresponding strategic agenda, we should begin the process of selecting the managerial indicators that will allow us to adequately measure and monitor the explanation of our selected strategy. Putting it in very simple terms, we should do the strategy first, and then we should design the Balanced Scorecard.

In practice, however, we notice that the Balanced Scorecard often becomes an independent project which has a life of its own. As illustrated in Fig. 7.4 (which is in the original reference of the Balanced Scorecard), each perspective is assigned objectives, measures, targets, and finally initiatives. That is quite puzzling because

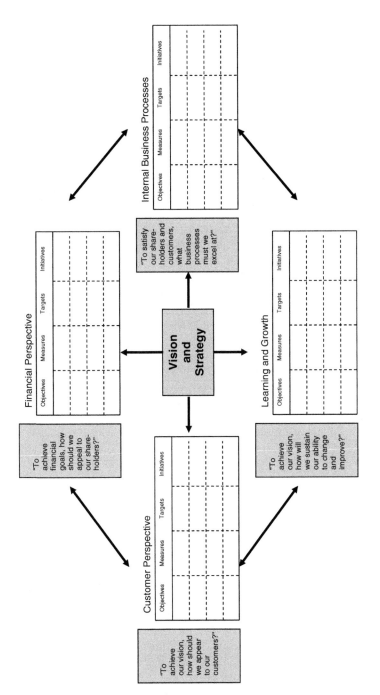

Source: "The Balanced Scorecard – Measures That Drive Performance," Robert S. Kaplan and David P. Norton, Harvard Business Review, January-February 1992.

Fig. 7.4 Balanced Scorecard and initiatives

the initiatives seem to call for action – in other words, it is a substitute for what should be the set of strategic action programs. It seems that anyone who is applying the Balanced Scorecard this way is putting the cart before the horse – namely the indicators decide the strategy and not the other way around.

The Delta Model and the Balanced Scorecard

We buy the argument espoused by the Balanced Scorecard that we need to complement the financial metrics with the three other dimensions. The easiest metrics to select are in fact those related to financial performance, since this subject has been thoroughly analyzed. Figure 7.5 provides a brief summary of meaningful financial indicators to pick for different relevant categories such as Capital Market Indices, Profitability Measures, and indicators related to Risk, Cost of Capital, and Growth. What we need to do is to decide on the most appropriate financial indicators from this list that address the specific business performance we are analyzing and to set up the appropriate targets for the expected results.

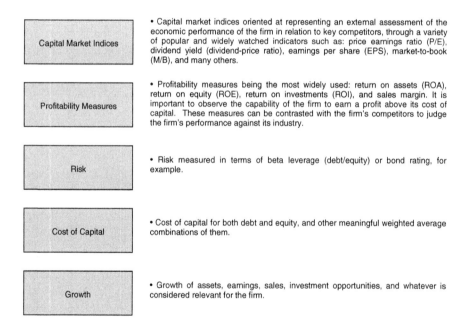

Fig. 7.5 Measures of performance related to the financial strategy

What concerns us is how to guide the selection of the metrics for the other three dimensions of the Balanced Scorecard in such a way that they are properly aligned with the strategy of the business.

In most cases of applications of the Balanced Scorecard, the metrics that are proposed tend to have a strong connotation of product-centric strategic positioning.

They are mostly inward-oriented, dealing with the internal business economies, the existing customer base, and the internal efforts that guide the organizational learning and innovation process. This is an unacceptable bias that we need to correct.

The Delta Model and the Adaptive Process

As the Balanced Scorecard tries to be properly balanced in the selection of the performance indicators of a business, the Delta Model attempts to achieve a similar balance in the way the strategy of the business is defined. We start the strategy formulation process with the Triangle, which opens our mind to three distinct options: Best Product, Total Customer Solutions, and System Lock-In. As we have argued throughout this book, a properly designed strategy often covers all these options depending on the way we are generating the individual value propositions for our customers. Therefore, we need to make sure that the Balanced Scorecard reflects the requirements that capture the breadth of the full spectrum of a strategy that covers all the relevant positions.

To accomplish this goal we define three business processes we believe that capture the core activities that are associated with the implementation of a strategy: operational effectiveness, customer targeting, and innovation. We have briefly introduced these processes in the previous chapter. We are going to cover them more extensively now. Their definitions are as follows:

1. *Operational Effectiveness* – This process is responsible for the delivery of products and services to the customer. In a traditional sense, this includes all the elements of the internal supply chain. Its primary focus is on producing the most effective cost and asset infrastructure to support the desired strategic position of the business. In a more comprehensive sense, operational effectiveness should expand its external scope to include suppliers, customers, and key complementors, thus establishing an extended supply chain. This process is the heart of a company's productive engine as well as its source of capacity and efficiency.
2. *Customer Targeting* – This process addresses the business-to-customer interface. It encompasses the activities intended to attract, satisfy, and retain the customers, and ensures that customer relationships are managed effectively. Its primary objectives are to identify and select attractive customers and to enhance their financial performance, either by helping to reduce their costs or increase their revenues. The ultimate goal of this process is to establish the best revenue infrastructure for the business.
3. *Innovation* – This process ensures a continuous stream of new products and services to maintain the future viability of the business. It mobilizes all the creative resources of the firm – including its technical, production, and marketing capabilities – to develop an innovative infrastructure for the business. It should not limit itself to the pursuit of internal product development, but should extend the sources of innovation to include suppliers, customers, and key complementors.

The heart of this process is the renewal of the business in order to sustain its competitive advantage and its period financial performance.

These three processes have a very different role depending on the nature of the strategy they are intended to support. Again, we find it is of particular concern that most managers implicitly define each process according to a Best Product strategy. Namely operational effectiveness seeks to establish an internally efficient cost infrastructure; customer targeting seeks maximum coverage through distribution channels; and innovation seeks the speedy development of the firm's products aided by appropriate platforms and first-to-market expectations. As recognized in Fig. 7.6, the situation is starkly different when the adaptive process supports the Total Customer Solutions and the System Lock-In strategic options.

In the Total Customer Solutions strategy, the key objective of operational effectiveness is the maximization of customer value, and this can only be achieved through direct consideration of the combined value chain of the firm and its customers. Customer targeting is aimed at developing individual customer bonding, by structurally enhancing the interface with the customer, by stimulating mutual learning of our joint capabilities, and by stimulating joint investments in our product and services. Innovation aims for the development of a composition of customized products jointly with the customer.

In the System Lock-In strategic position the role of each process continues to change. Now, operational effectiveness is concerned about enhancing the overall system performance, by consolidating strong partnerships with complementors. Customer targeting attempts to consolidate harmonized system architecture through a network of complementors and complementor interfaces. The ultimate goal of innovation is to develop and appropriate an industry standard, facilitating the breadth and range of the applications it enables.

Once more, a primary objective is to raise awareness of an excessive product-centric mentality and to expand alternatives open to managers. Rivalry and competition may not be the winning strategies.

The Adaptive Processes and Aggregate Metrics

Just as activities need to vary by strategy, so do the measures of success. Performance measurements and quantifiable indicators are essential for the development, execution, and monitoring of the desired strategy. The Delta Model aligns performance metrics to the strategic options selected, and it recognizes that these metrics will be fundamentally different depending on the strategic position they intend to support.

The aggregate metrics we propose are a direct by-product of the adaptive processes just discussed. Since these processes are the instruments for the execution of each strategic option, they also serve as the guidelines to define the strategy performance. Figure 7.7 provides a summary of a selected set of generic metrics

Adaptive Process	Strategic Positioning		
	Best Product	**Total Customer Solutions**	**System Lock-In**
Operational Effectiveness	*Best Product Cost* • Identify product cost drivers • Improve stand alone product cost	*Best Customer Benefits* • Improve customer economics • Improve horizontal linkages in the components of total solutions	*Best System Performance* • Improve system performance drivers • Integrate complementors in improving system performance
Customer Targeting	*Target Distribution Channels* • Maximize coverage through multiple channels • Obtain low cost distribution • Identify and enhance the profitability of each product by channel	*Target Customer Bundles* • Identify and exploit opportunities to add value to key customers by bundling solutions and customization • Increase customer value and possible alliances to bundle solutions • Select key vertical markets • Examine channel ownership options	*Target System Architecture* • Identify leading complementors in the system • Consolidate a lock-in position with complementors • Expand number and variety of complementors • Whenever possible create ownership of direct distribution channels

Innovation	*Product Innovation*
	• Develop family of products based on common platform
	• First to market, or follow rapidly – stream of products
		Customer Service Innovation
		• Identify and exploit joint development linked to the customer value chain
		• Expand your offer into the customer value chain to improve customer economics
		• Integrate and innovate customer care functions
		• Increase customer lock-in through customization and learning
			System Innovation
			• Create customer and system lock-in, and competitive lock-out
			• Design proprietary standard within open architecture
			  - Complex interfaces
			  - Rapid evolution
			  - Backward compatibility

Fig. 7.6 Role of the adaptive processes in supporting the strategic options of the triangle

	Best Product	Total Customer Solutions	System Lock-In
Effectiveness (Cost Drivers)	• Cost performance 　- Unit cost 　- Lifecycle cost 　- Variable and total cost • Cost drivers • Quality performance • Degree of differentiation	• Customer value chain 　- Total cost 　- Total revenue and profit • Customer economic drivers • Impact on customer profit due to our service vs. competitors	• Description of system infrastructure • Total system costs/revenues • Complementor's investments and profits • Complementor costs of adhering to your standard • System performance drivers
Customer Targeting (Profit Drivers)	• Product market share • Channel cost • Product profit 　- By product type 　- By offer 　- By channel • Profit drivers	• Customer share • Customer retention • Our profitability by customer 　- Individual and by segment • Customer bonding 　- Switching costs	• System market share • Our share of complementors 　- % of investments tied to our proprietary standard • Our profit by complementor
Innovation (Renewal Drivers)	• Rate of product introduction • Time to market • Percent of sales from new products • Cost of product development • R&D as % of sales	• Relative involvement in customer value chain • Percentage of product development 　- From joint development 　- Customized • Degree of product scope 　- Current vs. potential bundling	• Switching costs for complementors and for customers • Rate of product development • Cost of competitors to imitate standard

Fig. 7.7 Performance metrics for the business drivers of the Delta Model

according to adaptive processes and strategic options. Of course, specific tailor-made metrics also could and should be introduced in each individual business situation.

Notice that the various processes carry on their defined charters: operational effectiveness is the depository of the cost drivers; customer targeting, of the profit drivers; and innovation, of the renewal drivers. Also notice that the Best Product options are product oriented; Total Customer Solutions are customer oriented; and System Lock-In options are system oriented. The logic is clear. However, we continue to find that most firms only concentrate their attention on product-oriented opportunities. It is yet another manifestation of the pervasive product-centric mindset.

The three adaptive processes we have described serve as effective proxies for the three dimensions (other than the financial measures) that are part of the various perspectives of the Balanced Scorecard. Operational effectiveness can be used as a surrogate of the business perspective; customer targeting as the customer perspective; and innovation as the organizational learning perspective. It you accept this proposition, Fig. 7.7 gives us a good overall framework for understanding how the measures associated with each perspective of the Balanced Scorecard change with the nature of the strategy they intend to support – that is, Best Product, Total Customer Solutions, or System Lock-In. This helps to resolve one of our major concerns with this tool.

The Balanced Scorecard of the Chemical Coatings Company

In the Delta Model, we do not limit the application of the Balanced Scorecard to just one single entity but we apply it to the business as a whole and to every one of the customer tiers we have developed for the business. This allows us to not only understand the performance of the entire business, but also to recognize that each customer tier has a very distinct strategic role that needs to be captured as well.

So you can see how to approach this task, we will return to the case of the Chemical Coatings Company, introduced in Chapter 5, where we discussed its customer segmentation and its mission, and again in Chapter 6, where we developed its strategic agenda. Figures 7.8 and 7.9 on the following pages are duplicated from Chapter 5 for your convenience to show the company's key players and the proposed customer segmentation that we suggested.

Figure 7.10 gives us the Balanced Scorecard for the company as a whole. The corresponding Balanced Scorecards for customer tiers 1, 3, 4, and 5, are respectively, Figs. 7.11, 7.12, 7.13, and 7.14. Remember that Tier 2 was just a "parking lot," meaning that we positioned as Tier 2 those large companies that we wish to move into Tier 1, but if we are unable to accomplish that successfully, we will transfer them to Tier 3.

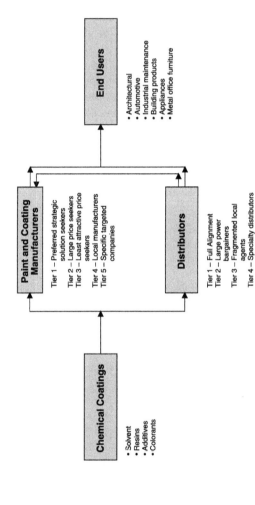

Fig. 7.8 The paint and coating industry: key players

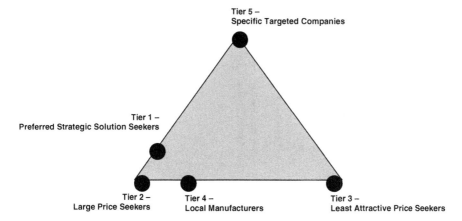

Fig. 7.9 The Chemical Coatings Company's customer segmentation

The figures are quite explicit in terms of how the performance indicators change with each dimension of the Balanced Scorecards and with each Customer Tier in accordance to their strategic options.

Value Creation by Each Strategic Option: Empirical Evidence

In conclusion, we want to examine the comparative economic value created by each of the strategic options of the Triangle. Our belief throughout the book is that the Total Customer Solutions strategy is superior to a Best Product strategy, and, in turn, the System Lock-In strategy is better than Total Customer Solutions. It is very hard to demonstrate this claim because of the inherent idiosyncratic differences that exist among businesses and firms. Economic results might depend on a host of complex behavioral and economic circumstances. Being conscious of these limitations, we attempt to address the issue.

Economic returns vary markedly by strategic position. We collected empirical evidence from over 100 companies occupying a range of strategic positions. Our sample included firms drawn from the Fortune 500 whose corporate-wide strategies could be clearly categorized as emphasizing one of the three alternatives in the Triangle.

The acid test in terms of the merits of each option is the economic value that the companies are able to create for their shareholders. We use two common, and very popular, performance measurements: market value added (MVA) and market-to-book ratio (M/B).

Market value added measures the difference between a company's total market value of equity and debt and its book value, which is the total amount that investors of equity and debt have contributed to the company. On this measure, System Lock-In businesses produce an MVA, which, on average, is over four times

Balanced Scorecard Framework	Financial Perspective (Shareholder Lock)	Business Processes (Operational Effectiveness)	Organizational Learning (Innovation)	Customer Perspective (Customer Targeting)

Corporate Level	• Volume, revenue, earnings, gross margin by product and/or market segment (actual vs. plan)
	• Revenue and earnings by service and business models
	  - Corporate ROI
	  - Complementor ROI
	• Revenue and earnings by specialty vs. commodity
	• Growth of volume, revenue, earnings, gross margin (Growth initiatives)
		• Capacity utilization by product categories or production site
		• Unit cost by product categories
		• % First pass quality by product categories
		• Budget vs. plan (Cost centers)
		• Specialty/ Commodity ratio of sales
			• Rate of product introduction by market segment
			• Percent of sales from new products by market segment
			• R&D as % of sales
			  - Resins
			  - Solvents
			  - Additives
			  - Formulations
			• Projected revenue vs. actual for tactical portfolio reaching commercialization
			• Projected revenue vs. actual for strategic portfolio reaching commercialization
				• Product market share
				• Customer market share by tier
				• Profitability by customer by tier

Fig. 7.10 The Balanced Scorecard dimensions (Corporate – The Chemical Coatings Company)

Balanced Scorecard Framework	Financial Perspective (Shareholder Lock)	Business Processes (Operational Effectiveness)	Organizational Learning (Innovation)	Customer Perspective (Customer Targeting)

Customer Tier Level – Tier 1	• Volume
	• Revenue
	• Gross Profit
	• Earnings from Operations
	• Return on Capital
	• Year over year sales and earnings growth
	• Working capital levels
	• Profitability of "customized" manufacturing revenue stream
		• Cost to serve the customer
		• Breadth of customer engagement (use +5 to −5 scale)
		• % of revenue from differentiated customer solutions
		  – Revenue from differentiated products
		  – Revenue from customer integrated solutions and services
		• % revenue from decommoditized products
			• Revenues emerging from R&D technology partnerships
			• Revenue emerging from customized technology solutions by customer
			  – Customers
			  – Complementors
			• Return on invested hours of technical support being provided to customer for product development and for process improvement
			• Rate of product introduction by market segment
			• Percent of sales from new products by market segment for each customer
			• Total R&D as a % of Total Tier 1 Sales
			• Projected revenue vs. actual for tactical portfolio reaching commercialization by customer
			• Projected revenue vs. actual for strategic portfolio reaching commercialization by customer
				• Product market share by customer
				• Solution revenue/earnings by customer
				• Cost to serve the tier
				• Value added integration level
				  – Customer ROI
				  – Corporate ROI
				• Joint revenue/ earnings from complementor relationship
				  – Customer ROI
				  – Corporate ROI
				  – Complementor ROI

Fig. 7.11 The Balanced Scorecard dimensions – Tier 1: preferred strategic solutions seekers

Balanced Scorecard Framework	Financial Perspective (Shareholder Lock)	Business Processes (Operational Effectiveness)	Organizational Learning (Innovation)	Customer Perspective (Customer Targeting)

Customer Tier Level - Tier 3	• Volume
	• Revenue
	• Gross Project
	• Earnings from Operations
	• Return on Capital
	• Year over year sales and earnings growth
	• Working capital levels
	  - Receivables
	• Cash flow contribution by customer
		• Time to complete the transaction from start to finish
		• Measure customer satisfaction with the transaction
		• % revenue, volume and earnings by channel
		  - Inside sales
		  - Distributor
		  - Self serve
		  - Direct
		  - Digital
		• % revenue from decommoditized products
			• Fees emerging from R&D technology wizards
			  - Customers
			• Cost of developing standardized low cost product solutions by product
			• R&D cost associated with providing non-customized differentiated products
			• Rate of product introduction by market segment
			• Total R&D as a % of total Tier 3 sales
				• Product market share by customer
				• Service fees generated
				• Cost to serve the customer by channel
				  - Inside sales
				  - Distributor
				  - Self serve
				  - Direct
				  - Digital
				• Unit delivered cost to customer

Fig. 7.12 The Balanced Scorecard dimensions – Tier 3: least attractive price seekers

Balanced Scorecard Framework	Financial Perspective (Shareholder Lock)	Business Processes (Operational Effectiveness)	Organizational Learning (Innovation)	Customer Perspective (Customer Targeting)

Customer Tier Level – Tier 4	(Data by Customer Group)
	
	• Volume
	• Revenue
	• Gross Profit
	• Earnings from Operations
	• Return on Capital
	• Previous year's month sales and earnings growth
	  – Quarterly
	  – Annually
	• Working capital levels
	  – Receivables
		Tier 1 metrics may apply to some subgroups and tier 3 metrics apply to other subgroups	(Data by Customer Group)
			
			• Feeds emerging from R&D technology wizards
			  – Customers
			• Cost of developing standardized low cost product solutions by product
			• R&D cost associated with providing non-customized differentiated products
			• Rate of product introduction by market segment
			• Total R&D as a % of total Tier 4 sales
			• Projected revenue vs. actual for tactical portfolio reaching commercialization by customer
			• Projected revenue vs. actual for strategic portfolio reaching commercialization by customer
				• Market share by customer group by product
				• Service fees generated by customer group (ROI justified)
				• Cost to serve by customer group
				• Value added
				  – Customer ROI
				  – Corporate ROI
				• Joint revenue/ earnings from complementor relationship by customer group
				  – Customer ROI
				  – Corporate ROI
				  – Complementor ROI

Fig. 7.13 The Balanced Scorecard dimensions – Tier 4: local manufacturers

Balanced Scorecard Framework	Financial Perspective (Shareholder Lock)	Business Processes (Operational Effectiveness)	Organizational Learning (Innovation)	Customer Perspective (Customer Targeting)

Customer Tier Level - Tier 5	• Total leveraged value across all customer tiers from tier 5
	  - Volume
	  - Revenue
	  - Gross Profit
	  - Earnings from Operations
	• Cost to manage the relationship
		• Breadth of technology and business innovation engagement (use +5 to - 5 scale)	• % of revenue from differentiated technology or business model solutions
			  - Revenue from differentiated technologies
			  - Revenue from customer integrated solutions and services
			• % revenues from decommoditized products
			• Revenues emerging from R&D technology partnerships
			  - Customers
			  - Complementors
				• Customer's relative market share in the niche
				• Size of market potentially impacted by tier customer
				• Size of additional revenue for the tier customer innovated (prepare these companies for acquisition by tier 1)

Fig. 7.14 The Balanced Scorecard dimensions – Tier 5: specific target companies

	Number of Firms	MVA (Market Value Added)			Market-To-Book Value		
		Mean	Standard Deviation	Index	Mean	Standard Deviation	Index
Best Product	74	14.26	16.57	1.0	5.88	9.33	1.0
Total Customer Solution	67	22.38	28.14	1.6	7.29	7.7	1.2
System Lock-In	16	57.15	48.67	4.0	11.98	5.86	2.0

Fig. 7.15 Value creation by each strategic option: empirical evidence

that of Best Product companies; Total Customer Solutions firms generate over 1.6 times the MVA of Best Product organizations. The results are shown in Fig. 7.15.

The market-to-book ratio compares the value that shareholders place in the business based upon their assessment of the expected future cash flows relative to the past resources that have been committed to the business. In other words, if a total of $1 million has been invested in a business that today the market values at $2 million, then the market-to-book ratio is 2. Obviously, the strategy and execution of the business has a multiplier effect that creates the additional value. The empirical data show that the System Lock-In companies had an M/B ratio that is on average twice as large as the Best Product companies. The Total Customer Solutions companies have an average M/B that is 20% higher than that of the Best Product firms (Fig. 7.15).

We have found a significant financial premium for companies that can achieve a Total Customer Solutions position, and a further enhanced premium for those attaining System Lock-In. However, there are important caveats. This conclusion reflects the performance of companies that have successfully arrived at these positions, it does not account for those that have attempted and failed. There may be added risk and greater difficulty in reaching for the brass ring of System Lock-In or the annuities attached to Total Customer Solutions. Furthermore, while there are striking rewards that can draw you to new strategies, we do not mean to imply that the strategic answer for all companies is the same.

Notes

1. The original references of the Balanced Scorecard are: Robert S. Kaplan and David P. Norton, "The Balanced Scorecard – Measures That Drive Performance," *Harvard Business Review*, Vol. 70, No. 1, January–February 1992; Robert S. Kaplan and David P. Norton, "Putting the Balanced Scorecard to Work," *Harvard Business Review*, Vol. 71, No. 5, September–October,

1993; Robert S. Kaplan and David P. Norton, "Using the Balanced Scorecard as a Strategic Management System," *Harvard Business Review*, Vol. 74, No. 1, January–February 1996; Robert S. Kaplan and David P. Norton, *The Balanced Scorecard – Translating Strategy into Action*, Harvard Business School Press, 1996.

Chapter 8
Putting It All Together: How to Integrate the Critical Tasks of Strategy – An Illustration[1]

Up to this point, we've carefully examined the Delta Model and laid out the primary concepts and tools you need to implement its customer-centric approach to business strategy. We have also provided some practical examples of its application in a number of different settings.

In this concluding chapter, we present one single case that pulls it all together. The case centers on the five strategic tasks of the Delta Model that we illustrated in Fig. 1.4, duplicated in this chapter for your convenience (Fig. 8.1).

Fig. 8.1 The strategic tasks of the Delta Model

A.C. Hax, *The Delta Model*, DOI 10.1007/978-1-4419-1480-4_8,
© Springer Science+Business Media, LLC 2010

The Case of DMK International

DMK is a software outsourcing provider located in Dalian, China, offering custom-built software applications and system maintenance. Their value proposition is based on offering high-quality IT solutions at low costs through off-shore teams based in China to companies in countries where IT labor is much more expensive. The low cost is achieved by leveraging top and well-trained talents that are available at much lower cost in mainland China. The high quality is achieved by operating the business and managing the projects at the stringent level and maturity of CMM5 (Capability Maturity Model 5) and Six Sigma.

DMK specializes in IT services, including application development, system integration, system migration and conversion, maintenance and support. Its technology competence covers Java, Oracle, .Net, AS400, ASP (Application Service Provider), as well as mainframe. Mainframe-based legacy technology is still extensively used in several industries, including banking and insurance, among others. DMK has achieved CMM5, the highest rank in software development quality, and has also embraced the Six-Sigma methodology in its business and software project management processes. DMK's major customers are large corporations with IBM, GE, Unisys, AIG, and NEC ranking as the top 5 clients by annual revenue. Starting out as Japanese-focused outsourcing provider, DMK developed US market capabilities and entered the US market in early 2003.

The modern city of Dalian, headquarters of DMK, is located in the northeast of China. It is considered one of China's major success stories and is a crucial economic zone in the country. It was the first technological development area to be approved by the central government and thus far the largest one in China in terms of development area.

Dalian has become one of the most overseas-oriented cities in China. Companies in Dalian, like DMK, continue to enhance relations with foreign partners, and cooperative partnerships have been created with a wide variety of industries. With the historical influence of Japanese culture, Dalian is unique among Chinese cities, with a large talent pool that has fluent Japanese-language capability and deep understanding of the Japanese culture.

A concerted effort by the Chinese government to build Dalian into the "Silicon Valley of Northern China," and the presence of several major universities and technical institutions in Dalian that provide a relatively inexpensive software talent pool, gives DMK a location advantage operating as an overseas software outsourcing provider.

Customer Segmentation and Customer Value Proposition of DMK

The first task of the Delta Model is the development of the Customer Segmentation and Customer Value Propositions.

Initially, DMK divided its market into three geographical segments – Japan, United States, and China – as businesses were being developed in the three regions. However, this way of segmenting the market does not seek to maximize value for both DMK and their clients, and it does not communicate which customers are of high value, and to what extent a customer contributes to its long-term profitability. Another criterion for segmentation was needed. Figure 8.2 shows the customer segmentation that was adopted as well as the main characteristics of the resulting four tiers. Each tier represents a different level of customer bonding. Tier 1 achieves the highest degree of bonding, tier 4 the lowest. A good validation for this segmentation is that the level of long-term profitability for DMK also aligns with the ordering implicit from tier 1 to tier 4. Given the strategic bonding and profitability significance, DMK should try to move customers from tier 4 toward 3, 2, and 1. More discussion on the tiers follows below.

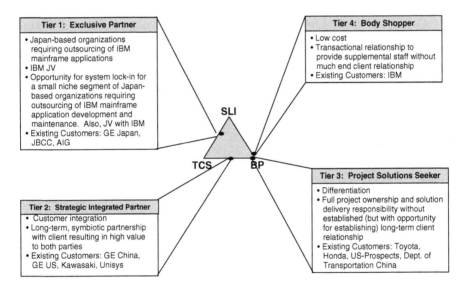

Fig. 8.2 Customer segmentation and its main characteristics

Tier 1 – Exclusive Partner

The Business Dimension

The niche market of IBM mainframe application development and maintenance in the Japanese business environment gives rise to this tier. DMK's key competency in Japanese language and culture and strong experience and expertise in IBM mainframe technologies are unique in China. The IT industry in China did not really take off until the early 1990 s. At that time, mainframe technology was no longer the IT trend, and therefore most engineers were only educated and had experience in newer technologies. DMK acquired its IBM mainframe expertise by assimilating entirely a large team of experts from a government department that was shut down with one of the only IBM mainframe installations in China. As part of this, DMK also acquired a fully operational IBM mainframe, which makes it feasible for off-shoring new mainframe development. This provides DMK with competitive advantage and creates an entry barrier to potential competitors.

In contrast to China, mainframe technology was adopted in Japanese industries when mainframe technology became available in the market in early 1970 s. Today, most of the banking and insurance industries continue to rely heavily on mainframe systems for critical business operations. The shift from mainframe to newer technologies in Japan is difficult because the relevant talent for system development is scarce and extremely expensive to maintain. For this reason, many Japanese companies are seeking lower costs of services and support for their mainframe systems. Offshore companies in India possess the mainframe technology expertise but have neither the language nor the cultural skills that are absolutely essential to working in Japan. This gives DMK an opportunity to lock in those customers.

A company like GE Capital in Japan falls into this tier. GE Capital has developed a deep relationship with DMK, including training DMK personnel on GE mainframe systems to have the expertise to support GE equipment. The lack of alternatives of comparable mainframe and Japanese knowledge, and the huge amount of money GE Capital has invested, make switching costs extremely high. DMK has successfully achieved customer lock-in and competitor lock-out in this tier. Another customer DMK has in this tier is JBCC, a joint venture between DMK and IBM Japan. Under this JV agreement, work from IBM through this JV has to go into DMK.

Accenture is a complementor in this tier. They bring deep business domain expertise and provide technology strategy at the high end of the IT consulting value chain. However, work that is needed in the lower end of the value chain is expected to be performed by a low-cost provider such as DMK. This creates a complementary relationship between Accenture and DMK and provides an end-to-end solution with the best ROI for clients. See Fig. 8.2 for more details.

The Value Proposition

This exclusive relationship is based upon extreme similarities between DMK and these customers. Both have dedicated teams enhancing lasting relationships, both understand each other's culture, and both have high-level management involvement, allowing for fast response to daily operational issues. Technology knowledge, methodology (Six-Sigma for the case of GE) and experience are shared and have become a common language. Teams of the two companies work together as one team, and infrastructure is merged into a common network for seamless connectivity. In some cases, GE can allow DMK to use corporate software licenses legally, thereby reducing costs to DMK. All these work toward providing the critical Japanese mainframe solutions at low costs. For tier 1 clients, DMK typically serves as a one-stop shop of a total solution provider by offering bundled hardware and software solutions.

In this tier of closely bonded relationships, DMK is considered a valued partner and enjoys long-lasting and secure business, and thus predictable revenue, and higher margin. Customers also benefit from controlled security, improved time-to-market through seamless operation, and superior ROI. See Fig. 8.3 for further details.

Customer Dimension	Description
Products Scope	Critical partner to client providing highly integrated, customer specific, high value-added turnkey solutions for legacy mainframe applications in Japanese market.
Services Scope	24x7 maintenance of mission critical mainframe legacy applications. Application extension through analysis, design and development of new, integrated modules.
Customer Scope	Japanese corporations in Financial Services, Insurance Industry, etc.
Channels Scope	Direct referrals from highly satisfied existing clients.
End Users Scope	Japanese corporations, Japanese government organizations.
Complementors Scope	IBM (as a hardware/software partner), existing clients, Accenture.
Unique Competencies Scope	• Combination of deep knowledge of mainframe applications and deep understanding of Japanese culture (not available to other companies in China). • Very high level of quality (only CMM level 5 and Six-Sigma company in China) combined with all the other cost advantages available to Chinese companies not available anywhere else in the world.

Fig. 8.3 Business dimension for tier 1 – "exclusive partner"

The Challenges from the Value Proposition of Tier 1

One challenge for tier 1 relationships is the need for continuous improvement year after year. If DMK does not improve its processes, then the high level of profits will provide a strong incentive for competitors to build the same required skills over a period of time. Every major mainframe system and operation change initiated by customers is a challenge in terms of technology transfer, speed of acquiring new knowledge, and new organization to cope with the change. Imperfection in coping with customer change may have significant negative results, as DMK is serving business critical systems for customers. Hiring and retention is another key challenge as DMK seeks to expand business in this tier. It is practically not possible to hire new graduates with mainframe knowledge as most new graduates choose to work on newer technology such as Java and Oracle. DMK also assumes the risk of training engineers on mainframe technology only to have them headhunted away by other Japan-focused outsourcing providers. However, acquiring the entire system development process and Japanese business domain knowledge is both difficult and time consuming.

Value Proposition Element	Description
Experiences	Seamless extension of client team with integrated culture, skilled technologies with deep understanding of client's business.
Value Delivery Systems	• Dedicated client-focused team immersed in all aspects of client's culture. • Network integration to seamlessly extend client environment. • Open communication of all relevant information on both sides. • Executive sponsor. CEO oversight and full corporate reach. • CMM and Six-Sigma delivery methodologies for delivery. • Value-added reselling of hardware and software for one-stop-shopping.

Value Appropriation	Value gained by customer:
	  Superior ROI, improved time-to-market, security, resource stability.
	Value gained by DMK:
	  Exclusive long-term relationship, higher margins, predictable revenue.
	Value shared by both:
	  Shared IP, shared learning, shared risk.

Fig. 8.4 Value proposition for tier 1 – "exclusive partner"

Figures 8.2, 8.3, and 8.4 provide good examples of the formats that we use in documenting the various tasks associated with Customer Segmentation and Customer Value Proposition.

Tier 2 – Strategic Integrated Partner

Business Dimension

DMK and customers have integrated teams, infrastructure, culture, methodology, and share knowledge extensively in this tier. This tier takes advantage of the integration to provide solutions to multiple business units, and multi-phase projects jointly with customers by re-applying the technical and business domain knowledge DMK has acquired for that customer. Kawasaki is an existing customer that falls into this tier. The DMK team that initially established a relationship with Kawasaki continues to provide services in multiple Kawasaki facilities, as well as in continuous project upgrades and maintenance.

GE is another customer here. Any business of GE US and GE China can choose to receive services from DMK under the Master Services Agreement (MSA) that already covers comprehensive contractual agreement on legal issues. All they have to do is to focus on the technical work contents and service level agreements for technical delivery. DMK has teams already knowledgeable about GE culture and the expectation that they could work for any GE business. DMK has succeeded in customer lock-in in this tier, but not competitor lock-out. See Fig. 8.5 for more details

Customer Dimension	Description
Products Scope	Long-term relationship with client to provide customized and integrated solutions across multiple business units.
Services Scope	• T&M and fixed price application development across multiphase projects • Joint application development enabled through deep understanding of client culture and methodology • Dedicated retained teams as extension of clients' IT organization
Customer Scope	GE US, GE China, Kawasaki, Unisys.
Channels Scope	Direct
End Users Scope	N/A
Complementors Scope	Other GE partners, IBM, other software partners, Accenture.
Unique Competencies Scope	• One of 12 exclusive outsourcing vendors for GE • Six-Sigma/CMM level-5 quality combined with China's cost advantage.

Fig. 8.5 Business dimension for tier 2 – "strategic/integrated partner"

Customer Value Proposition

In this level of integration, both DMK and the customers invest in periodic two-way training and knowledge transfer. Relationships are sponsored by high-level management in both organizations. Dedicated business relationship managers are in place to manage day-to-day operations and business relationships. DMK teams that have specific knowledge, experience, and a cultural understanding of the customers are readily available to serve business needs with short ramp-up time and low risk. This provides superior ROI and time-to-market for the customer, reduces security risks, and provides a dedicated team of resources for the customers. DMK wins new orders via referrals within the customer organizations, thereby reducing cost of new sales. See Fig. 8.6 for more details.

Challenges

The key challenge is in maintaining quality of services and processes (Six-Sigma, CMM5) as DMK grows its business and customers. Maintaining quality standards is a requirement for growth of the business, yet it is growth that puts significant stress on the ability of the organization to maintain CMM level 5 and Six-Sigma quality standards. Consider a large corporate such as GE: if a DMK team does not perform well in any one division of GE, word spreads, and other business units in addition to future opportunities from the same division might disappear entirely.

Hiring could be another challenge, as DMK is not a big national brand in China, and has been able to recruit mostly in the northeast part of China, in and around Dalian. DMK competes with numerous other outsourcing organizations around the world for people with customer relationship management skills and experience in the United States and Japan.

Value Proposition Element	Description
Experiences	Integrated teams of skilled technologists with deep understanding of client's business.
Value Delivery Systems	• Dedicated client teams fully trained in client's methodologies and processes • Joint development plans • Cross-training and periodic two-way knowledge transfer • Business Relationship Manager, CEO oversight, and full corporate reach
Value Appropriation	Value gained by customer: Superior ROI, improved time-to-market, resource stability, shared risk, continuous improvement. Value gained by DMK: Access to client network as sales channel, credibility, learning. Value shared by both: Co-development of shared standards and processes.

Fig. 8.6 Value proposition for tier 2 – "strategic/integrated partner"

Tier 3 – Project Solution Seeker

Business Dimension

Customers in this tier typically do not have a fixed set of predefined outsourcing partner relationships. They have well-bounded discrete needs and select a set of outsourcing companies to bid out each project based on the needs of that project. They judge on provider's delivery capabilities for their specific needs, and pay on Time & Material (T&M, i.e., hourly or monthly rates), or Fixed Price for those deliverables. Long-term relationships, and therefore integration or bonding, is minimal in this tier. DMK wins those projects by offering high-quality and matured process experience (Six-Sigma and CMM5) at low costs that are perceived by customers as the differentiators in this tier. IBM Japan and NEC are currently such customers in this tier. See Fig. 8.7 for more details.

Customer Value Proposition

DMK delivers high-quality results that meet customer expectations at low costs. Dedicated teams learn about the customer culture, work style, and requirements for the project, and team managers oversee project progress and delivery. Besides high-quality and low-cost deliverables, customers gain from understanding DMK capability, and they often learn from DMK on the CMM5 and Six-Sigma methodology in practice. DMK gains new learning from customer domain and knowledge, and also opportunities of establishing long-term relationship. See Fig. 8.8 for more details.

Customer Dimension	Description
Products Scope	Individual project solutions without committed long-term relationship.
Services Scope	T&M and Fixed price application development for discrete projects.
Customer Scope	Toyota, Honda, Department of Transportation China, U.S. prospects.
Channels Scope	• Direct • Consulting partners such as IBM • Strategic partners such as GE
End Users Scope	N/A
Complementors Scope	IBM, GE, other software partners, Accenture.
Unique Competencies Scope	Six-Sigma/CMM level-5 quality combined with China's cost advantage.

Fig. 8.7 Business dimension for tier 3 – "project solution seeker"

Value Proposition Element	Description
Experiences	End-to-end delivery of project with high quality and competitive price.
Value Delivery Systems	• Structured processes and teams with high quality of performance • Ability to quickly ramp-up on clients business and culture • Process for seamless transition at end of project • Dedicated project team manager with executive oversight
Value Appropriation	Value gained by customer: Experimentation, learning, flexibility, reduced time-to-market, high quality, ROI. Value gained by DMK: Opportunity for long-term relationship, ROI, learning. Value shared by both: Shared learning in business domain and new technology.

Fig. 8.8 Value proposition for tier 3 – "project solution seeker"

Challenges

The challenge is in the timely development of expertise in new industry verticals to increase market share, maintaining high project management skills, and working well with different customers that have distinct processes and culture. Mobilizing resources that are capable and flexible enough to work with new customers and new projects is also a challenge. This requires DMK to assign their scarce high-end caliber talents to meet the needs. Having a pool of such personnel increases idle time and is costly to DMK.

Tier 4 – Body Shoppers

Business Dimension

Customers in this tier are known as body shoppers. That is, they have transactional needs to fill in their skill or labor gaps. Customers own and manage the projects and approach DMK with skill specifications and expect DMK to assign personnel that meet the needed specifications. The requirement of work is a specific duration, and payment is done based on the T&M for that period. Since the provider selection criteria is based on the ability to offer the personnel meeting a set of technical skills, DMK's differentiated capabilities in software development process and methodology with CMM5 and Six-Sigma do not add significant value. Cost is a major driver. The company that provides the personnel with the lowest cost wins the deal. The relationship experience is not repeatable. If the same customer approaches DMK again next time, they are likely to have different personnel skill set requirements. Therefore, the experience gained in the previous project has limited applicability. See Fig. 8.9 for more details.

Customer Dimension	Description
Products Scope	Individual resources to supplement existing project teams and fill skill gaps (transactional)
Services Scope	• T&M and retained resources for fixed time durations • Provide specific technology development skills on projects
Customer Scope	IBM Japan, NEC
Channels Scope	Consulting partners such as IBM, Direct.
End Users Scope	Corporations
Complementors Scope	N/A
Unique Competencies Scope	Consulting partnerships, technology skill differentiation.

Fig. 8.9 Business dimension for tier 4 – "body shopper"

Customer Value Proposition

Skills expertise and a flexible, on-demand resource pool is the primary value proposition for customers. Customers resolve their skill set gap and resource issues at that specific time. DMK uses such engagements as a "foot-in-the-door" for targeted prospective clients and can use the opportunity to build credibility and trust to migrate the client into higher tiers. Also, the body shopping approach by customers offers the ability for DMK to gain experience in specific industry verticals, new technologies, and innovative processes that can be leveraged in future client work. See Fig. 8.10 for more details.

Value Proposition Element	Description
Experiences	Supplement team with individual resources and fill gaps with skill expertise
Value Delivery Systems	• Strong branch that can be tapped on demand • Mix of skills and expertise

Value Appropriation	Value gained by customer:
	    Resources on demand and skills on demand.
	Value gained by DMK:
	    Opportunity to up-sell, learning, improved bonding.
	Value shared by both:
	    Exchange of skills.

Fig. 8.10 Value proposition for tier 4 – "body shopper"

Challenges

Key challenge is maintaining the low-cost structure because customers go for cost. Also, since customer requirement is unpredictable, DMK needs to have a pool of resources on bench ready to meet the requirements. This creates unpredictable personnel idle time which hurts DMK's profitability.

The Firm as a Bundle of Competencies

The previous task – customer segmentation and customer value proposition – allows DMK to define how they are going to treat their customers and the content of the offering that is provided. Now is a time for management to reflect on the existing competencies of DMK, which are listed according to the eight strategic positions of the Triangle in Fig. 8.11 – and the desired competencies that will supplement

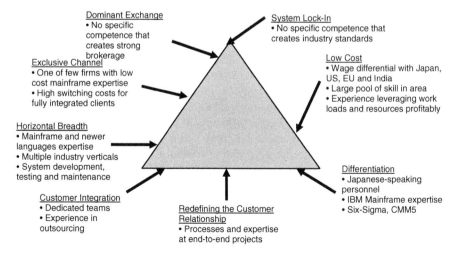

Fig. 8.11 Bundle of competencies analysis (current)

DMK's current capabilities to assure that the intended value propositions will be delivered. This last task is presented in Fig. 8.12.

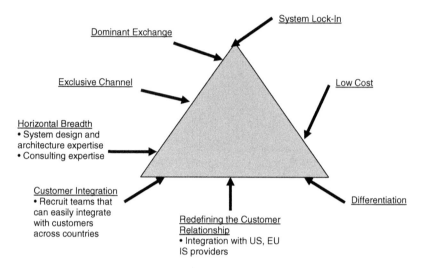

Fig. 8.12 Bundle of competencies analysis (desired)

Cataloging the competencies of the firm is a rather straightforward exercise. The picture that emerges, however, could be very helpful in helping the executives visualize the depth and breadth of the firm's capabilities and what efforts are needed to reinforce them. Figures 8.13, 8.14, and 8.15 give us a sense of the overall combined competencies that DMK has in each of the three strategic options of the Delta Model – Best Product, Total Customer Solutions, and System Lock-In, respectively.

From Fig. 8.13 we can see that the initial foundation of DMK business resides on its extremely competitive low-cost infrastructure and its differentiation capabilities due to the familiarity of the Japanese culture and language possessed by its consultants. Notice that there are also important non-location-specific competencies associated with both the low cost and differentiation.

Figure 8.14 helps us in grasping the more subtle set of capabilities that DMK needs to nurture to attain a strong position in Total Customer Solutions. This is what will allow DMK to transfer unique knowledge to their customers in a most efficient way.

Finally, Fig. 8.15 brings the claims DMK has in seeking some form of System Lock-in as an Exclusive Channel or the provider of a Dominant Exchange. The full set of competencies that DMK has been able to consolidate in such a short period of time is quite remarkable. They assure DMK a strong standing in the business they are pursuing.

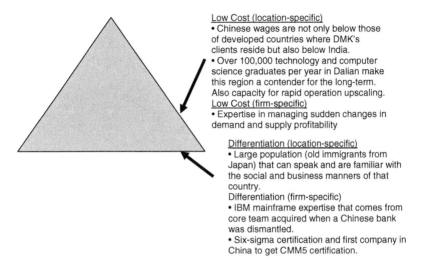

Low Cost (location-specific)
• Chinese wages are not only below those of developed countries where DMK's clients reside but also below India.
• Over 100,000 technology and computer science graduates per year in Dalian make this region a contender for the long-term. Also capacity for rapid operation upscaling.
Low Cost (firm-specific)
• Expertise in managing sudden changes in demand and supply profitability

Differentiation (location-specific)
• Large population (old immigrants from Japan) that can speak and are familiar with the social and business manners of that country.
Differentiation (firm-specific)
• IBM mainframe expertise that comes from core team acquired when a Chinese bank was dismantled.
• Six-sigma certification and first company in China to get CMM5 certification.

Fig. 8.13 Bundle of competencies analysis – the best product option

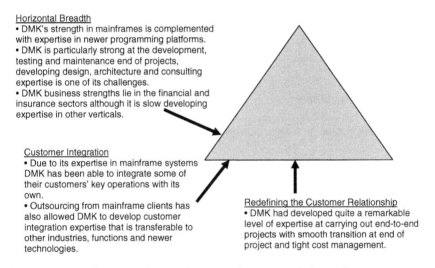

Horizontal Breadth
• DMK's strength in mainframes is complemented with expertise in newer programming platforms.
• DMK is particularly strong at the development, testing and maintenance end of projects, developing design, architecture and consulting expertise is one of its challenges.
• DMK business strengths lie in the financial and insurance sectors although it is slow developing expertise in other verticals.

Customer Integration
• Due to its expertise in mainframe systems DMK has been able to integrate some of their customers' key operations with its own.
• Outsourcing from mainframe clients has also allowed DMK to develop customer integration expertise that is transferable to other industries, functions and newer technologies.

Redefining the Customer Relationship
• DMK had developed quite a remarkable level of expertise at carrying out end-to-end projects with smooth transition at end of project and tight cost management.

Fig. 8.14 Bundle of competencies analysis – the total customer solutions option

The Challenges from the Existing and Desired Bundle of Competencies

It is obvious that the successful entry of DMK into the IT supplier business in Japan resulted from its low-cost infrastructure – due primarily to the lower wage of China – and the Japanese cultural and language knowledge residing in Dalian. Their major challenge is to add to these obvious strengths more qualifications in the vast

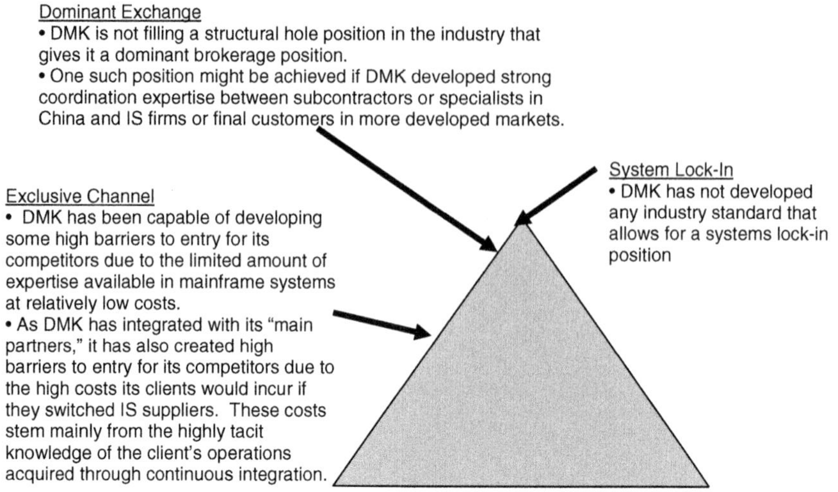

Dominant Exchange
• DMK is not filling a structural hole position in the industry that gives it a dominant brokerage position.
• One such position might be achieved if DMK developed strong coordination expertise between subcontractors or specialists in China and IS firms or final customers in more developed markets.

System Lock-In
• DMK has not developed any industry standard that allows for a systems lock-in position

Exclusive Channel
• DMK has been capable of developing some high barriers to entry for its competitors due to the limited amount of expertise available in mainframe systems at relatively low costs.
• As DMK has integrated with its "main partners," it has also created high barriers to entry for its competitors due to the high costs its clients would incur if they switched IS suppliers. These costs stem mainly from the highly tacit knowledge of the client's operations acquired through continuous integration.

Fig. 8.15 Bundle of competencies analysis – the System Lock-In option

professional knowledge required in the IT outsourcing business and to geographically expand eventually to Europe and the United States, where the most important global markets reside. This is not an easy task, but it is required if DMK wishes to extend its presence beyond a rather confined segment of the IT business.

The Mission of DMK

The following statement defines the mission of DMK

DMK – Building the Outsourcing Model of the Future

Become the #1 provider of Business Process Outsourcing and IT Services in China:

- Analyzing, designing, developing, deploying, and maintaining software systems and solutions
- Delivering the highest quality of service and unparalleled value
- Seamlessly integrating with complementary local service providers
- To service large- and mid-sized corporations, government departments and non-profit organizations
- Through experienced, passionate, and hard-working associates driven to provide outstanding service
- Focusing first on Japan, China, and United States and expanding next into Europe and Latin America markets

The definition of DMK transformation according to the eight dimensions of the Mission is presented in Fig. 8.16.

	Now	**Future**
Product Scope	Technology-based such as J2EE framework, Microsoft, NET framework, etc. for rapid code development/	• Horizontal application framework such as portal toolkits, content management toolkits, etc. • Solutions frameworks such as wealth management solutions for financial services, employee portals as HR solutions, etc. that leverage competencies/expertise of strategic and exclusive partners.
Service Scope	Lower-end of software services value chain: application development, system integration, system conversion/migration, maintenance and support.	Integrated service that captures the entire value chain through strong collaboration with complementors at the high-end of the software services value chain.
Customer Scope	Primarily large corporations, government departments in China	Expand to include service providers at the high-end of the software services value chain
End-User Scope	Large corporations, government departments in China	Expand to include mid-sized corporations, state and federal government departments, non-profit organizations.
Channel Scope	Direct, joint venture	Exclusive offshore service delivery partnerships that allow white labeling of DMK services.
Complementor Scope	Hardware and software product companies	Business consulting, IT strategy/architecture consulting firms.
Geographical Scope	Japan and China with limited presence in the US	US, UK. Expand into countries where language of business is non-English and where cost of IT services is higher than China. (Indian firms do not have language advantage while China-based firms have significant cost advantage.)
Unique Competencies Scope	• High maturity in software development processes – First company to obtain SEI CMM level 5 certification in China. • Six-Sigma certified project and operational managers to ensure data-driven analysis and predictability. • Low cost of China-based delivery. • Japanese language and cultural strength.	• Ability to build teams that can integrate seamlessly to form extensions of other service organizations. • Develop familiarity and comfort in business/professional relationships with other cultures based on geographic expansions. • Develop strength in technical design and knowledge of specific business domains for solutions development.

Fig. 8.16 The mission of the business

Challenges from Changes in the Mission of DMK

Identifying the challenges we face in stretching an organization from its existing state to build new capabilities and achieve a new business scope is an important pre-cursor to identifying new strategic thrusts for the business. These are the challenges DMK identified.

Challenges from changes in Product Scope
- Deeper expertise in industry verticals required to build solutions sets
- Focused effort required to build horizontal application frameworks

Challenges from changes in Service Scope
- Ability to build teams that can integrate seamlessly to form extensions of other service organizations
- Lack of strength in technical design
- Lack of network of complementors at high end of software services value chain

Challenges from changes in Customer Scope
- Ability to build teams that can integrate seamlessly to form extensions of other service organizations
- Develop familiarity and comfort in other foreign cultures

Challenges from changes in End-User Scope
- Need to build intermediary channel to gain access to mid-sized corporations
- Need to build partnerships with service providers focused on servicing state and federal governments
- Need to build intermediary channel to access non-profit organizations

Challenges from changes in Channel Scope
- Need new sales and marketing strategy that targets services organizations in high end of services value chain

Challenges from changes in Complementor Scope
- Need new sales and marketing strategy that targets services organizations in high end of services value chain

Challenges from changes in Geographical Scope
- Develop familiarity and comfort in business/professional relationships with new foreign cultures

Challenges from changes to Unique Competencies Scope
- Lack of knowledge in European and Latin American cultures
- Lack of dominant technical design strength

The Strategic Agenda

The three tasks that we have completed – Customer Segmentation, Bundle of Competencies, and Mission – should provide all the necessary input to create a comprehensive and effective Strategic Agenda.

At this point, the executive team that was engaged in the process of developing the agenda recognized 10 major strategic thrusts (see Fig. 8.17) by following the format explained in Chapter 6. The thrusts have been grouped according to four major themes the executives found to be central driving forces: Building Internal Capabilities, Solidify Core Markets, Building US Market, and Expand into Other

#	Strategic Thrusts	CEO	CFO	RP US	RP China	RP Japan	VP Operations	VP HR	VP Sales	VP Marketing	Business Processes	Performance Measures
Build Internal Capabilities												
1	Invest in people, train and motivate. Hire outstanding talent. Develop strong technical design capabilities.	2	2		2		1	1		2	OE	Attrition, number of recruits, performance
2	Expand nationally leveraging government programs to develop global delivery centers throughout China.	1	2		1		1	2	2	2	OE	Growth in GDC, number of employees, utilization profit margin
3	Work with exclusive channel partners to develop horizontal frameworks (portals, content/doc management) and industry specific solution sets (energy, publishing, financial services) for rapid development.	1		2	2	2			2	1	I	Decrease in project execution time, increase in client satisfaction, increase in sales competitiveness
Solidify Core Markets												
4	Dominate IBM mainframe outsourcing market in Japan through aggressive sales and marketing programs.		2			1	2	2	1	1	CT	Increase in profitable market share
5	Strengthen strategic relationships (e.g. IBM, GE, Kawasaki, Unisys) through deep customer understanding/integration and continuous improvement.	1	2		1	1	1		2		OE	Increase in client satisfaction, increase in size of relationship and profitability
Build US Market												
6	Develop strong direct-marketing program to target the intermediary service provider channel.	2	2	1			2		2	1	CT	High quality sales leads into US based consulting and IT services firms.
7	Actively pursue US based consulting/high-end IT service firms to become their exclusive provider of design, development, and maintenance services.	2		1			2		1	2	CT	Increase in US market share and profitability. Number of exclusive partners and projects.
8	Develop an engagement program with processes to ensure long-term, successful integration of offshore DMK team with local service firm.			1			1	2	2		I	Client satisfaction, increase in revenue/profits, profitability of client.
Expand to Other Markets												
9	Expand to UK and test EU (Germany, France, Italy) using an intermediary partnership network similar to US strategy.	1	1	2			2	1	1	2	B	Increase in UK market share, targeted partners/projects.
10	Enter and test the Latin American market (Brazil, Mexico, Chile) also through an intermediary partnership network.	1	1	2			2	1	1	2	B	Targeted relationships/projects in specific geographies

1 – Key role in formulation and implementation
2 – Important role of support and concurrence
▢ - "Champion," Leadership role in execution of Strategic Thrust

B - Business Model
CT – Customer Targeting
OE – Operational Effectiveness
I- Innovation

Fig. 8.17 Strategic agenda of DMK

Markets. Figure 8.17 shows how the thrusts are mapped into the existing organizational structure of DMK in order to be able to assign the proper responsibilities for their execution, identify the resulting business processes that cut across organizational units, and select key performance metrics. Moreover, DMK ran the following tests to assure that the strategic agenda is the appropriate one at this stage of its evolution.

1. Comprehensiveness: Does the agenda extend across all of DMK's services, geographies, and market segments including customers, end-users, channels, and complementors?
2. Stretch: Do performance measures for each thrust provide achievable but involve highly demanding goals for the organization?
3. Monitoring and Control – Ease of implementation: Are milestones established throughout the process to allow for continuous monitoring and change in strategy if and as required?
4. Motivation – Quality of Working Environment: Will the mission, combined with clear strategic thrusts, energize the organization with the common set of goals and flexibility required to innovate and grow?
5. Vulnerability: No material vulnerabilities were identified at this time.

Aligning execution with this strategic agenda will be critical to the success of DMK.

The Intelligent Budget and the Balanced Scorecards

We indicated in Chapter 7 that the two main instruments used by the Delta Model to wrap-up the full strategic analysis are the budget – which provides the financial implications of the strategy and the economic value created – and the Balanced Scorecards – which allow us to monitor the performance of the business as a whole and each of its customer tiers. This is how DMK proceeded.

The Intelligent Budget

DMK International is going to allocate its financial resources mainly to four strategic areas. (Please note that this budget does not reflect DMK's actual numbers to protect company confidentiality.)

1. Increase in building-up business relations with selected key existing clients or potential clients. The ability to move clients from tier 4 (body shopping category) to tier 1 or 2 (bonded relationship categories) greatly increase DMK's revenue stream, as cost of acquiring new clients is reduced. Such expenses include a combination of training, recruiting, marketing, and administrating costs.

2. Innovation offering customized portfolios of bundled products and services that enhance our client capabilities and can open up new revenue potential for DMK. Selling products requires different market insights and skills, and all relevant costs are considered.
3. Fixed costs and variable costs dedicated to developing centers of excellence to provide customers with top-quality solutions that will generate high margins, further relationship bonding, new complementors, and improved efficiency through centralized knowledge management.
4. Investment in several key technologies such as ERP and collaboration tools that will serve high-value customer better, while bringing operation costs down. The implementation will require costs in tangible assets, project trials, new recruits, and training of people.

Figure 8.18 gives a compact presentation of the DMK budget, which splits the strategic and operational expenses as we have recommended in Chapter 7. It also gives the expected growth to be realized in the future projections.

Historical and Projected P/L (Million $)

	History			Current	Projections		
	2005	2006	2007	2008	2009	2010	2011
Sales Revenues	13.00	16.00	18.00	20.00	23.00	26.00	30.00
Operating COGS	8.61	10.15	10.50	10.33	11.20	11.90	12.60
Gross Operating Margin	4.39	5.85	7.50	9.68	11.80	14.10	17.40
Operating SG&A	3.69	4.35	4.50	4.43	4.80	5.10	5.40
Operating Margin	0.70	1.50	3.00	5.25	7.00	9.00	12.00
Strategic Expenses	0.20	0.25	0.50	0.88	2.00	3.38	5.50
EBITA	0.50	1.25	2.50	4.38	5.00	5.63	6.50
Taxes	0.10	0.25	0.50	0.88	1.00	1.13	1.30
Net Income	0.40	1.00	2.00	3.50	4.00	4.50	5.20

Growth Ratio

	History			Current	Projections		
	2005	2006	2007	2008	2009	2010	2011
Sales Revenue		+ 0.23	+ 0.13	+ 0.11	+ 0.15	+ 0.13	+ 0.15
Operating COGS		+ 0.18	+ 0.03	- 0.02	+ 0.08	+ 0.06	+ 0.06
Gross Operating Margin		+ 0.33	+ 0.28	+ 0.29	+ 0.22	+ 0.19	+ 0.23
Operating SG&A		+ 0.18	+ 0.03	- 0.02	+ 0.08	+ 0.06	+ 0.06
Operating Margin		+ 1.14	+ 1.00	+ 0.75	+ 0.33	+ 0.29	+ 0.33
Strategic Expenses		+ 0.25	+ 1.00	+ 0.75	+ 1.29	+ 0.69	+ 0.63
EBITA		+ 1.50	+ 1.00	+ 0.75	+ 0.14	+ 0.13	+ 0.16
Taxes		+ 1.50	+ 1.00	+ 0.75	+ 0.14	+ 0.13	+ 0.16
Net Income		+ 1.50	+ 1.00	+ 0.75	+ 0.14	+ 0.13	+ 0.16

Fig. 8.18 Strategic funds programming and operational budgets

The Balanced Scorecards

We developed the balanced scorecards for the entire firm and for each customer tier. The balanced scorecard will show DMK to have established the proper indicators for business performance for the four relevant perspectives: financial perspective, operational effectiveness perspective, technology (organization learning) perspective, and customer perspective. The Balanced Scorecard for DMK as a whole is

Balanced Scorecard Framework	Financial Perspective (Shareholder Look)	Business Process (Operational Effectiveness)	Organizational Learning (Technology)	Customer Perspective (Customer Targeting)
Company	• Volume, revenue, earning, gross margin by tech. segment and/or market segment (actual vs. plan) • Revenue and earnings by geographical segment (China, US & Japan) • Revenue and earnings by business domain (Capital, Industrial & Government)	• Capacity utilization by engineer idle time • Saving derived from six sigma productivity • Six sigma penetration • Budget vs. plan (facility in China, US & Japan) • Number of employees passing language tests	• Percent of sales from new tech. domain by market segment • Training as percent of sales • ERP/CRM/ Collaboration Tool implementation timeline	• Customer market share by tier • Profitability by customer tier • Customer satisfaction by tier

Fig. 8.19 Balanced scorecard dimensions – DMK

Balanced Scorecard Framework	Financial Perspective (Shareholder Look)	Business Process (Operational Effectiveness)	Organizational Learning (Technology)	Customer Perspective (Customer Targeting)

Tier 1
 	
Exclusive Partner
 	
Japanese companies requiring outsourcing of mainframe applications
	• Volume, revenue, earning, gross margin by individual clients (actual vs. plan)
	• Year over year sales and earnings growth by individual clients (actual vs. plan)
	• Return on Business Relationship investment
	• ROI on mainframe total investment
		• Cost to serve clients
		• Saving derived from six sigma joint projects with clients
		• Budget vs. plan (facility in Japan)
			• Percentage revenue from projects using in-house IBM Mainframe
			• Percentage revenue from projects using client IBM Mainframe
			• Number of clients on DMK ERP
				• Value-added from six sigma
				• ACFC (GE "At Customer For Customer") initiatives
				• Process reengineering joint revenue/earnings from complementor relationship (customer ROI)
				• Customer satisfaction in
				  - Project deliverables
				  - Relationship

Fig. 8.20 Balanced scorecard – tier 1, exclusive partner

presented in Fig. 8.19. Figures 8.20, 8.21, 8.22, and 8.23 illustrate the Balanced Scorecard for each of the four customer tiers of DMK.

The Four Perspectives

Financial Perspective: Financial indicators such as revenue, earnings, and growth rate should be monitored by technology segments, customer segments, geographical diversity, and business domains (capital, industrial, and

Balanced Scorecard Framework	Financial Perspective (Shareholder Look)	Business Process (Operational Effectiveness)	Organizational Learning (Technology)	Customer Perspective (Customer Targeting)

Tier 2
 	
Strategic/ Integrated Partner
 	
Long-term, symbiotic partnership with client resulting in high value to both parties
	• Volume, revenue, earning, gross margin by individual clients (actual vs. plan)
	• Year over year sales and earnings growth by individual clients (actual vs. plan)
	• Return on Business Relationship investment
		• Cost to serve clients
		• Saving derived from six sigma joint projects with clients
		• Budget vs. plan (facility in Japan, US, China)
		• Percentage revenue sales derived from DWH
			• Number of clients on DMK ERP
			• ROI on EAI initiatives
			• ROI on collaboration tools per selected client
			• ROI and percentage revenue on center of excellence establishment
				• Value-added from six sigma
				• ACFC (GE "At Customer For Customer") initiatives
				• Process reengineering joint revenue/earnings from complementor relationship (customer ROI)
				• Customer satisfaction in
				  - Project deliverables
				  - Relationship

Fig. 8.21 Balanced scorecard – tier 2, strategic integrated partner

Balanced Scorecard Framework	Financial Perspective (Shareholder Look)	Business Process (Operational Effectiveness)	Organizational Learning (Technology)	Customer Perspective (Customer Targeting)

Tier 3
 	
Project Solutions Seeker
 	
Full project ownership and solution delivery responsibility without established (but with opportunity for establishing) a long-term client relationship
	• Volume, revenue, earning, gross margin by individual clients (actual vs. plan)
	• Return on Marketing investment
	• Percentage revenue from clients moved into Tier 3
		• Marketing cost per client
		• ROI on collaboration initiatives
		• Percentage revenue, volume, earnings by channel:
		  - Referral by clients
		  - Referral by JBCC
		  - Direct: pull & push
		  - Cross-selling
		• Cost of training per project
			• ROI on collaboration tools per selected client
			• ROI on software license per project
				• Cost to serve clients per channel
				• Customer satisfaction in
				  - Project deliverables
				  - Relationship

Fig. 8.22 Balanced scorecard – tier 3, project solution seeker

governmental). In addition, because DMK International is in an emerging offshore outsourcing industry, it is more significant to measure planning gaps in order for the firm to recognize required level of capability to serve clients, than it is for firms in a matured and stable industry.

Operational Effectiveness: Six-Sigma activities that DMK International has already introduced will provide the firm with key indicators of operational effectiveness (OE). In addition, the penetration and productivity of foreign language capability of employees, which are measured by the number of

Balanced Scorecard Framework	Financial Perspective (Shareholder Look)	Business Process (Operational Effectiveness)	Organizational Learning (Technology)	Customer Perspective (Customer Targeting)

Tier 4
 	
Body Shopper
 	
Transactional relationship to provide supplemental staff without much end client relationship
	• Volume, revenue, earning, gross margin by individual clients (actual vs. plan)
	• ROI by head
	• Percentage revenue from new clients
		• Time to complete the transaction from start to finish per project
		• ROI on collaboration initiatives
		• Percentage revenue, volume, earnings by channel:
		   - Referral by clients
		   - Referral by JBCC
		   - Direct: pull & push
		   - Cross-selling
		• Cost of training per project
			• Cost of collaboration tool to facilitate knowledge transfer	• Cost to serve clients per channel
				• Customer satisfaction in
				   - Project deliverables
				   - Relationship
				   - Cost

Fig. 8.23 Balanced scorecard – tier 4, body shopper

passing language tests, affects OE significantly. In tier one and two, which are in the stage of system lock-in of the Delta Model, "cost to serve clients" is regarded as a dimension of OE rather than that of customer targeting (CT), due to the nature of the service industry, in which it is difficult or meaningless to detach the cost to serve clients from delivery costs of OE.

Technology (Organization Learning): The sustainable growth of DMK as a whole depends on how effectively the firm acquires new technologies and enhances its core capabilities that provide competitive advantage, such as ERP, CRM, and collaboration tools. In tier 1, the customer segment of exclusive partners, the percentage of revenue of a project using an in-house IBM mainframe in Dalian shows technological strength for DMK International's ability to serve them without IBM supports. If possible, this firm also needs to create long-term relationships from its great pool of temporary clients in tier 4.

Customer Targeting: The wallet share and the level of customer satisfaction in each tier indicate the degree of customer bonding with DMK International. Because of DMK's long-term relationships with their customers in tiers 1 and 2, the outcome of Six-Sigma activity in dedicated client teams (ACFT: At Customer For Customer initiatives) and the entire re-engineering process are significant not only for OE perspective but also for CT perspective. In addition, since DMK International needs to reinforce its technological capability with consultants like Accenture, its profit share with complementors shows how it is able to provide enough total solutions to satisfy clients.

Notes

1. Professor Arnoldo C. Hax and Harry Reddy along with graduate students (Hideo Uchida, Paul Lin, Priya Iyer, Richard Chao, and Yoshiro Fujimori) prepared this case. MIT Sloan School of Management cases are developed solely as the basis for class discussion. Cases are not intended to serve as endorsement, sources of primary data, or illustration of effective or ineffective management. Copyright © 2004 MIT Sloan School of Management.

Chapter 9
Managing Small- and Medium-Sized Enterprises (SMEs) – Lessons from the Delta Model

Most of what we have discussed in this book applies without much adaptation to any kind of organization. After all, every firm, regardless of its nature and specific circumstances, has customers and competencies – the two pillars of the Delta Model. However, there are two types of organizations that, because of their importance and singularity, deserve special attention. They are the small- and medium-sized enterprises (SMEs) and the not-for-profit organizations (NFPs). We will devote the next two chapters to the analysis of these institutions, examining what lessons can be derived if we approach them from the perspective of the Delta Model.

The Importance of SMEs

There is no uniform and widely accepted definition of what constitutes an SME. The standards vary from country to country. Typically, SMEs are defined by an upper limit in the headcount and/or the sales revenues. An agreement is emerging, particularly within the United States, to classify a company as small if it has less than 50 employees and medium if the headcount is below 250. This gives you a sense of what kind of organization we are addressing here.

Regardless of its definition, we know that the overall impact of SMEs is overwhelmingly large. Uniformly, 95–99% of the total companies in any country are SMEs; they employ between 40% and 60% of the workers; and they contribute between 40% and 50% of the GDP. In addition, they play a central role as a leading source of innovation and creativity.

For these considerations, we feel the SMEs deserve special treatment.

The Challenges of Managing SMEs

We believe that the Delta Model can guide us in defining a successful strategy for SMEs by looking at how an SME can adopt each of the strategic positions represented in the Triangle.

A.C. Hax, *The Delta Model*, DOI 10.1007/978-1-4419-1480-4_9,
© Springer Science+Business Media, LLC 2010

It may seem odd that most of the examples that we use in this chapter are large, successful companies. We do this for two reasons. First, at one point, all companies were small, and it is interesting to understand how our chosen examples were able to make the successful transition from very embryonic companies to the large organizations they became. Second, we want to use companies that are universally well known to greatly simplify the communication process.

The Best Product Strategy

Generally, SMEs are born with a product-centric mindset. Typically, the founder is an entrepreneur with a smart idea that has some potential to be developed into a successful business. This idea – more often than not – is based upon a product that is judged to have unique attributes that make founding a business on the initial product concept to be attractive. When you accept this premise – which we find quite prevalent – it means that at least in its early stages of development, the relevant strategy followed by an SME is the best product option.

Unfortunately, if this is the case, most SMEs start with a very shaky foundation. Why is that? Remember that there are two ways to develop a successful Best Product strategy: low cost or differentiation. The problem is that most SMEs do not have the cost infrastructure that allows them to compete effectively with large corporations or with cheap imports, which means that the low-cost strategic position is either non-viable or inaccessible. With regard to differentiation, we find a seemingly insurmountable obstacle. Remember that a differentiation option does not imply only that the product is somehow unique. It also requires that the customer both recognize this uniqueness and is willing to pay a significant premium for it. This is not easy for an SME to accomplish.

From what we have said, it might be easy to conclude that for an SME to play the Best Product strategy is a sure recipe for certain failure. This is the great dilemma. SMEs almost invariably are Best Product oriented, and that seems to lead nowhere. Therefore, it is not surprising that there is such a great mortality rate among SMEs. The statistic varies from country to country but about 90% disappear in a very short time span.

What can we do? Abandoning the Best Product position is not the obvious answer because, as we have demonstrated throughout this book, the other strategic options – Total Customer Solutions and System Lock-In – not only are more demanding, but they also require the solid foundation of the Best Product positioning. Let us look into this a bit further.

The Low-Cost Positioning

The major issue with this strategic positioning is how an SME, which does not have access to major economies of scale, could compete with those who do. The answer resides in two very critical qualities that the cost infrastructure of a successful SME strategy should possess: modularity and scalability. Modularity means that we are able to operate extremely effectively with small quantities, which implies that we do not need large economies of scale to be productive. Scalability means that we can expand the volume of our operations by reproducing the same successful modular format, while maintaining our cost-effectiveness without constraining our possible growth.

A remarkable example of the effective use of these two attributes is Southwest Airlines, a company that has experienced 36 uninterrupted, consecutive years of profitability in an industry where most of its competitors have dismal performance or are facing bankruptcy. The winning formula is easy to describe: they fly to secondary airports of major cities to avoid crows and delays, using only one type of aircraft, the Boeing 737, to reduce training and maintenance costs; while offering lowest prices and no-frills service. In 1971 they started serving three secondary airports in Dallas, Houston, and San Antonio, with three 737-200 planes. As they increased in popularity, growth became an easy task by gradually adding new cities in secondary airports, and more Boeing 737s to their fleet.

In Southwest Airlines, we can detect unequivocally modularity and scalability in action! We believe that every SME should pay close attention to these two basic requirements to define the proper cost infrastructure. If you do, you can compete effectively with the large established firms, sometimes from a position of strength. How can American Airlines and United Airlines – to mention the two largest airline companies in the United States – counteract the winning formula of Southwest Airlines? The fact of the matter is, they cannot. By establishing a new and effective way to operate the company from the outset, Southwest enjoys a 20% cost advantage over their large rivals, which is unassailable.

If you do not pay attention to the requirements of modularity and scalability, you are going to face a very steep uphill battle to succeed with a Best Product strategy.

The Differentiation Strategy

We know that differentiation is both hard to establish and, even worse, extremely difficult to sustain when it is only based upon the characteristics of the product itself. This involves another great challenge for an SME seeking a Best Product strategy. What is the way to resolve this dilemma? The answer sounds very trivial but we believe it contains some elements of wisdom: Do not directly confront an important competitor; search for niches where you can occupy a secured space that can be filled by creativity and originality.

A company that excelled in this dimension was Digital Equipment Corporation (DEC). It was founded in 1957, and in a very quick time span, about 10 years, became the second largest computer company in the world, after IBM. DEC invented the minicomputer, and it provided individual users an opportunity to "own" such an important device for the first time. Initially, its customer base was intended to be engineers and scientists, who were to develop their own software applications. Consequently, DEC concentrated all its innovative capabilities in designing and manufacturing the unique hardware needed to support its sophisticated customers. In the process, DEC never directly confronted IBM, which was busy establishing a dominant position in the mainframe computer segment. DEC's creativity was spectacular, legendary. It produced an unrelentingly stream of products – PDP1, 2, 3, . . ., and 16 – that enhanced the performance of its predecessors but was fully compatible in terms of software applications. By doing so, DEC produced enormous entry barriers to any possible competitor. In fact, during a significant period of time, DEC totally dominated the minicomputer market. It was only after the creation of the microcomputer – introducing the personal computer industry – when this domination began to be challenged.

DEC was a brilliant company which unfortunately was not flexible and adaptable enough to face the challenges emanating from a changing environment. As IBM seemed not to understand the huge impact of the minicomputer, DEC was oblivious to the challenge of the microcomputer. The moral of the story is that you cannot stick to a winning formula forever. To make the tragic ending of DEC almost ironic, Compaq bought DEC in 1998 – at the time, one of the leading PC companies. The triumph of Compaq, however, was short-lived because in 2002 Hewlett-Packard ended up acquiring it.

To conclude, Fig. 9.1 shows the position in the Triangle of the two companies we have discussed in this section – Southwest Airlines and DEC; Fig. 9.2 summarizes the implications of the Best Product strategy for the SMEs.

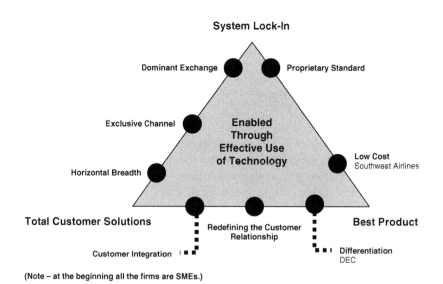

Fig. 9.1 The triangle: the positions of selected SMEs following a best product strategy

Best Product	Definition	Comments
Low cost	Focus on being the lowest cost provider in an undifferentiated product category	The cost infrastructure of the SMEs should be based on modularity and scalability. This means doing things well with small quantities, but having the possibility to develop an effective expansion in volume (one store, one client, one city at a time), e.g. Southwest Airline.
Differentiation	While maintaining effective production economies focus on key differentiation in the product features and functionalities such that the products are uniquely desired and command price premiums	Do not confront an important competitor but establish a different strategic positioning. Search for niches and originality in a space that is not central for key competitors, e.g. DEC.

Fig. 9.2 SMEs and the best product strategy

The Total Customer Solutions Strategy

It might seem obvious – and therefore unnecessary to point out – that the customer is the driving force to every business. Nonetheless, because of the extreme product-centric mentality that resides in most SMEs, this basic fact of life is taken for granted and not been recognized as a central management concern. Thus, SMEs are born in a state that is fairly vulnerable for commoditization, because the customers are not targeted in a different way and are regarded as a single, amorphous mess. We have insistently warned against the dangers of commoditization and explained why it is such an undesirable state for a business. If this can be a serious cause for lack of performance in a large corporation you can well imagine how devastating consequences could be for an SME, which inherently faces much more challenging environments. Our claim is, therefore, that from the outset an SME should become customer-centric mentality and offer a value proposition that has the four attributes we have identified in previous chapters of this book: it should be unique; it should be hard to imitate and be substituted for; it should produce significant value added both for the customers and the firm; and, consequently, it should generate unbreakable customer bonding.

This, of course, is easier said than done. To help understand how the SME can adopt a Total Customer Solutions strategy, we will review the three positions which are relevant to this approach: Redefining the Customer Experience; Customer Integration; and Horizontal Breadth. Once more, we will be using examples of large companies that succeeded in the difficult transition from their origins as an SME.

Redefining the Customer Experience

This task is probably the most demanding and the most important for achieving a Total Customer Solutions strategy. It involves not only knowing your customer base deeply and what their needs are, but also approaching the customer with a different and exciting offer that differentiates you from the rest of the field. One of the most brilliant examples illustrating this point is the entry of Dell in the personal computer (PC) industry. Michael Dell, then a freshman at the University of Texas at Austin, founded the Dell Computer Company in 1984 with $1,000 in capital that he had borrowed from his parents. By that time, the PC industry was fairly mature, with extremely strong companies – such as IBM, Hewlett-Packard, and Compaq – engaged in strong rivalry. However, the key players in the industry were not the computer manufacturers but two leading suppliers: Microsoft and Intel. These two companies had developed Wintel, the industry standard, consisting of the Windows operating system, made by Microsoft, and the computer chip, made by Intel. As a result, the PC business was considered a complete commodity and all of the players were experiencing losses or dismal profits. Who could have possibly considered entering into the PC business under these seemingly impossible conditions? Michael Dell did, but he deviated in three fundamental ways from the industry practices:

First, Dell configured each PC according to the individual specifications of the customer. Far from being a commodity, the computer would differ widely in processing speed, memory capabilities, portability, software configurations, modem speed, and screen sizes – to mention just a few options. Surprisingly, the first customers of Dell were major corporations such as Exxon and Mobil, which needed not off-the-shelf computers but properly designed systems and solutions to satisfy their specific needs.

Second, Dell decided to sell directly to the final customer, by-passing all the intermediate channels – retailers, distributors, and value-added resellers. This allowed him to eliminate the mark-up required by the channels – which significantly reduced his total cost – and, most importantly, he gained direct access to the customer. It is well known that who owns the channel, owns the customer relationship. Figure 9.3 presents the contrast between Dell's Direct Model and the distribution

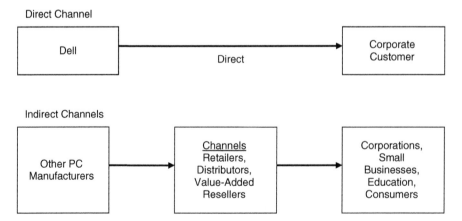

Fig. 9.3   The contrast between Dell and the other PC manufacturers distribution model

model employing indirect channels used by the other PC manufacturers. The difference has gigantic consequences. Dell targeted major business corporations, those requiring the customized solutions. The singularity of that offer gained Dell an enormous degree of customer loyalty and customer bonding. The other manufacturers have the channels as their customers, and they, in turn, own the end-user interface. As a consequence, the commoditization of the PC became a fact of life for the other PC manufacturers, and there was no way to differentiate and gain customer loyalty.

Third, from the very beginning, Dell decided to embrace a strong relationship between itself, its customers, and key suppliers. This is what we call the Extended Enterprise. Figure 9.4 describes the nature of the relationship among the key players.

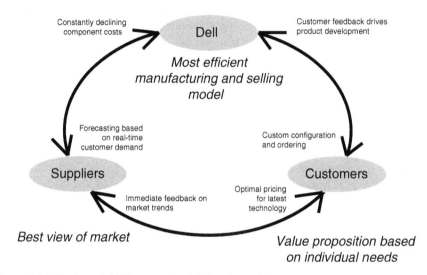

Source: Kevin Rollins, former Dell CEO, presentation at MIT Sloan School of Management.

Fig. 9.4 Dell's extended enterprise

Obviously, it took time to consolidate what is referred to in the figure as the "Virtual Integration" of customers and suppliers. But this was the form of operation that was pursued from the early states of Dell's evolution. It was facilitated by the use of Internet technology that allowed both the full integration of a relevant network of players, as well as the treatment of each customer with a totally unique value proposition that satisfied the specific need of each one.

The contrast with the PC manufacturers was outstanding. Dell targeted individual customers to offer customized solutions; the opposite was the case with the commoditized offer of the PC manufacturers. Dell established a strong cooperation among the key players, while the remainder of the industry was fragmented and engaged in serous rivalry. Dell was using direct channels; the other PC manufacturers were relying on indirect channels.

The results of the unique positioning of Dell in the PC industry were outstanding. In the first year of business, Dell's revenues exceeded $70 Million. During the 1990 s, Dell became one of the fastest growing companies in America. In the long-run, Dell became the only profitable company in the industry.

Dell is a perfect example of how to pursue a successful and original Total Customer Solutions strategy: targeting the customer individually offering a unique customized value proposition, while seeking the support of the Extended Enterprise in its implementation.

Customer Integration

The second task to accomplish the Total Customer Solutions strategy, which, incidentally, Dell fulfilled exceedingly well, is customer integration. The idea is not just to offer a product alone, but to transfer to the customer some expertise, knowledge, or capabilities that allow the customer to perform better in its own business. If an SME can develop this kind of attribute in its value proposition from the start, the degree of customer bonding is greatly enhanced.

The case of DMK, which we discussed in detail in the previous chapter, is a good illustration of an SME that has customer integration from its birth to solidify a strong strategic positioning. DMK is a Chinese company that uses the language and cultural affinity of their citizens of Japanese ancestry – who have developed expertise in mainframe computer technology – to outsource information technology services to Japanese corporations at extraordinary competitive prices.

Try to nurture and develop unique expertise from the very beginning of the SME, and you could have the basis for a successful business.

Horizontal Breadth

Achieving horizontal breadth means that the firm is able to provide a complete set of products and services that satisfy all the needs of the customer in the particular field in which the firm operates. It will be extremely unlikely that an SME would be able to deliver this feast all by itself. It is in this situation where the complementors play an important role. The main question, however, is who is complementing and who is being complemented? In other words, who is playing the leading role in this initiative? Most likely the SME will be the complementor to a large organization. This, however, is far from being a demeaning role; in fact, sometimes it is essential for the SME's survivability that it aggressively seeks a constructive and enduring association with a major partner that could benefit from some singular capabilities the SME could provide. This kind of cooperation is commonly encountered in technology-intensive industries, where small companies can begin to experiment with innovation in areas that could have enormous future potential and can add significant value to a large organization in need of that expertise. Often, these relationships end up with the large company acquiring the small one – which, again, is not such an undesirable outcome. The owners of the SME normally receive a handsome financial reward and still remain in the larger organization, this time enjoying much more abundant resources and capabilities to push the original business idea to its full, successful potential.

Cisco is a company that has distinguished itself for adopting this practice in quite effective ways. It has been said that Cisco has replaced the traditional R&D activity, meaning the internal process of Research and Development, with a more singular A&D, meaning Acquisition and Development strategy. The idea is to target small companies working in the advanced technological edge of their fields, buy them, and integrate them into the major Cisco organization without disrupting the freedom and creativity of the acquired SME. It is a win-win approach to technology procurement.

To conclude, Fig. 9.5 shows the position in the Triangle of the three companies we have discussed in this section – Dell, DMK, and Cisco; Fig. 9.6 summarizes the implications of the Total Customer Solutions strategy for the SMEs.

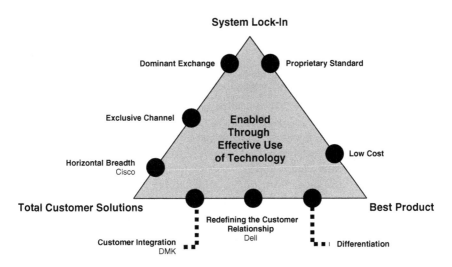

(Note – at the beginning all the firms are SMEs.)

Fig. 9.5 The triangle: the positions of selected SMEs following a total customer solutions strategy

The System Lock-In Strategy

A firm that has reached System Lock-In enjoys an uncontested dominance in the market place; it possesses what is commonly referred to as monopolistic power. Needless to say, this is the most coveted strategic position you could ever aspire

Total Customer Solutions	Definition	Comments
Redefining the Customer Experience	Focus is placed on considering the full experience of the customer from the point of acquisition through the complete lifecycle of ownership of the product.	The value proposition of the SMEs should be different than the traditional competitors and the way to attract the customer should be original. Provide an experience to the customer that no one else is offering. We are not seeking a mere transaction, e.g. Dell.
Customer Integration	This strategy seeks to provide full support to customers' activities by transferring knowledge to improve their performance. It involves a high degree of outsourcing which develops a complex web of connections with the customer that enhances their ability to do business and to use your product.	If possible the customer should be given a customized offering. It is key to add services to obtain this goal, e.g. DMK.
Horizontal Breadth	A complete set of customized product and service offerings that fulfill the entire range of customer need are provided. "One-stop shopping for a unique solution."	It is unlikely that the SMEs can obtain by themselves a large horizontal breadth; they need complementors. The dilemma is who complements whom; is the SME the complementor or is it the complementee? This provides great opportunities for value creation, e.g. Cisco.

Fig. 9.6   SMEs and the total customer solutions strategy

to achieve, which guarantees extreme customer bonding, spectacular financial performance, and – unless something highly unpredictable takes place – an enduring sustainability. As expected, this is a most demanding accomplishment that only few firms can claim. How could one pretend, therefore, that a System Lock-In could be a possible strategic positioning for an SME? The obvious answer is that a System Lock-In is extremely unlikely to be obtained by a small upcoming company. Nonetheless, it is important to address in this section for two reasons. First, it could be very useful to think about this option as a final objective, even in the most embryonic stages of a company development, because it establishes an ultimate aspiration that can influence the trajectory we follow in a most constructive way. Not only are we aiming at having an exceptional product – supported by an intelligent cost infrastructure founded on the principles of modularity and scalability; not only are we recognizing from the outset the centrality of identifying our intended customers, and providing them with a unique value proposition; but we also are asking whether there is something that we could begin to do to seize and make opportunities for System Lock-In. It is the mindset that we want to create to manage the business in search of leadership. Second, although a System Lock-In cannot be consolidated for the overall network in which we operate, it might be achievable one customer at a time. As we have said before, System Lock-In is all about barriers – barriers for our customer to exit from us, and barriers for the competitors to enter our customer base. If we have this objective clear in front of us, we might in fact be able to aspire and gain System Lock-In gradually, customer by customer. Let us be more specific by analyzing each of the strategic positions associated with our System Lock-In option.

Restricted Access

This is a kind of System Lock-In that can be acquired by targeting one customer at a time, as we have indicated before – by encircling the customer with barriers of entry and exit. The paramount example of how to carry this strategy to successful completion is Wal-Mart, which today is the largest employer in the United States with annual revenues above US$400 billion. Sam Walton founded the company in 1962 and carried out a very focused strategy: to open stores in rural areas with populations below 25,000, where no discount retail stores were in existence. By moving it into these towns, Wal-Mart assures a de facto monopoly on retail activities in areas within a 25-mile radius.

What is remarkable is to realize how long it took for Wal-Mart to consolidate its dominance. Its relevant competitors were K-Mart and Target, because they use similar approaches to the retail business by heavily discounting prices in their department stores. The three companies – Wal-Mart, K-Mart, and Target – were founded in 1962. Figure 9.7 tells us this incredible story. You could see that K-Mart enjoys a very quick start; in 1966 it reaches more than $600 million in sales, while Target only has $85 million, and Wal-Mart an unimpressive $6 million. During

		Sales	# of Stores
	K-Mart	$637 million	277
1966	Target	$85 million	7
	Wal-Mart	$6.25 million	16
	K-Mart	$2.02 billion	488
1970	Target	$302 million	24
	Wal-Mart	$30.86 million	32
	K-Mart	$6.15 billion	903
1975	Target	$512 million	48
	Wal-Mart	$335 million	125
	K-Mart	$14.20 billion	2,242
1980	Target	$1.70 billion	138
	Wal-Mart	$1.60 billion	330
	K-Mart	$22.42 billion	2,180
1985	Wal-Mart	$8.40 billion	859
	Target	$4.25 billion	226
	Wal-Mart	$26.02 billion	1,573
1990	K-Mart	$22.5 billion	2,200
	Target	$8.2 billion	420
	Wal-Mart	$104.8 billion	3,190
1997	K-Mart	$31.44 billion	2,261
	Target	$19.54 billion	735

Fig. 9.7 The evolution of the three major discount stores: Wal-Mart, K-Mart, and Target

1970, 1975, and 1980, the superiority of K-Mart, and secondarily Target, over Wal-Mart is quite impressive. It is only in 1985 that Wal-Mart surpasses Target; and it takes until 1990 – 25 years! – for Wal-Mart to assume the leadership position. However, these numbers can be very misleading. What is important to understand is that every store in Wal-Mart's column is a quasi-monopoly, sustained by a System Lock-In position; while K-Mart and Target are competing against each other in highly contested urban areas. K-Mart filed for bankruptcy in 2002 and merged with Sears in 2005, a de facto disappearance as a company. Figures can be deceiving. The overwhelming strength of Wal-Mart was there all along; it took time to make it from a rural, into a regional, and finally into a national dominance. Now they are expanded globally!

Wal-Mart was a very small company at the beginning – as all companies are – by playing the System Lock-In strategy at the store level, and expanding by using the modularity and scalability concepts that we have discussed in this section, Wal-Mart became one of the most successful companies that has ever existed.

Dominant Exchange

Think of the companies that have acquired dominance in their respective markets – Amazon, eBay, Google, Yellow Pages, Sotheby's; all of them provide a critical interface for their customers that is unique and very hard to substitute. The exchange connects buyers and sellers providing an option that is not available by any other alternative. It constitutes a most powerful way to achieve System Lock-In, but is not an option very accessible for a small firm. As always, there are exceptions to any rule, and Amazon is perhaps one of the most outstanding examples of a small company that was born with the intent of establishing a Dominant Exchange. Jeff Bezos, the founder of Amazon, thought that the Internet provided opportunities in retailing, but was not clear what that business could be. Then it occurred to him that books represented an ideal target; they were products that people could buy without the need to touch or try them. He developed a business that from the beginning was positioned quite distinctly from the conventional bookstore, particularly in terms of convenience and breadth of offering. While a large bookstore could accommodate a rather limited number of items in inventory, Amazon could offer more than a million titles. The first 300 employees of Amazon were almost exclusively information technology specialists who worked on the development of the exchange – bringing publishers, who want to sell books – to readers, who want to buy them. In addition, these specialists designed a system that registered the past history of purchases of each individual customer so Amazon could suggest a customized recommendation of new titles to buy. This is the basis of the Dominant Exchange: building a bridge between buyers and sellers, and offering a unique and customized value proposition. Amazon subsequently expanded into a wide, diversified set of product lines – music, computer software, DVDs, video games, electronics, apparel, furniture, food, toys – there seems to be no end to what they can offer to the client. In addition, they created the Extended Enterprise by establishing exclusive partnerships with other retailers to incorporate them into the web – such as Target, Sears Canada, Benefit Cosmetics, Timex, Mark and Spencer, Toys-R-Us, etc. Now Amazon is a remarkably successful company with over $19 billion of sales.

This story is not easy to replicate, but it is important to reflect on the benefits of providing system support to your customer base, even if you can only do it one customer at a time.

Proprietary Standard

Of all the ways to achieve System Lock-In, Proprietary Standard is usually the one that provides the highest and most enduring rewards; think of Microsoft and Intel, that constitute the ultimate paradigm in this field. As can be expected, this is also the most elusive and most difficult strategic position to capture. In fact, most industries do not have standards, and those that do, do not have proprietary ones. It is therefore almost presumptuous to address this topic in the context of a viable strategy for an SME.

However, if you are in a situation when – even remotely – you could have a chance to develop an appropriate standard for your industry, it is imperative that you are alert to this option, consider it as an ultimate goal, and take the necessary steps to accomplish it.

I can recall only one personal experience in this area. I was a consultant for PictureTel, a company founded by engineers with MIT connections and that became the leader in the videoconferencing business. From the outset, I was concerned not only with excelling in our immediate business, but also with attempting to develop the standards. In 2001, PictureTel was acquired by Polycom, which was started by former employees of PictureTel. We discussed this company in Chapter 4, where we contrasted it with Sony. In that chapter, we noticed that Polycom did indeed develop the communication protocol that all firms in the industry have to adopt. It was not impossible, after all!

To conclude, Fig. 9.8 shows the positions in the Triangle of the three companies we have discussed in this section – Wal-Mart, Amazon, and Polycom; Fig. 9.9 summarizes the implications of the System Lock-In strategy for the SMEs.

Final Comments

We have purposely used throughout this chapter examples of fairly successful and large companies to draw some lessons from their winning performance, as well as their remarkable evolution from initial SME starts to organizations of great prosperity. We should bear in mind that it is much more likely that an SME will fail than succeed. That is exactly why we believe it is mandatory for an SME to have a

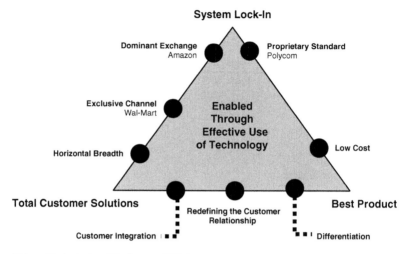

Fig. 9.8   The triangle: the positions of selected SMEs following a System Lock-In strategy

System Lock-In	Definition	Comments
Restricted Access	Significant barriers are in place that makes it difficult for competitors to even compete for the acquisition of customers.	Modularity is the key. This position is achieved one customer at a time, e.g. Wal-Mart.
Dominant Exchange	With this strategy the company provides an interface between buyers and sellers that is very hard to displace once it achieves critical mass.	This position is based on the availability of information systems that provide a bridge between customers and suppliers, e.g. Amazon
Proprietary Standard	The customer is drawn to your product because of the extensive network of third party complementors that are designed to work with your product.	In the great majority of the industries this option is not available. If you can successfully achieve it, the rewards are enormous, e.g. Polycom.

Fig. 9.9   SMEs and System Lock-In strategy

carefully laid out strategy from the very beginning, rather than being carried by the prevailing forces of the industry.

A winning strategy for an SME is not an easy pursuit, but it could be a highly exciting and rewarding task. Much has been said about the inherent weaknesses of SMEs because of their limited size and influence. However, those weaknesses can be transformed into major assets. While it is true that SMEs do not have large economies of scale and negotiation power, they enjoy enormous flexibility and the adaptability to respond effectively to changes in the external environment, giving them the potential to be enormously creative and innovative. It is also claimed that SMEs have difficulty in attracting top talent. This is easy to reverse. On the contrary, it is the large corporations that project an image of large bureaucracy that are not viewed as attractive places to work anymore. SMEs, particularly if they use intelligent incentives, profit sharing, and equity partnership mechanisms, are in an exceptional situation to attract young, creative talent. Therefore, not everything is working against the SMEs; one could say that it is quite the opposite.

We hope that the examples we have offered on the application of the Delta Model to small and medium enterprises can be of assistance in defining a winning strategy. We feel that the dangers of commoditization – that we have been constantly addressing in this book – are even more devastating to a small company, for whom differentiation is the key to survival. Also, majority of the SMEs need to grow to allow them to reach a size that allows future stability. These are two major concerns that most affect the SME strategy.

Chapter 10
The Challenges of Managing Not-for-Profit Organizations

We have not yet dealt specifically with the not-for-profit organizations (NFPOs), an important institutional segment, whose objective is not the creation of economic wealth but the pursuit of activities that will positively affect society at-large. The immediate problem we face when attempting to develop a cohesive strategy for NFPOs is their enormous diversity. The term not-for-profit seems to encompass a wide array of totally different institutions that only share the negative attribute that making money does not motivate them. Is it possible to conduct a coherent analysis of these institutions? We believe so. Moreover, we feel that the Delta Model can give us penetrating insights into how to manage them, based on conclusions that are quite different from the for-profit business sector.

Who Is the Customer?

Sometimes the word "customer" antagonizes those who are involved in not-for-profit environments. It sounds mercantile and somehow demeaning to the noble purposes of some organizations. This is simply an issue of semantics. It should be clear by now that by "customer" we mean one who occupies the center of attention of the organization, whom it is our duty to serve as effectively as possible. The customer here is not necessarily the one who pays the bill, but the one who receives the output that the organization generates. Maybe a better word would be "stakeholder" or "constituent" to designate that person in a not-for-profit setting. Depending on the nature of the organization this stakeholder takes many different names: Teachers think of students, churches think of parishioners, sporting clubs think of fans, symphony orchestras think of audiences, armies think of soldiers, and so on.

The concepts of "customer" should also be amplified to include not just the recipients of the final offerings of the organization, but also those who contribute to their funding. NFPOs often depend on the generosity or support of external parties, who somehow seem aligned with the purpose of the organization and are willing to contribute either financial or personal resources for its advancement. These donors can either be private individuals, other institutions, or government agencies.

A.C. Hax, *The Delta Model*, DOI 10.1007/978-1-4419-1480-4_10,

Once we define the nature of the relevant customers of an NFPO, we believe that, without much adaptation, we can apply the concepts and tools presented in Chapter 3 to segment the customer base and define creative customer value propositions.

Which are the Competencies?

Before we embark on the analysis of the development of a strategy for an NFPO, we must further refine the Delta Model language used to summarize the eight strategic positions that characterize the competencies of a business firm, as seen in Fig.4.1 in Chapter 4. The NFPO version of the eight strategic positions that designate the competencies of not-for-profit organizations is presented in Fig. 10.1 using slightly modified terms. They include:

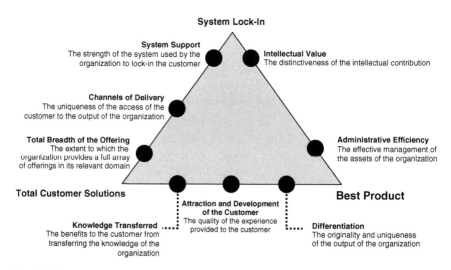

Fig. 10.1   Renaming the strategic positions for non-business organizations

- **Administrative Efficiency:** Instead of Low Cost, we prefer to call this position Administrative Efficiency. This simply denotes the undeniable need that any organization has, regardless of its nature, to be careful about the way in which its assets are employed and managed. Being not-for-profit doesn't mean that we have to be careless and ineffective. It simply means that the cost infrastructure has a slightly different connotation in terms of the role it plays, but it is still a highly relevant managerial issue. Focus on achieving a high level of efficiency in every aspect of the administrative duties, and in the management of business, physical and financial assets.
- **Differentiation:** We decided not to change the definition of this position, because it underscores the need for a certain sense of originality and uniqueness in what we do and the services that we produce. That challenge is always there.

The dangers of commoditization are as real in a for-profit as well in a not-for-profit environment. Establish a sense of uniqueness and creativity in what the organization does and the final products and services it offers.

- **Attraction and Development of the Customer:** Altered slightly from Redefining the Customer Relationship, this competency reflects the same need for all firms, which is to attract, satisfy, and retain the customer, culminating in a strong customer bonding. The concept of customer bonding is, in our opinion, as relevant in the non-profit world as it is in the business environment.

- **Knowledge Transferred:** Formerly Customer Integration, Knowledge Transferred makes it clear that what we are after in this strategic position is to recognize our knowledge base, and not only keep it inside the organization, but transfer it to the customer. In many not-for-profit organizations this is of paramount centrality. Think, for instance, about a university and other educational institutions where this is unquestionably at the heart of what these organizations provide to their constituencies. The key is to recognize the knowledge that resides in our organization, and not to keep it only for the internal administrative role. Transfer it to the customers in a way that enriches them.

- **Total Breadth of the Offering:** We have slightly modified "Horizontal Breadth" while retaining the same spirit of our original intent, which is to assess our capacity to offer our customers a proposition that is all encompassing and intended to satisfy as many of their relevant needs as possible. We should also consider whether we could accomplish this objective alone or should resort to the Extended Enterprise, meaning all of the relevant complementors that could assist us in this effort.

- **Channels of Delivery:** Rather than labeling this position Restricted Access, which is the proper designation for thinking about a System Lock-In option, we focus our attention on the means by which we would reach our customers. The search for a lock-in, of course, requires us to determine the degree to which these delivery channels would be exclusive to us or not, whether significant barriers are in place, which make it difficult for other organizations to compete for the acquisition of our customers.

- **System Support:** This is what we have been calling "Dominant Exchange." By changing it to System Support, we put the emphasis on the development and transfer of systems to help the customers do a better job. Therefore, we ask the organization to reflect on the centrality that systems play in the conduct of its activities, and consequently, the extent to which they might give us a certain sense of exclusivity that produces lock-in. This form of lock-in is based upon the deployment of exclusive systems that connect with our customers in unique ways that are not available elsewhere. It could also generate a network that integrates all parties interested in the service we are offering. In the for-profit world, eBay is an example of that.

- **Intellectual Value:** Known as "Proprietary Standard" in a business setting, Intellectual Value stresses on generating something that has a certain sense of uniqueness in the ideas, the values, and the distinctiveness of the output of the organization. It calls for us to focus on the caliber of our intellectual pursuits, and the degree of distinctiveness that they would attach to our institution. It is extremely hard to claim the full dominance of intellectual outputs that could create a system lock-in, though it might be created by gaining exclusive rights for the certification of intellectual value, such as the US Patent and Trademark Office.

The strategy formation process is fundamentally a dialog among the key executives of a firm or the key players of an organization. This dialog should allow the proper exchange of ideas, the debates that will be useful to clarify our commitments, and the eventual achievement of a consensus on the direction we would like the organization to pursue. However, in order to have a dialog we need a language. Therefore, semantics are not peripheral. They are at the center of strategy formation. This is why spending the time to clarify critical concepts is of the utmost importance.

The Delta Model can really be thought of as a set of concepts and ideas that constitute an approach to strategy reflection. In the process of building that approach, we define terms, and we construct a language. What we have done here is to facilitate the interpretation of language originally intended to support business decisions in order that it more accurately reflect a non-business setting.

Reflecting on the Strategic Challenges of the Not-for-Profit Organization

We will be using the Delta Model to guide our thinking in addressing the challenges associated with managing NFPOs. As we did in the previous chapter when we were discussing small- and medium-sized enterprises, we follow each strategic position that is represented in the Triangle, and address the lessons we can extract from them.

To illustrate our point, we will use examples of well-known government and non-government NFPOs.

Best Product Strategy

Although the pressures acting upon the not-for-profit organization might not be as great and the performance benchmarks not as clear as those prevailing in the for-profit business environment, the challenge is to be extremely conscious of the need to manage the asset and cost infrastructure in a highly effective manner. Similarly, the dangers of commoditization are as real in the not-for-profit as they are in a for-profit environment, which requires organizational determination to seek a position of leadership and uniqueness in the final offering.

To achieve a Best Product Strategy, the NFPO should concentrate on the two strategic positions that are relevant for this option: Administrative Efficiency and Differentiation.

Administrative Efficiency

The competitive pressures that are brought to bear on for-profit organizations are enormous, and managers have to concentrate a great deal of attention to be cost competitive. This pressure is not as strong in the not-for-profit environment. Therefore, it is imperative that managers develop the appropriate metrics for performance and promote cost consciousness throughout the organization. In a for-profit business we know when we are succeeding or failing. In the not-for-profit organization, it is often not that clear.

Some charity organizations have had fairly bad press due to their lack of efficiency in managing donor contributions. In some cases, it has been reported that only 20 cents out of every $1 donated goes to the beneficiaries; the rest is consumed in overhead. Obviously, this can have a strong negative impact on fund solicitation. Former Presidents George H.W. Bush and Bill Clinton established in July 2007 the Bush-Clinton Katrina Fund to improve the lives of those harmed by Hurricane Katrina, pledging that 100% of the contributions received would be used for grants. In this particular example, the intent was to recapture the trust of the donors by assuring efficient administration.

Differentiation

In the for-profit business commoditization occurs when there is no differentiation in the product offering, which often results in a price war. In the not-for-profit environment, there might not be equivalent product or service offerings against which we could compare ours. Therefore the detection of commoditization might not be as obvious. Essentially, in this environment, commoditization means mediocrity, and lack of originality – quite undesirable attributes of the final output of the organization. The challenge is to come out with an offering that brings unique excitement to the customers.

A good example of this strategic position is the Peace Corps. It started in 1961 when then President John Kennedy challenged young Americans to serve their country in a time of peace by living and working in undeveloped countries. The Peace Corps has produced more than 200,000 volunteers who served in about 140 countries with an enthusiasm and energy that is legendary. The beauty of this initiative is that it started with a sense of deep generosity, to help countries in need. In practice, it has been reported that the greatest beneficiaries were the volunteers themselves who returned to America with a personal understanding of parts of the world population they never recognized before. The experience made them better men and women; those who wanted to help ended up receiving the best deal!

Figure 10.2 shows the positions in the Triangle of the two NFPOs we have discussed in this section: Bush-Clinton Katrina Fund and the Peace Corps.

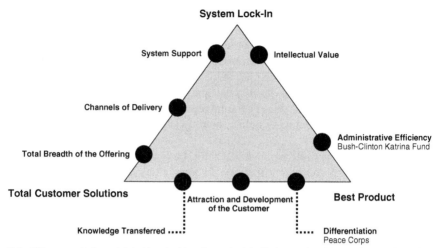

Note: All these organizations might legitimately claim a System Lock-In. We have assigned them to the strategic position that we think is most revealing of their external image.

Fig. 10.2   The triangle: the positions of selected NFPOs following a best product strategy

The Total Customer Solutions Strategy

The proper identification and targeting of customers is even more important in a not-for-profit environment than a for-profit one. The concept of "the customer" should also be amplified to include not just the recipients of the final offerings of the organization, but also those who contribute to their funding. Innovative and creative value propositions should be crafted for each relevant constituency. Fight the "faceless customer" syndrome.

To help our understanding of how the NFPO can adopt a Total Customer Solutions strategy we will review the three positions that are relevant to this effect: Attraction and Development of the Customer, Knowledge Transferred, and Total Breadth of the Offering.

Attraction and Development of the Customer

What is central in this strategic position is to define the customer properly and to identify the different segments that help us to produce a differentiated value proposition. We have already discussed at least two important clusters of customers: beneficiaries and donors. To attract and develop these customers, we need to offer excitement, originality, and uniqueness and go beyond the conventional; fight the trivialization the customer might be receiving in similar organizations.

An interesting example that comes to mind is the Patrons of the Museum of Fine Arts in Boston – one of the largest and most attractive museums in the country. If you are a patron, you give an annual donation that is not excessive but collectively helps to cover a big part of the operating costs of the museum. What you get in return is a very special treatment. You are invited to exclusive openings of every new special event, where you can see the exhibition after being properly educated on its merits, without fighting big crowds. In these special social activities you meet very interesting people. There are trips abroad that you can join which are spectacular experiences, providing access to places not normally available to the common tourist and guided by world-class curators. These are not the normal activities in which you might normally expect to participate when you acquire a conventional membership in a regular museum.

Another institution that offers something truly unique is the National Guard. This organization is part of the first-line defense of the United States. Their members can be called for federal active duty in times of Congressionally sanctioned wars or national emergencies, such as floods or hurricanes. Their members receive military training and, when they are not on call, live a normal civilian life. What is important for most of the recruits is that they are recipients of the GI Bill, which allows them to get tax-free benefits to pay for college or trade school education. This opens university doors for people who might not otherwise be able to afford a college degree on their own resources.

Knowledge Transfer

In many not-for-profit organizations this is of paramount importance. Think, for instance, of universities and other educational institutions where this is unquestionably at the heart of what they can provide to their constituencies. Once you think about this issue, you will be surprised how relevant knowledge transfer becomes part of a winning strategy.

We said in the treatment of the Delta Model for business firms that they should not think of themselves as just an engine for this development, making, and delivery of products; but rather consider themselves as a bundle of competencies which can be transferred with great benefit to their customers. We believe this observation applies equally well to NFPOs.

I beg your indulgence by allowing me to make a reference to my beloved institution, MIT – the Massachusetts Institute of Technology. I should not show off, but unarguably we can claim that we attract some of the best students in the world, and we engage them in a process of knowledge discovery that has made the university system in America the envy of the world.

Total Breadth of the Offering

The issue here is the creative identification of all those customer needs that we can effectively satisfy, even anticipating the customer detection of those needs, to give a full exciting experience. This can be accomplished alone or with the support of the

Extended Enterprise, meaning all the relevant complementors that can assist us in this effort.

I could have used the example of the Patrons of the Museum of Fine Arts in Boston as a model for this strategy because in addition to the obvious – namely giving access to their customers to a great museum – they extend the offer to include more intangible benefits such as socialization, convenience, and excitement.

Another great example of total breadth is the Library of Congress of the United States. Its collection is unmatched, including more than 32 million cataloged books. It developed a system of book classification that is used in most university libraries.

Figure 10.3 shows the positions in the Triangle of the NFPOs we have discussed in this section: Patrons of the Museum of Fine Arts in Boston Patrons, National Guard, MIT, and the Library of Congress.

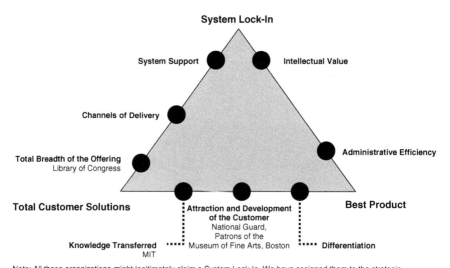

Note: All these organizations might legitimately claim a System Lock-In. We have assigned them to the strategic position that we think is most revealing of their external image.

Fig. 10.3 The Triangle: the positions of selected NFPOs following a total customer solutions strategy

System Lock-In Strategy

This is a position that is often not available or feasible for a for-profit business. It requires achievement of such a strong competitive standing that it culminates in a dominance of the market being served. However, many government as well as not-for-profit organizations are given a unique status that either eliminates direct competitors or diminishes the intensity of rivalry among them. This means that some not-for-profit organizations are born with a quasi or total monopoly. In this case, enormous care has to be taken to reach the level of excellence comparable to those of extremely successful companies in highly competitive environments.

To help our understanding of how the NFPOs can adopt the System Lock-In strategy we will review the three positions relevant to this effect: Channels of Delivery, System Support, and Intellectual Value.

Channels of Delivery

Many government institutions and several not-for-profit organizations are granted the exclusive rights to undertake a specific activity, which provides the exclusive channels for their constituencies to avail themselves of their services. Think of organizations such as the Red Cross – an international humanitarian movement consisting of approximately 97 million volunteers worldwide that was created to protect human life and health without any discrimination regarding nationality, race, religion, or political belief. Think of NASA, the National Aeronautics and Space Administration of the United Stages – an agency of the U.S. government responsible for the nation's public space program. Think of all the branches of the Armed Forces – including the Army, Navy, Air Force, Coast Guard, and more recently the Homeland Security Department. All of these organizations have unique charters that are practically not replicated by any other national organization.

Other NFPOs might not have a complete exclusivity but still might enjoy a singular position in their respective fields that gives them a dominant presence. We refer to organizations such as the Bill and Melinda Gates Foundation, or special institutions such as Amnesty International. The Bill and Melinda Gates Foundation is the largest private foundation in the world. The primary aims are, globally, to enhance health care and to reduce extreme poverty and, in America, to expand educational opportunities and to increase access to information technology. Amnesty International is a non-government organization that defines its mission as "to conduct research and generate action to prevent and end grave abuses of human rights and to demand justice for those whose rights have been violated." These organizations, to some extent, are born with exclusive rights that endow them with, if not a full, at least a partial System Lock-In.

System Support

This form of lock-in is based upon the deployment of exclusive systems that generate a network that integrates all parties entrusted in the service being offered. Good examples of these kinds of networks in the international arena are the United Nations, the World Bank, and the International Monetary Fund. The United Nations is an international organization to promote international peace, security, and cooperation. The World Bank is an international banking organization established to control the distribution of economic aid among member nations, and to make loans in times of financial crisis. The International Monetary Fund was founded in 1945 to promote international trade, monetary cooperation, and the stabilization of the exchange rates among their member countries. It also offers financial and technical assistance to its members, making it an international lender of last resort.

All these organizations are extremely powerful and influential, being the depositary of exclusive System Lock-In positions.

Intellectual Value

The focus of this form of System Lock-In is the generation of unique values and ideas that provide an intellectual distinction to the organization. We thought of two examples of NFPOs enjoying this position. One is the US Patent and Trademark Office – which is an agency of the US Department of Commerce that issues patents to inventors and businesses for their inventions, and trademark registration for products and intellectual property identification. There is no other institution in the United States that is allowed to do that. The second example, fairly different in nature, is the Nobel Prize Committee that awards the coveted distinction in six categories every year: physics, chemistry, medicine, literature, peace, and economics. The Nobel Prize is widely regarded as the most prestigious award one can receive in those fields. Those who are so recognized immediately achieve a distinction that elevates them to the absolute top of their professions.

Figure 10.4 shows the position in the Triangle of the NFPOs we have discussed in this section: Red Cross, NASA, all the branches of the Armed Forces, United Nations, World Bank, International Monetary Fund, Bill and Melinda Gates Foundation, Amnesty International, U.S. Patent and Trademark Office, and Nobel Prize Committee.

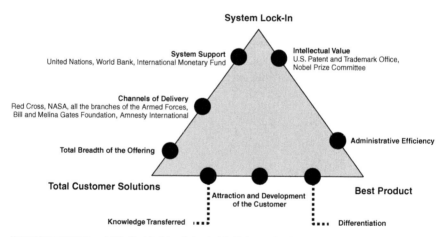

Note: All these organizations might legitimately claim a System Lock-In. We have assigned them to the strategic position that we think is most revealing of their external image.

Fig. 10.4 The Triangle: the positions of selected NFPOs following a System Lock-in strategy

The Unconventional Dynamics of Evolution of the Not-for-Profit Organizations

Most, if not all, of the organizations that we have discussed in this chapter could legitimately claim that they enjoy some form of System Lock-In. This is because they are either government organizations – such as the Armed Forces or NASA – which are being given a unique charter that only they are able to carry out; or they are delivering a rather special service – such as museums or foundations – that make them oblivious to the intense competitive forces that business firms have to face. This is not to ignore the often-severe challenges that NFPOs face to attract customers and donors. It is simply a recognition that the environment they live in is more benign than the one prevailing in cutthroat business climates. If you accept this premise – and we are aware that it could be rather debatable – the recommendations emerging from the Delta Model to assure a healthy evolution of the NFPOs are quite different from the conventional dynamics of the for-profit business.

As should be evident from the applications of the Delta Model to business firms that have been discussed throughout this book, we have advocated a dynamics of evolution, as presented in Fig. 10.5. In this chart, we illustrate the evolution of a firm that starts as a product-centric organization adhering to a Best Product strategy. We feel this company should consolidate an effective cost infrastructure to assure that it is capable to develop, produce, market, and distribute a stream of differentiated products of great quality. Once this is accomplished, it should pursue a transformation toward a Total Customer Solutions strategy, adding services to a properly integrated portfolio of products to provide complete, customized solutions to satisfy the customer needs. The proximity to the customer and the originality of the customer value proposition is critical to realize this goal. And finally – if we

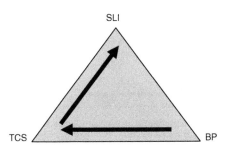

- **Start with a solid position in the Best Product option - supported by an effective low cost infrastructure and a stream of innovative products.**
- **Continue toward a Total Customer Solutions option - getting closer to the customer offering a full set of unique value propositions that contribute to strong customer bonding.**
- **And seek opportunities for System Lock-In - either through the realization of Restricted Access, Dominant Exchange, or Proprietary Standards.**

Fig. 10.5 The conventional evolution of the strategic positions for the for-profit organizations

possibly can – we need to identify and seize opportunities for a System Lock-in either via Restricted Access, Dominant Exchange, or Proprietary Standards. The prescription is clear, the challenge is well defined, and a proper execution is quite demanding.

If we turn our attention to NFPOs, the message is quite different, as illustrated in Fig. 10.6. We have claimed that most NFPOs do not face the same competitive forces that affect the business firms. Rather, they enjoy – not always but often enough to make this point significant – a protected environment which can be characterized as a quasi-monopoly. That is to say that they start at a System Lock-In position in the Triangle – as opposed to a Best Product position which is the common starting point of a business firm. The problem is that they might not have achieved the degree of internal excellence that is mandatory in the for-profit environment to enjoy a System Lock-In. This means that we believe that the NFPO should first move toward a Best Product strategy. What does this mean? It simply implies that the organization has to be conscious of its possible inefficiencies and be prepared to make the changes that allow it to achieve an effective cost infrastructure and deliver truly differentiated products. We have said, repeatedly, that these are the foundations of a well-run company. However, if we are given a unique and protected role, it is very likely that we do not give enough attention and effort to "getting rid of the fat." Therefore we need to move toward a Best Product strategy to acquire the cost infrastructure and product quality that we are missing. After consolidating this position, then we should adopt the Total Customer Solutions strategy. This means the careful identification of all the relevant customers and the development of exciting and customized value propositions to serve each of them. It is after we conclude

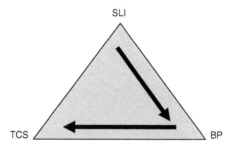

- **Often Not-For-Profit Organizations occupy a position close to a System Lock-In not because they have gained it, but because it has been regulated or for lack of direct competition.**
- **Move first toward a Best Product option - to achieve the administrative efficiency and the excellence in product offering that might be lacking or need to be reinforced.**
- **Then move toward Total Customer Solutions option - identifying clearly the unique value propositions to be offered to the full customer base, resulting in differentiated treatment to the individual customer tiers.**

Fig. 10.6 The unconventional evolution of the strategic positions for the not-for-profit organizations

this transformation that we can move to achieve what now will be a well-deserved System Lock-In.

What follows is a case detailing an application of the Delta Model by the Economic Development Board of Singapore, a very exciting and successful not-for-profit organization. For the reader's convenience we are duplicating here Fig.1.1 that shows the five tasks of the Delta Model that we will cover in the next section (Fig. 10.7).

Fig. 10.7 The strategic tasks of the Delta Model

The Case of Singapore Economic Development Board – An Application of the Delta Model to a Not-for-Profit Organization

Founded in 1961, the Singapore Economic Development Board (EDB) has led the nation-state through a period of phenomenal growth that propelled the country from third-world to first-world status in less than five decades. As a statutory board under the Ministry of Trade and Industry, the EDB is charged with the mission to create sustainable GDP growth for Singapore with good jobs and business opportunities for its people.[1]

Singapore, a country founded in 1965 without any natural resources or technological know-how, faced serious unemployment issues, with many people even questioning whether it could survive independently as a nation. For economic survival, the country opened its door to foreign investments from day 1, hoping that these investments in manufacturing and services would create jobs and economic output for the country. EDB was formed in 1961 to undertake this huge responsibility. While the modus operandi has not changed for more than four decades, the operating environment has transformed tremendously, with competition heating up for the same investment dollars.

In today's world, many countries are opening their doors to foreign investments. They offer attractive support such as tax holidays and free land for global MNCs to build their manufacturing operations. EDB cannot afford to compete by positioning Singapore as a low-cost manufacturing location in Asia, as it was in the 1960s and 1970s. Rather, it has to continuously move up the value chain and focus on technology-intensive and knowledge-intensive industries in order to justify Singapore's more expensive talented workforce and business infrastructure.

Customer Segmentation

The first task of the Delta Model is to analyze how to segment EDB's customers. With thousands of investors making investments, ranging from tens of thousands to multi-billion dollars in Singapore every year, it is only prudent that EDB prioritize its client list into different categories. The resulting customer tiers are depicted in Fig. 10.8.

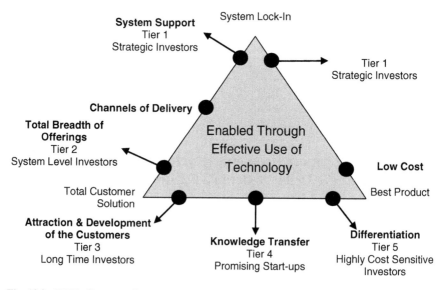

Fig. 10.8 EDB's Customer Segmentation

- Tier 5 – Highly Cost-Sensitive Investors
  The category includes highly cost-sensitive investors who are only going after Singapore's existing cost advantage, with no long-term view or intent to become more entrenched. For example, the company may just want to take advantage of the lower skilled manpower cost compared to the United States or Europe. EDB could attract Tier 5 investors by offering low-cost opportunities, such as tax holidays. In addition, the EDB can also point them to the fastest way to set up the business in Singapore, or facilitate their liaison with other key agencies such as industrial land developer or recruitment agencies.
- Tier 4 – Promising Start-Ups
  Another smaller, but important category of customers is the technology start-up enterprise, which may become the big corporations of the future. For this group of companies, the EDB should spend time to keep them engaged and nurture them. While they may not be big contributors in terms of investment or jobs created today, they have the potential to grow. EDB could even consider providing them with seed investments and other assistance such as access to technology or knowledge transfer to engage them.
- Tier 3 – Long-Time Investors
  Another category of investors is those who are in Singapore for a long time, employ a significant pool of employees, are highly profitable and stable, but have little intention to extend their breadth of activities. For this group of companies, EDB should focus on helping them to enhance their efficiency and reduce their cost of operation. Over time, the profitability of this group of companies should climb, which will help them maintain their competitiveness in Singapore. Otherwise, they will have the tendency to move to other, cheaper locations once they find more cost-effective sites.
- Tier 2 – System-Level Investors
  The Tier 2 category is comprised of investors who are not just cost conscious, but are in Singapore to capture the advantage of what Singapore can offer at the system level – for those seeking total solutions. For example, the company is not concerned that Singapore's land cost may be more expensive, because of the advantage of the total system. Once the company takes into consideration the efficient logistics, availability of skilled manpower, and so on, the overall cost may be more attractive than other competing locations. EDB should work together with this group of customers to develop a broader investment plan, ensuring that the different aspects of the customers' needs are taken care of. Most importantly, EDB must continue to ensure that Singapore is able to offer the Tier 2 investors the most cost-effective solutions.
- Tier 1 – Strategic Investor
  The most important category of customers for EDB groups is the strategic investors in Singapore. These are global MNCs that are deeply entrenched in Singapore, employing thousands of people and holding a long-term view for their multi-billion dollar investments. In fact, customers in this category normally view Singapore as a key node in their global operations and have, so far, taken significant interest in the general well-being of the country. These companies have

become a group of key corporate citizens, who play an integral role not only in helping to shape the progress of Singapore's economy, but also in the social and education aspects. For these clients, EDB should invest resources to constantly engage them in strategic dialogs, to get a good sense of what else the Singapore government can do to help them grow in Singapore.

EDB's Existing and Desired Competencies

We can now catalog EDB's competencies according to the eight strategic positions of the Triangle, as presented in Fig. 10.9.

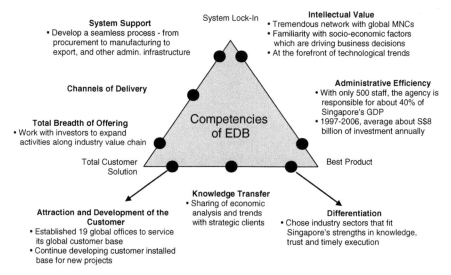

Fig. 10.9 EDB's existing and desired competencies

As an organization with about 500 staff, EDB is a relatively lean organization given the level of responsibility and contribution it makes to the Singapore economy. The two key sectors are manufacturing and business services, which together contribute about 40% of the country's GDP, amounting to about US $200 billion in 2008. In addition, being the leading investment promotion agency, EDB's team managed to bring in on average, more than US $8 billion of fixed asset investment (FAI) from 1997 to 2006.

EDB is also the agency that works on developing more attractive products for potential investors. Ranging from tax incentives for high value-added investments to R&D grants for cutting-edge research projects, EDB continues to listen to the needs of its customers. For example, in early 2003, EDB launched a series of programs that catered to companies pursuing knowledge-based activities in Singapore, such as research, patent filing, patent licensing and technology development. The programs were aimed at developing Singapore as the intellectual property hub of Asia. By leveraging on Singapore's unique image in integrity, EDB hopes to differentiate Singapore as a business hub for investments in knowledge intensive projects.

With a population of 4.6 million, Singapore is limited by its small domestic market and relatively small talent pool when compared with many of its competitors. Thus, it is not possible for the country to develop every industry. It has to select certain key industries that fit its long-term strategy and endowment. With one of the highest literacy rates in the world, Singapore's workforce is highly skilled. Thus, it makes sense for EDB to lead the country into focusing on high-tech sectors, such as electronics, petrochemicals, and biomedical.

Another area in which the EDB has managed to differentiate Singapore from its competitors is system integration. Efficiency is critical to the profitability of an investment. EDB positions itself as the one-stop center for investors, assisting them in linking up with other agencies to expedite most of the operational matters. From registering for a business license, to bring in foreign executives, to getting permits for facility construction, EDB ensures that investors have a smooth and efficient experience. It is similar to the case where Singapore Airlines wants its first-class passengers to experience its superb hospitality from the moment they step onto the curbside of the airport, till they disembark from the plane at their destination.

EDB has a network of 19 offices located in major cities around the world, especially in the United States, Western Europe, Japan, China, and India. Akin to the McKinsey model, this global network is able to feel the pulse of the global market and signal emerging trends. The ability to gather information, translate it into knowledge, and formulate it into executable strategies has long become a core competency of EDB. On many occasions, key partners will have dialogs and conduct strategic exchanges with EDB to keep abreast with the latest developments. This is indeed a great way for EDB to keep its strategic clients engaged.

EDB is a customer-oriented organization. In fact, the primary objective of its network of global offices is to be close to its customers. Nothing beats knocking on the door of your key clients and having a face-to-face discussion (not even the best videoconferencing facility). In fact, this level of intimate engagement with customers creates a critical channel for direct communication and expedient resolution of any urgent operational issues. It is what we call "concierge" service at your doorstep anywhere in the world.

The ability to build close relationships with the customer is another key competency of the EDB. The strong relationship with the customers allows EDB to understand not only what the customers need today, but also anticipate what the customers look for tomorrow. With a pool of more than 6,000 MNCs in Singapore, EDB has developed a great relationship with a global network of companies. By consolidating the customers' needs, EDB is able to project forward, plan with greater certainty, and anticipate how the industry landscape will change and evolve. This competency is critical for a small nation like Singapore in order to deploy scarce resources and compete effectively.

EDB can also leverage the close ties with its customers to extend into new investment partnerships – the competency we call Total Breadth of Offering. For example, a company with manufacturing operations in Singapore may consider branching upstream into product development or downstream into distribution and supply chain management. Having this huge installed base of key customers is a strategic advantage, which when managed carefully, will enhance the "stickiness" to further entrench the companies in Singapore.

Over the decades, the EDB has developed in-house expertise in many different industries, such as semiconductors, supply chain management, digital media, software and IT, and petrochemical. But, more importantly, a key competency in EDB is its ability to integrate across the various sectors and capture the synergies between them, offering its customers a unique value proposition. While the logistics sector is a business of its own, its presence actually differentiates Singapore as a regional hub that offers world-class logistical connectivity. This is an extremely important downstream activity for many manufacturing operations. Thus, a total system support can be created to add value for the investors. In fact, once a company establishes its presence in Singapore, it is able to tap into the support across the entire value chain. This system moves Singapore a step closer to having a System Lock-In on the investors. From the financial perspective, customers are attracted to the cost savings at the system level, derived from the efficiency and reliability. This allows Singapore to move beyond low-cost competition.

The last but more desirable competency that will enable Singapore to lock-in its customers is intellectual value. While EDB does not file for patent or copyright, the organization's immense business know-how and knowledge in high-tech industry makes it a valuable partner for many investors. In fact, EDB is one of the main reasons investors choose Singapore as their Asian location. Many companies in Singapore look to EDB for direction as to where the industries are heading. In fact, the various industrial working groups formed between investors and government agencies are great platforms where some of these intellectual values are shared with investors and partners. This continuous building of trust and relationship is a self-reinforcing mechanism that will further enhance EDB's competencies and increase the level of comfort for investors.

EDB's Mission

The mission of EDB is to create sustainable GDP growth for Singapore with good jobs and business opportunities for its people.

Toward this goal, the Board's vision is to develop Singapore into a compelling global hub for business and investments. As a government statutory board, it is serving the interest of the people of Singapore. However, it is fully aware that as the customer-facing agency that promotes investment, understanding the needs of its customers and ensuring that they are successful in Singapore are imperative for the ultimate growth of Singapore's economy. This leads us to the following product and services scope on which the organization should focus (Fig. 10.10).

It is important that the EDB position itself as a forward-looking organization, focusing on what customers are looking for in the future and not just the present. This is because policies, programs, and infrastructures take years to develop and

	Now	Future
Product Scope	Government incentives for investment ranging from tax holidays, R&D grants and manpower training grants.	Compelling business propositions where investments are driven primarily by value creation.
Services Scope	One-stop agency that facilitates investors' needs to establish operations in Singapore.	In addition to facilitation, establish closer links to proactively engage investors in forward planning.
Customer Scope	Singapore hosts more than 7000 global companies.	In addition to large Multi-National Corporations (MNCs), EDB will consider increasing its outreach to smaller high-tech enterprises.
End-User Scope	While relationships with existing investors are good, some of the partnerships could be strengthened.	Further understanding the future needs of the investors, pre-empting their requirements and be ready for them.
Geographical Scope	EDB operates a network of 19 international offices globally.	As the global economic landscape changes, EDB will selectively adjust the distribution of its offices or even consider expansion into new countries.
Unique Competencies Scope	EDB has many unique competencies, especially in system integration and working with its customers to deliver the results.	Develop the competency to identify new emerging opportunities at the cross section of industries or different fields of knowledge.

Fig. 10.10 Statement of product and services scope

build. Having a good sense of what customers' desire in the future allows EDB to mobilize resources to build in advance, giving Singapore the first-mover advantage, and always staying ready to catch the next wave. To strengthen its competitive base, it is strategic for EDB to focus on creating investment incentive programs that are relevant to customers' needs in the future, cultivating strategic customers that fit into Singapore's economic model and development strategy, developing emerging geographies, and fostering innovative capabilities across various industry sectors.

EDB's Strategic Agenda

The Strategic Agenda of EDB is presented in the following chart, where the strategic thrusts are listed in order of priorities (Fig. 10.11).

The various strategic thrusts in the EDB are each led by one champion and supported by other divisions related to the activity. The chairman and managing director are primarily the leaders for both strategic customer engagements and for programs delivering changes to the organizational structure and core values. It is clear that the group of cluster directors is responsible for keeping each cluster at the forefront of emerging trends and for charting the direction in which each of the clusters should move toward. The clusters represent the major vertical markets that EDB is supporting such as electronics, chemicals, biomedical sciences, information, communications and media, logistics, and transportation. This allows each cluster to develop in-depth knowledge and expertise in their respective markets.

In fact, Global Operations plays a lead role in seeking out new developments in foreign geographies and making sure customers are being cultivated.

Corporate Strategic Thrusts	Organizational Units											Business Processes	Performance Measurements
	Chairman	Managing Dir	Cluster Dir	HR	CIO Office	Finance	Resource Dev	Global Ops	New Business	Planning	Admin Div		
Value proposition development and delivery mechanism for investors		1	1			2	1	2	2			CT	Completion of Assignment
Develop domain knowledge in specific industry sectors		1	1			2	1	2	2			I	Progress Report
Strategic engagement of key investors (Tier 1 & Tier 2)	1	1	1						2	2		CT	Customer engagement scorecard and tools
Alignment of organizational structure, process, measurement and rewards		1	1	1	2	2		1	2	2		OE	Progress report of alignment and completion of restructuring
Developing corporate values and norms	1	1	1	1				2			1	OE	Delivery of corporate values and standard operating procedures
Developing new markets (geographical)		2	1			2		1	1			CT	Level of investment activities from each geographical region. Progress reports of customer engagement
Innovation program to crate new industry and business focus		1	1			2	2	1	1	2		OE/B	Number of new sectors engaged. Level of business activities in each new industry
Strengthening engagement of Strengthening engagement of customer through global operations	1	1	2						1			CT	Progress report on number of customers engaged and potential outcome
Strengthening global IT support for business activities		1	2		1	2		2				OE	Progress report on system downtime and usage level
Talent attraction to build up internal capability		1	1	1		2						OE	Operational manning level and turnover rate

1 – Key role in formulation and implementation
2 – Important role of support and concurrence

1 - Identifies the "Champion" who takes leadership for the Strategic Thrust

B - Business Model
CT – Customer Targeting
OE – Operational Effectiveness
I- Innovation

Fig. 10.11 Corporate strategic thrusts

Other functions across the organization are responsible for different strategic thrusts, ranging from human resource, finance, CIO, resource development, planning, and administration. Another point worth noting is the strategic thrust led by the New Business group. It is a deliberate design to have a business group that is independent from the existing clusters. This allows officers in this group to think outside of the current parameters and not feel curtailed by limited resources deployed in supporting existing businesses. Thus, the number of new areas uncovered and new businesses created can independently measure this group.

Monitoring the Strategy Execution

Besides the performance measurements identified in the Strategic Agenda, there are many other high-level indicators that the EDB tracks to monitor its performance at the national level. For its role as an investment promoter, EDB is being measured by the total fixed asset investment and total business spending committed each year in Singapore. In addition, EDB is also measured on the number of new skilled jobs created annually.[2]

As the architect of Singapore's economic development, EDB is responsible for almost 40% of the country's GDP. Thus, the annual GDP growth rate is also an indicator of how well EDB has been performing. However, given that GDP is an output indicator, which typically has a delay effect over a few years, it is important to note that it is used more as an indicator to measure how successful EDB is in attracting the right investment projects that create greater contributions of value added to the economy.

In addition to quantitative measurement, qualitatively, EDB's qualitative performance is also directly linked to Singapore's international standing as a business hub. Indicators such as competitiveness of its economy, business friendliness, and ease of doing business are also used to measure EDB's performance. This is linked to the quality of both types of investments attracted to Singapore, the type of jobs created, workers' productivity, and how efficient the business infrastructure of the country is. See the global competitiveness report from the World Economic Forum 2008/2009 below (Fig. 10.12).

The EDB Culture

Since its founding in 1961, the EDB has been recognized as one of the most important of the government statutory boards that hold the responsibility to grow an economy. Thus, it has been able to attract not only good talent to join the board, but has also been typically led by strong and capable leaders. Over the decades, a strong culture has been developed in the organization, which in a way guides the value and work ethics of the staff, both locally and internationally. The "can do" spirit of the organization has been cited not only by political leaders of the country, but also by foreign investors who were impressed by the efficiency and professionalism of the EDB team. This has created a reinforcing effect in the organization's ability to attract good people and keep the team motivated.

Country/Economy	GCI 2008-2009		GCI 2008-2009 rank (among 2007 countries)	GCI 2007-2008 rank
	Rank	Score		
United States	1	5.74	1	1
Switzerland	2	5.61	2	2
Denmark	3	5.58	3	3
Sweden	4	5.53	4	4
Singapore	5	5.53	5	7
Finland	6	5.50	6	6
Germany	7	5.46	7	5
Netherlands	8	5.41	8	10
Japan	9	5.38	9	8
Canada	10	5.37	10	13
Hong Kong SAR	11	5.33	11	12
United Kingdom	12	5.30	12	9
Korea, Rep.	13	5.28	13	11
Austria	14	5.23	14	15
Norway	15	5.22	15	16
France	16	5.22	16	18
Taiwan, China	17	5.22	17	14
Australia	18	5.20	18	19
Belgium	19	5.14	19	20
Iceland	20	5.05	20	23

Fig. 10.12 Global competitiveness report

On many occasions, EDB has wowed investors by delivering the impossible. For example, when it was leading a project to reclaim land (Jurong Island) to build a petrochemical island, EDB was already selling "industry land parcels" (still water, in the process of being reclaimed) to investors. Investors who trusted Singapore's ability to deliver what was being promised went ahead with full confidence that the EDB would deliver the reclaimed land on time.

Establishing strong partnerships with customers and delivering what has been promised to investors has earned the EDB the trust and loyalty of thousands of its customers. These qualities and values will continue to be EDB's trademark, deeply ingrained into the culture of the team, which differentiates the organization as a respected investment promotion agency internationally.

Conclusion

With decades of success behind it, EDB continues to be a driving force in transforming Singapore's economic landscape. However, what continues to make it successful is its ability to change and adapt to the rapid evolution of new trends and global competition. From this perspective, EDB is a new organization every day, facing brand new challenges and customer demands. Thus, we believe the Delta Model is a great tool to facilitate the continuous analysis of EDB's changing customers, which helps guide the agency in repositioning its value propositions, developing the necessary competencies, formulating new strategic thrusts, and measuring the appropriate indicators to track its performance.

Notes

1. This presentation is based upon the work of former Sloan Fellow Jayson Goh, 2008, as part of the requirements of the MIT Sloan School Strategic Management course. It does not intend to represent the views of the Singapore Economic Development Board on how to manage its customer base.
2. Tables on FAI, TBS and Employment extracted from EDB Annual Report 2007/2008.

Chapter 11
A Comparison Among the Three Strategic Frameworks: Porter, the Resource-Based View of the Firm, and the Delta Model

In spite of the enormous proliferation of competing schemes in the business strategy literature, there are two fundamental paradigms that have emerged as the most influential in the last two decades. First, Competitive Positioning, as proposed by Michael Porter[1] from the Harvard Business School in the 1980s, and, second, the Resource-Based View of the Firm[2] that evolved during the 1990s.

Porter's arguments are drawn from the work of organizational economists who place the industry as the central focus of strategic attention. According to Porter's framework, structural characteristics of a firm's industry best explain variations in firm performance. In other words, Porter sees good industries, such as pharmaceuticals, where most players enjoy high margins; he also sees bad industries, such as trucking, where most participants suffer from low profitability.

Using the language of economics, a successful firm is one that appropriates monopolistic rents. In other words, in the industry as a whole or in a segment of the industry, the firm establishes itself as the dominant (or sole) competitor.

Porter's logical conclusion from this perspective is that there are only two ways to compete: through Low Cost or Product Differentiation. Cost leadership is achieved through the aggressive pursuit of economies of scale, product and process simplification, and significant product market share that allows companies to exploit experience and learning effects. Differentiation calls for creating a product that the customer perceives as highly valuable and unique. Approaches to Differentiation can take many forms: design of brand image, technology, features, customer service, and dealer networks.

The strategic positions of Low Cost and Differentiation are centered on product economics. The resulting mentality of this approach, which is widely apparent in the business world, has enormous implications that we have addressed throughout this book.

Instead of looking at the industry as the source of profitability, the Resource-Based View of the Firm argues that the attention should turn to the firm. Instead of seeking profitability at the intersection of the products and markets, the Resource-Based View looks for value derived from resources, capabilities, and competencies. Instead of relying on monopoly rents, premium returns depend upon what economists refer to as "Ricardian rents." What makes one firm different from another is its ability to appropriate resources that are valuable, rare, and difficult

A.C. Hax, *The Delta Model*, DOI 10.1007/978-1-4419-1480-4_11,   207
© Springer Science+Business Media, LLC 2010

to substitute or imitate. The roots of this perspective go back to David Ricardo,[3] a British economist who lived in the early 1800s. Ricardo tried to explain variations in farm profitability by pointing to differences in the supply of fertile land. Proponents of the Resource-Based View had the insight to recognize that management skills, information capabilities, and administrative processes can also be regarded as scarce factors able to generate Ricardian rents.

Porter's framework and the Resource-Based View of the Firm basically perceived the primary role of strategy as achieving a unique competitive advantage. We underline the word competitive because that seems to us to be the common principle. In this sense, the objective of strategy becomes beating your competitor either by excelling in the activities of your value chain that allows you to establish a dominant position in your industry, or through the mobilization of unique resources and capabilities.

Although these frameworks have often been presented as conflicting views, since they emphasize different dimensions of strategy, they can richly complement each other. However, they both can be enhanced by adding a missing perspective: the Customer. Surprisingly the customer does not emerge as the key player in either of these two frameworks. If you take Porter literally, the customer is represented by the "Buyer" – one of the Five Forces Model – whose bargaining power we should resist or diminish. In that respect, the customer constitutes an additional element of the rivalry that we need to overcome. In the Resource-Based View of the Firm, there is no explicit mention of the customer.

By contrast, the Delta Model places the customer at the center of strategy, and defines the essence of strategy to be achieving customer bonding. We felt that the new technology surrounding the Internet provides novel and effective ways to link to the customer and to the extended enterprise, opening up new sources of strategic positioning that should be properly evaluated.

We will now briefly describe the two frameworks. Our treatment is not intended to be exhaustive. We will deal with the frameworks at a level sufficient for the reader to allow comparing them with the Delta Model.

Porter's Competitive Positioning Framework

According to Michael Porter, there are two basic determinants of the profitability of a business: the structure of the industry in which the business operates and the competitive positioning of the business within that industry. These are the inputs that determine the Strategic Agenda of the business and that lead to the formulation and implementation of its strategy. Figure 11.1 captures the essence of the framework.

Industry structure explains the value generated by the economic activity of the industry participants, as well as their ability to share in the wealth created. Michael Porter postulates that there are five forces that typically shape industry structure: intensity of rivalry among competitors, threat of new entrants, threat of substitutes, bargaining power of buyers, and bargaining power of suppliers. These five forces determine prices, costs, and investment requirements, which are the basic factors

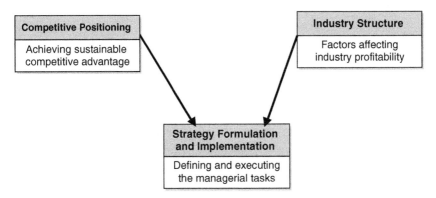

Fig. 11.1 The basic framework for explaining the profitability of a business

driving long-term profitability, and henceforth industry attractiveness. Figure 11.2 illustrates the generic structure of an industry as represented by its main players (competitors, buyers, suppliers, substitutes, and new entrants), their interrelationships (the five forces), and the factors behind those interrelationships that account for industry attractiveness.

Figure 11.3 shows the application of the Five-Forces Model to describe the characteristics of the pharmaceutical industry in the early 1990s. What the simple example reveals is the power of the framework to capture the key elements that explain the degree of attractiveness of an industry, and the role that the key players are having. In a very succinct way, we are able to grasp a host of fairly complex interactions and obtain a feeling for the nature of the overall industry. This is quite a remarkable feature of the Five-Forces Model.

The *competitive position* establishes the basis for achieving a sustainable advantage, which is a business' relative standing against its key competitors. According to Porter, the value chain model is the guiding framework for assessing the competitive position of a business. The underlying principle is that all the tasks performed by the business organization can be classified into nine broad categories. Five of them are called *primary activities* and the other four, *support activities*. Figure 11.4 provides a full representation of the value chain.

The primary activities involve the physical movement of raw materials and finished products and the marketing, sales, and servicing of these products.[4] They can be thought of as the classical management functions of the firm, where there is an organizational entity with a manager in charge of a very specific task, and with full balance between authority and responsibility. The support activities are more pervasive. Their role is to provide support not only to the primary activities but also to each other. They provide the managerial infrastructure of the business: all processes and systems intended to ensure proper coordination and accountability – and include human resource management, technology development, and procurement.

Since the value chain is composed of the set of activities performed by the business unit, it provides a very effective way to diagnose the position of the business against its major competitors, and to define the foundations for action aimed at

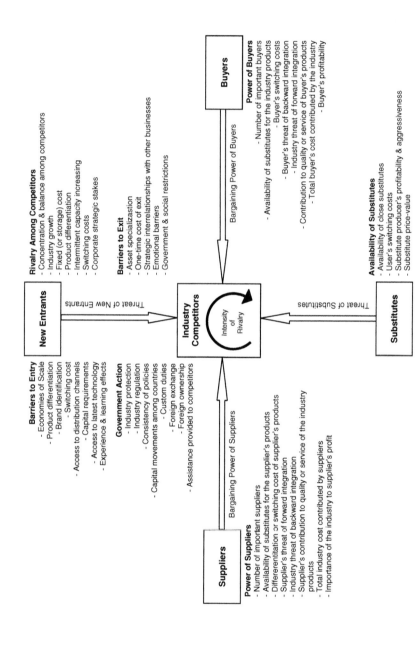

Fig. 11.2 Elements of industry structure: Michael Porter's five forces

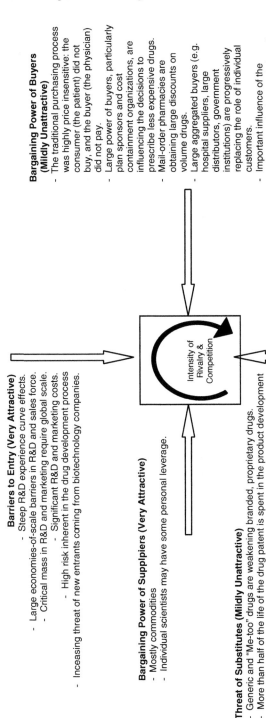

Barriers to Entry (Very Attractive)
- Steep R&D experience curve effects.
- Large economies-of-scale barriers in R&D and sales force.
- Critical mass in R&D and marketing require global scale.
- Significant R&D and marketing costs.
- High risk inherent in the drug development process
- Inceasing threat of new entrants coming from biotechnology companies.

Bargaining Power of Buyers (Mildly Unattractive)
- The traditional purchasing process was highly price insensitive: the consumer (the patient) did not buy, and the buyer (the physician) did not pay.
- Large power of buyers, particularly plan sponsors and cost containment organizations, are influencing the decisions to prescribe less expensive drugs.
- Mail-order pharmacies are obtaining large discounts on volume drugs.
- Large aggregated buyers (e.g. hospital suppliers, large distributors, government institutions) are progressively replacing the role of individual customers.
- Important influence of the government in the regulation of the buying process.

Bargaining Power of Supplpiers (Very Attractive)
- Mostly commodities
- Individual scientists may have some personal leverage.

Threat of Substitutes (Mildly Unattractive)
- Generic and "Me-too" drugs are weakening branded, proprietary drugs.
- More than half of the life of the drug patent is spent in the product development and approval process.
- Technological development is making imitation easier.
- Consumer aversion to chemical substances erodes the appeal for pharmaceutical drugs.

Intensity of Rivalry (Attractive)
- Global competition concentrated among fifteen large companies.
- Most companies focus on certain types of disease therapy.
- Competition among incumbents limited by patent protection.
- Competition based on price and product differentiation.
- Government intervention and growth of "Me-too" drugs increase rivalry.
- Strategic alliances establish collaborative agreements among industry players.
- Very profitable industy, however with declining margins.

Intensity of Rivalry & Competition

SUMMARY ASSESSMENT OF THE INDUSTRY ATTRACTIVENESS (Attractive)

Fig. 11.3 Michael Porter's five-forces model applied to the pharmaceutical industry in the early 1990s

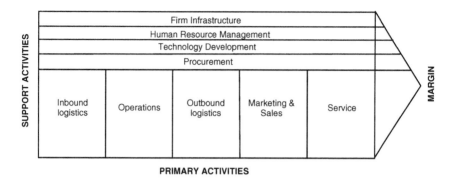

Fig. 11.4 Michael Porter's value chain

sustaining a competitive advantage. As opposed to the forces that determine the industry structure of the business – which are largely external and not controllable by the firm – the activities of the value chain are factors that companies can control as they strive to achieve competitive superiority. By analyzing these activities, managers can identify the success factors central to competing well and to understanding how to develop the unique competencies that provide the basis for sound business leadership.

Figure 11.5 shows the description of the key activities of the value chain for Merck, a leading pharmaceutical company during the 1990s. Merck had been for many years voted the most admired company in America for the Fortune 500 CEOs. Once again, the simple description of Merck's activities illustrated in Fig. 11.5 serves to understand how powerful this framework is. In a very brief space, we are able to penetrate the major attributes of Merck and visualize why it has obtained such a strong position in the pharmaceutical industry.

Low Cost or Differentiation – Michael Porter's Only Two Strategic Options

As we have indicated previously, Porter postulates that there arc only two ways to compete – either Low Cost or Differentiation. Even he goes beyond that, claiming that attempting to do both things simultaneously is the worst we can do – we get "caught in the middle."

The rationale of this argument is explained in Fig. 11.6. We can see in the figure that there is an "average player," who has a given cost and margin for the product that determines the price this player charges. The "Low-Cost player," however, has an insurmountable advantage due to being able to price the product below the average player and, therefore, dominating the market. What is the alternative? In Porter's view, the only option is to differentiate the product – through initiatives like additional features, functionality, brand image – that allow you to charge a higher

MARGIN

Management Infrastructure
Very strong corporate culture
One of America's best managed companies
Superb financial management & managerial control capabilities
Very lean structure
Highly concerned about ethics, ecology, and safety

Human Resources Management
Friendly & cooperative labor relations
Strong recruiting programs in top universities
Excellent training & development
Excellent rewards & health-care programs

Technology Development
Technology leader; developer of break-path drugs (e.g., Vasotec, Sinement, Mevacor)
Intensive R&D spending
Strengthening technological & marketing capabilities thorough strategic alliances (Astra, DuPont, and Johnson &
Johnson) Fastest time-to-market in drug discovery and drug approval processes

Procurement
Vertical integration in chemical products

Inbound logistics	Manufacturing	Operations	Marketing & Sales	Service
	- Increasing manufacturing flexibility and cost reductions - Stressing quality and productivity improvements - Global facilities network	- Acquisition of Medco provides unique distribution capabilities and information technology support - Medco is the number one mail-order firm	- Marketing leadership - Large direct sales staff - Global marketing coverage - Leverage through Medco, including powerful marketing groups and salesl forces, and proprietary formulary - Medco IT infrastructure and database, covering patients, physicians, and drug uses - Strategic alliances	- Medco's service excellence has attracted major corporations and health-care organizations as clients

Fig. 11.5 Merck's value chain

There are two ways to compete: Low Cost or Differentiation

The efficiency of the low cost provider's cost structure allows pricing below the average competitor, which in the long run may put average competitors out of business.

This is why the alternative to low cost needs to be differentiation, offering unique product attributes that the customer values and will pay a premium for.

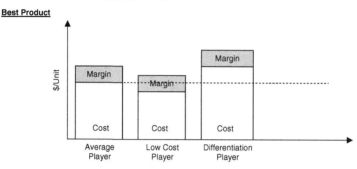

Fig. 11.6 Low cost or differentiation

price since the customer appreciates those added features and is willing to pay a premium for the product. Sounds pretty convincing, doesn't it?

The fallacy of this argument is that we are looking only at the product economics, which is typical of the Best Product option. Instead, if we consider not just the additional cost that the customer has to absorb, but the additional benefits – in either cost reduction and/or additional revenues – that the customer will receive from a Total Customer Solutions, the situation is quite different – as can be seen in Fig. 11.7. In there are the customer economies that matter. The "negative cost" that

However, the Total Customer Solutions positioning offers a possible preferred alternative by introducing significant cost savings (and/or revenue increases) to the customer.

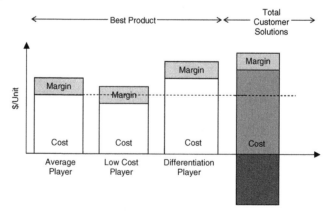

Fig. 11.7 Total customer solutions – a possible preferred option

is portrayed in the figure allows for even higher costs to be incurred and still produce a better alternative for the customer.

Porter's Winning Formula

Porter's framework offers a simple approach to business success: pick an attractive industry in which you can excel. The framework and the language Porter uses to describe it: stress rivalry and competition. Therefore, an attractive industry is one in which a business can achieve as close to a monopolistic position as possible. The message of the value chain model to managers is that they must achieve sustainable advantage by beating their competitors in as many key activities as possible. According to Porter, then, strategy is war!

Comments on Michael Porter's Frameworks

Porter's influence in the business and academic communities has been enormous. It is not an exaggeration to say that he has become the most prominent business academic of our generation. As a result of that, his ideas and lessons have been applied extensively in all kinds of different settings. Professors and consultants teach his ideas and business people apply them. There are many laudatory comments that we could make about his work. We would like to address those that we find most significant.

- Porter has provided a rigorous methodology that permits to carry on a systematic review of industry structure and competitive positioning. It has given the field of strategy a solid foundation and a professorial language that allows us to communicate in much more coherent and precise terms.
- The Five-Forces Model addresses the issue of the appropriation of the "rent" generated by the industry players. An industry is formed by a collection of firms engaged in an economic activity that generates wealth – what economists refer to as the "rent." Porter is interested in identifying who is appropriating that rent, which is why the model stresses rivalry, threats, and bargaining power rather than cooperation and support.
- The value chain is a way to describe the major activities of a business and the way that the firm can acquire competitive advantage over its rivals. The value chain is a brilliant way of decomposing the business activities, to allow for a comprehensive understanding of the business capabilities.
- The final observation that we want to make is that Porter's model aggregates and diffuses the role of the customer. The customer is presented as "the buyer" who is in conflict with the firm, threatening with a bargaining power. This is all part of the intent of Porter's framework that, as we have said, attempts to describe the appropriability of the rent. This is, however, a critical character of this framework, very much antagonistic to the ideas of the Delta Model that regards the customer as the central positive driving force of the business.

Caveats to Porter's Framework

From the perspective of the Delta Model, if you are not careful, Porter's framework might talk you into reaching the wrong conclusions.

- Putting the competitor as the driving force. As we see in Fig. 11.2, the center of the Five-Forces Model is the "intensity of rivalry among competitors," which plays the most prominent role. Instead, we believe that the customer should be the major thrust of the business initiatives.
- The excessive concern about your competitor leads to imitation, congruency, and eventually the commoditization of the business. Instead, we recommend studying your competitors – not to imitate them but to try to find a new, creative, unique value proposition to offer your customer which will set you apart from your competitors.
- The Five-Forces Model not only presents the firm in conflict with its competitors, but also creates a rivalry attitude among all the key players. Instead, we believe you should embrace the Extended Enterprise, establishing a strong collaboration, if not with all, with a select set of suppliers, customers, and complementors.
- Limiting the strategic options to either Low Cost or Differentiation is a very narrow set. Instead, we suggest you open your options to include the alternative represented in the Best Product, Total Customer Solutions, and System Lock-In strategies.

The Resource-Based View of the Firm

The Resource-Based View of the firm represents a major departure from Porter's approach that is based on market-driven factor considerations. Porter posits that industry structure plays a central role in creating opportunities for superior profitability. The Resource-Based View, on the other hand, argues that the central forces of competitive advantage are factor-driven; that is, they depend on the firm's development of resources and capabilities. Figure 11.8 illustrates the essence of the Resource-Based View, which has four key components:

1. Competitive advantage is created when resources and capabilities owned exclusively by the firm can generate unique core competencies.
2. The resulting advantage can be sustained due to the lack of substitution and imitation capacities by the firm's competitors.
3. The benefits derived from these advantages are retained inside the firm: they are not appropriated by others.
4. The timing of the acquisition of the necessary resources and capabilities is so opportune that their cost will not offset the resulting benefits.

If all these conditions are met, then the competitive advantage that is created will generate economic value for the firm.

Building on Fig. 11.8, we will now explore the components of the Resource-Based View in more detail.

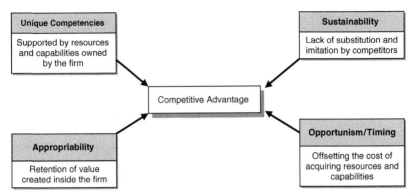

Source: Adapted from Margaret A. Petaraf, "The Cornerstones of Competitive Advantage: A Resource-Based View of the Firm," Strategic Management Journal, March 1993, and Pankaj Ghemawat, *Commitment, The Dynamics of Strategy*, Free Press, 1991.

Fig. 11.8 The resource-based view of the firm – elements of competitive advantage

Unique Competencies

The firm's resources and capabilities are the sources of its unique competencies. Resources can be tangible (e.g., financial and physical assets) or intangible (e.g., reputation, customer orientation, and technological superiority). Resources are converted into capabilities when the firm develops the necessary routines to use them effectively. Often, resources and capabilities are the results of investment in durable, specialized, and non-tradable factors.

This is what Pankaj Ghemawat has defined as commitment. In his view, commitment explains the persistence in an individual firm's performance, and the differences in profitability enjoyed by different firms competing in the same industry. These investments represent both sticky factors that are not easily lost to competition, and major bets that are not easily reversed.

Sustainability

For a business unit's competitive advantage to be sustainable, its resources must be valuable, scarce, and difficult to imitate or substitute.

Appropriability

A strategy that is both unique and sustainable generates significant economic value. The issue of appropriability addresses the question of who will capture that value. Sometimes the owners of the business do not appropriate all the value created because of a gap between ownership and control. Non-owners might control complementary and specialized factors that divert the cash proceeds away from the business. This type of dissipation of value is called *hold-up*. A well-known example of hold-up took place in the personal computer industry, in which Intel and Microsoft captured 80% of the total market value of the industry, value lost to the computer manufacturers themselves.

The second threat related to the appropriability of economic value is referred to as *slack*. It measures the extent to which the economic value realized by a business is significantly lower than what it could have been. Slack is often the result of inefficiencies that prevent the accumulation of economic rents by a business. One of the major sources of slack in the United States has been confrontations between management and labor unions. It has been reported, for example, that General Motors loses $2 billion annually to its bottom-line due to strikes.

While hold-up changes the distribution of the total wealth created, slack reduces the overall size of this wealth.

Opportunism and Timing

The final necessary condition for competitive advantage comes (or fails to come) prior to the establishment of a superior resource position. The cost incurred in acquiring the resources must be lower than the value created by them. In other words, the cost of implementing the strategy should not offset the value generated by it.

Core Competencies and the Resource-Based View of the Firm

C.K. Prahalad and Gary Hamel popularized the Resource-Based view of the firm, particularly with their prominent article in the *Harvard Business Review*.[5] They establish three main ideas in their paper. First, that competitive advantage derives from an ability to build, less expensively and more rapidly than competitors, the core competencies that spawn unanticipated products. The real source of advantage is to be found in management's ability to consolidate company-wide technologies and production skills into competencies that empower individual businesses to adapt quickly to changing opportunities. Second, the tangible link between identified core competencies and end products is what they call the core products, the physical embodiment of one or more core competencies. And third, senior managers should spend a significant amount of their time developing a corporate strategic architecture that establishes objectives for competency building. Strategic architecture is the road map to the future; it helps determine which core competencies to build and helps identify their constituent technologies.

The Resource-Based View of the Firm's Winning Formula

Based on the original Resource-Based View, unmodified by Prahalad and Hamel, the winning formula is very simple:

- Develop resources and capabilities that are unique, valuable, and non-tradable, and that constitute the unique competencies of the firm
- Make the resulting advantages sustainable by preventing imitation or substitution by competitors
- Appropriate the resulting economic rent by preventing negative hold-up and slack conditions
- Ensure that the implementation process is done in such a way that its associated costs do not overwhelm the resulting benefits.

In other words, it is strategy by real estate, in the sense that the corporate assets are the sources of competitive advantages.

If we further extend the winning formula to account for Prahalad and Hamel's message, we would add three more elements: develop core competencies at the corporate level; apply them to create core products as opposed to end products; and use a strategic architecture to guide competence building.

Porter's framework and the Resource-Based View differ in explaining the sources of profitability. Porter associates it with monopolistic rent that flows from industry structure. The Resource-Based View of the Firm ties it to the corporation's internal capabilities. They share the perspective that business is akin to war and that designing business strategy is akin to playing a zero-sum game. Profitability accrues to those who are superior to their competitors. The Delta Model takes issue with this almost obsessive focus on competition.

A Practical Framework of the Application of the Resource-Based View of the Firm

Figure 11.9 reproduces the approach that Robert Grant has proposed for the application of the Resource-Based view of the Firm for the development of its strategy. Notice that the recommended approach starts with the identification and classification of the firm's resources, followed by a similar analysis of the firm's capabilities. Then an appraisal is made on the rent-generating potential of these resources and capabilities to further select the strategy which best exploits those resources and capabilities. As is stressed in the center of the diagram, the objective is to generate competitive advantage.

Some Caveats to the Resource-Based View of the Firm

To us, the most concerning element of this approach is that it starts with the development of resources and capabilities, and then defines the strategy which makes best use of these assets. Shouldn't it be the other way around? Shouldn't we nurture and develop those capabilities that are needed to support the preferred strategy? Otherwise, how do we know what resources and capabilities to acquire? Are we putting the cart before the horse?

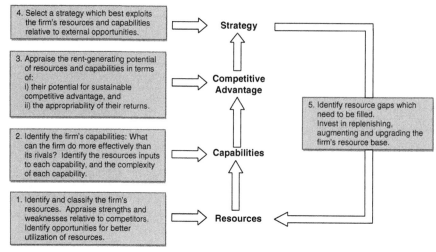

Source: Adapted from Robert H. Grant, "The Resource-Based Theory of Competitive Advantage: Implications of Strategy Formulation," California Management Review, Vol. 33, No. 3, 1991.

Fig. 11.9   A resource-based approach to strategy analysis: a practical framework

There is a great degree of vagueness in the Resource-Based View of the firm regarding the nature of the resources and capabilities that play such a critical role in the definition of the strategy. It seems to us that this framework seems to work better to explain how a firm has achieved competitive advantage (ex-post), rather than to help us to acquire a sustainable one (ex-auto). It seems that this is a framework in search of a framework.

The Delta Model does provide an answer to this dilemma. One important task of the Delta Model is the identification of the Existing and Desired Competencies of the Firm, which we have treated in some length in Chapter 4. There we propose that the Eight Strategic Positionings of the Triangle are the ones which should guide us to both assess our existing capabilities and detect the required competencies we need in the future to develop a successful strategy.

Comparisons Among Porter, the Resource-Based View of the Firm, and the Delta Model Frameworks

Now that we have been exposed to the three frameworks, we can make proper comparisons among them. As we present in Figure 11.10, they are three relevant dimensions to reflect upon the differences that these frameworks bring to the study of strategy.

First, the focus of strategic attention of Porter's framework is the industry in which the business participates that the Five-Forces Model is applied to, and the

	Porter	Resource-Based View	Delta Model
Focus of Strategic Attention	Industry/Business	Corporation	**Extended Enterprise** (The Firm, The Customer, The Suppliers, The Complementors)
Types of Competitive Advantage	Low Cost of Differentiation	Resource Capabilities, Core Competencies	Best Product, Total Customer Solutions, System Lock-In
Strategy As	Rivalry	Real Estate	Customer Bonding

Fig. 11.10 Comparison among strategy frameworks

business itself that is the depository of the Value Chain analysis. The Resource-Based View of the Firm expands the scope of attention to the full corporation, with a possible full portfolio of business, since that is where the Core Competencies reside. Finally, the Delta Model extends the scope even further to include the Extended Enterprise – composed by the firm and its key Suppliers, Customers, and Complementors.

In Porter's framework, there are two alternative ways to achieve competitive advantage, and these are Low Cost or Differentiation; the Resource-Based View of the Firm seeks to achieve competitive advantage through the use of Resources, Capabilities, and Core Competencies; the Delta Model expands the options to consider Best Product, Total Customer Solutions, and System Lock-In strategic positionings.

Finally, we have attempted to capture the strategy espoused by each framework by identifying Porter as Rivalry, the Resource-Based View of the Firm as Real Estate, and the Delta Model as Bonding. While we have emphasized the differences among these frameworks – and we believe those differences are quite strong and real – this should not prevent us from exploiting the positive messages they convey. Porter is remarkably effective in describing the industry characteristics and the activities surrounding the business. The Resource-Based View of the Firm has added an important and critical dimension of strategy, which is quite relevant. The Delta Model, we believe, puts the right emphasis on the customer, an element that is somehow neglected in the other frameworks. From this perspective, the three frameworks should be regarded as complementary to one another. Each in its own right carries a relevant message to take into consideration. Each provides a different lens from which to understand the great complexities that surround the business practice. Finally, we contrast in Fig. 11.11 how the three frameworks addressed the issues of Environmental Scan and Internal Scrutiny.

The Environmental Scan process deals with those elements which pertain to the external environment of the firm, that are to a great extent outside the firm's control but critical to understand its strategic positioning and guides its strategic actions. Porter responds to that concern by offering his famous Five-Forces Model, which gives us an understanding of the attractiveness of the industry the firm is in. The

	Porter	Resource-Based View	Delta Model
Environmental Scan	Five-Forces Model	None	Customer Segmentation and Customer Value Proposition
Internal Scrutiny	Value Chain	Resources, Capabilities, Core Competencies	The Firm as a Bundle of Competencies – The Eight Strategic Positionings

Fig. 11.11 How the strategy framework deals with environmental scan and internal scrutiny

Resource-Based View of the Firm is mute on this issue. It concerns itself with the internal capabilities of the firm. The Delta Model puts the emphasis in understanding the customer and how to provide the customer a unique, sustainable, value-added proposition that generates a high degree of bonding. Surprisingly, the customer is not a major actor in the other two frameworks.

The Internal Scrutiny process looks at those factors that are controllable by the firm. Porter proposes the Value Chain and claims that the activities of the chain should by that focus achieve competitive advantage. The Resource-Based View emphasizes the issue of resources and capabilities, but doesn't offer a guiding framework or how to identify and nurture them. The Delta Model follows the spirit of the Resource-Based View of the Firm, but offers eight Strategic Positionings as the perspectives from which to catalog the firm's capabilities.

It should be clear now what each framework offers, how they differentiate from one another, and what could be the role they play in the development of the strategy of a business.

Reinterpreting Porter's Five-Forces Model Through the Delta Model: Thinking Out of the Box

The conventional interpretation of Porter's framework has emphasized rivalry and competition as the key components of strategy. We start by analyzing the industry that we are in, namely the one that is shaped by our competitors. Not only are we concerned with the incumbent firms, but also with those that could enter either directly or indirectly, by means of substitutes. In addition, we are concerned about the amount of wealth that can be appropriated by our buyers or suppliers. The strategic focus is internal, the prevailing climate is friction, and the way to win is by defeating and outsmarting those who could have a claim on the industry wealth. Whether Porter intended it or not, the legacy has been a product-central mentality; strategy is war.

Let's put to work the lessons of the Delta Model to reinterpret Porter's Five Forces Model in a fundamental new way that will move us out of the Best Product positioning toward Total Customer Solutions and System Lock-In (Fig. 11.12). The

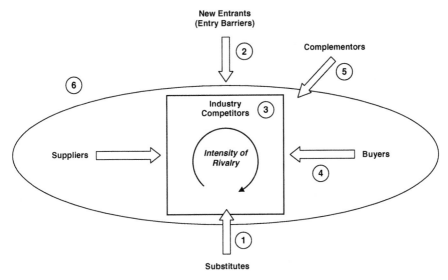

Fig. 11.12 Reinterpreting Porter's five forces through the Delta Model

trick is not to take this industry as a given. Think of the five forces as a way to identify actions that will lead to a very strong positioning for you, and for all of your
relevant partners: customers, suppliers, and complementors. This is the process of
business transformations that we can engage in.

Search for the 10X Force

In his book *Only the Paranoid Survive*, Andy Grove, the Chairman of Intel, introduces the concept of the 10X Force. This goes well beyond assessing the potential

substitute product in a given industry, and requires searching for a change of such magnitude that it will transform the rules of competition and the playing field. This is a 10X Force because it is an order of magnitude larger than the existing forces in the industry. This concept is both provocative and, at times, quite practical. It requires a completely open mind, rejecting the stereotypes of the industry, not emulating, not taking anything for granted, and, above all, rejecting the product-centric mentality and commoditization mindsets.

Generate Barriers Around Your Customers

Don't think of barriers to entry as those forces that prevent an outsider from penetrating the overall industry. Rather think about building barriers around your key individual customers so as to establish customer lock-in. This is not based on an abusive behavior; on the contrary, it is built on a relationship so strong and so mutually beneficial that both parties will never break apart. The key to achieve this position is to gain a deep customer and consumer understanding through careful segmentation and targeting. Having acquired this knowledge, we can develop unique economic value propositions to the customer, which is the source of the barriers to change. It is interesting to note that it is not your industry knowledge that is most critical to achieve this state of relationship with the customer. It is rather the customer's industry that is most relevant. You need a deep knowledge of the profit and cost drivers of your customer so that your capabilities and product offerings measurably enhance your customer performance.

Your Competitors Are Not the Relevant Benchmarks

This could be seen as heretical; after all, your competitors are at the center of Porter's Five Forces. We do not suggest that you should ignore your competitors. Study them intensely; from this you can learn both what and what *not* to do. If you use them as an across-the-board, unquestioned benchmark, your standards will decline. Merck, the pharmaceutical company, collects extraordinary detailed competitor intelligence, but not to simply follow or imitate. As we have said before, competitor imitation leads toward commoditization and congruency, which is the opposite of leadership.

It is not your industry that is the most relevant when you pursue a Total Customer Solutions or System Lock-In strategy. The key industries that you need to comprehend are those of your customers and complementors. It is the overall system and how to influence it that is critical.

Develop and Nurture the Intrated Value Chain

Your customers and your suppliers are your natural partners, which you need to cultivate around the jointly structured value proposition to your customer. Those relationships can be greatly enhanced by the use of e-business and e-commerce technology. The chain of interrelationships often extends beyond the customer to include the final consumer, as depicted in Fig. 11.13.

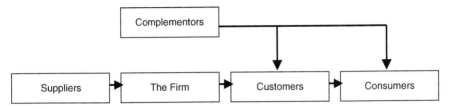

Fig. 11.13 The elements of the extended enterprise

If you do not reach the consumer directly, you have to make a concerted effort to have as much understanding of the end-user as possible. The consumer, the final user, the ultimate player in the chain is absolutely critical. With today's technology, it is possible to understand individually each and every one of the consumers and tailor services to his/her needs in a highly customized way.

Add a New Player; the Complementors

Why has Microsoft been so successful? Because Bill Gates has an army of people working for him who are not on his payroll. These are the complementors: software producers, CD/ROM developers, and a cadre of professionals whose primary work is to extend the usefulness of the Windows operating system. Suppliers and customers are critical to achieve customer lock-in. Complementors go even further; they are the instruments for seeking competitor lock-out and system lock-in. Identify key potential complementors. Incidentally, many could be in your own backyard. They are other businesses in your company portfolio that have not been integrated in a well-conceived corporate (not business) strategy. Make the complementors be your loyal partners, by providing them a mutually exciting value proposition. Have them invest in your business. Make the relationship stable and long-lasting.

Fragmented Industries Offer Big Opportunities

If your customers, suppliers, and complementors are numerous, fragmented, and somehow "ignored" by the top industry players, you could have a golden opportunity to serve as the "glue" in bonding the industry together and emerge as a key powerful leader. The beauty of network technology is that one can access directly the fragmented players and create a virtual entity that could enjoy the economies of scale that have been otherwise reserved for the major players. Also, one could provide them with state-of-the-art managerial capabilities that would have been impossible to acquire under the old circumstances.

Notes

1. Michael E. Porter's primary work in Competitive Positioning are in his books, *Competitive Strategy* (New York: The Free Press, 1980) and *Competitive Advantage* (New York: The Free Press, 1985).
2. The seeds for this view originated in the work by E. Penrose, *The Theory of the Growth of the Firm*, Basil Blackwell, 1959. This approach was substantially developed among others by B. Wernerfelt, *A Resource-Based View of the Firm*, Strategic Management Journal, Vol. 5, pp. 171–180, 1984; J.B. Barney, *Firm Resources and Sustained Competitive Advantage*, Journal of Management, Vol. 17, pp. 99–120, 1991; M. Peteraf, *The Cornerstones of Competitive Advantage: A Resource-Based View*, Strategic Management Journal, Vol. 14, No. 3, pp. 179–192, March 1993. C.K. Prahalad and Gary Hamel popularized the approach in their now classic paper, *"The Core Competence of the Corporation,"* Harvard Business Review, May–June, 1990, pp. 71–91.
3. D. Ricardo, *Principles of Political Economy and Taxation*. (London, J. Murray. 1817).
4. This applies to services as well as products.
5. C.K. Prahalad and Gary Hamel, "The Core Competence of the Corporation", *Harvard Business Review*, May–June 1990, pp. 79–91.

About the Author

Arnoldo C. Hax is the Alfred P. Sloan Professor of Management Emeritus at the Sloan School of Management of the Massachusetts Institute of Technology. He served as Deputy Dean of the Sloan School from 1987 through 1990. During his career at the Sloan School, Professor Hax has been the Chairman of the Strategy Group, the Program for Senior Executives, and the Sloan Fellows Program at MIT.

Dr. Hax is a native of Chile, where he received his undergraduate degree in industrial engineering, with highest honors from the Catholic University. Subsequently, he received his M.S. at the University of Michigan, and his Ph.D. at the University of California, Berkeley. Prior to joining MIT in 1972, he was a member of the faculty at the Harvard Business School and a senior consultant for Arthur D. Little, Inc. He has been in the MIT faculty since 1972.

He has published extensively in the fields of strategic management, management control, operations management, and operations research. He has authored and co-authored 10 books and some 100 journal articles. An accomplished teacher, he won the Salgo Award for Excellence in Teaching at the Sloan School of Management. He has participated in a great many executive programs at MIT, in many US universities and corporations, and in most countries in Europe and Latin America, as well as Japan, China, and the former USSR.

He has a wide consulting experience, specializing in the development of formal strategic planning processes. His corporate clients include Advanced Micro Devices, Synthess, Siemens, Eastman Chemical, Merck, EDS, Saturn, Coca-Cola, Motorola, General Motors, Citibank, Searle, Analog Devices, Unilever, 3 M, Michelin, Teléfonica, Johnson and Johnson, Ford, Codelco, Icatu-Hartford, and Molymet, among others.

His books include *The Delta Project: Discovering New Sources of Profitability*, coauthored with Dean Wilde (Palgrave, 2001); *Strategic Management: An Integrative Perspective* (Prentice-Hall, 1984), and *The Strategy Concept and Process: A Pragmatic Approach* (Prentice-Hall, 1995), both coauthored with Nicolas Majluf; *Production and Inventory Management*, coauthored with Dan Candea (Prentice-Hall, 1983), which received the Institute of Industrial Engineers-Joint Publishers Book-of-the-Year Award; *Applied Mathematical Programming*, coauthored with Stephen Bradley and Thomas Magnanti (Addison-Wesley, 1977); and he edited *Readings in Strategic Management* (Ballinger, 1984) and *Planning*

A.C. Hax, *The Delta Model*, DOI 10.1007/978-1-4419-1480-4,
© Springer Science+Business Media, LLC 2010

Strategies That Work (Oxford, 1987). He contributed a chapter on corporate strategy, with Nicolas Majluf, to the *Encyclopedia of Operations Research and Management Science*, 2/e (Gass and Harris, eds., Kluwer/Springer, 2001). He is strategic management editor for *Interfaces*, and former editor of *Operations Research* and *Naval Research Logistics Quarterly*. He is on the editorial board of the *Journal of Manufacturing and Operations Research* and the *Journal of High Technology Management Research*.

Dr. Hax has been granted from the Catholic University of Chile an Honorary Doctorate Degree. He has also been granted a Doctor Honoris Causa from the Universidad Politécnica de Madrid. He has been awarded the Ramon Salas Edwards Award by the Chilean Engineering Institute, an award given every 3 years to the best research contribution across all fields of science and technology. He has been granted a Dean's Award for Excellence at the Sloan School of Management, MIT. He has been listed in *Who's Who in America*, *Who's Who in American Education*, *Who's Who in the World*, and *Who's Who in Science and Technology*.

Index

Printed by Printforce, the Netherlands